After Neoliberalism:
THE KILBURN MANIFESTO

Edited by Stuart Hall,
Doreen Massey & Michael Rustin

A SOUNDINGS COLLECTION

Soundings
A journal of politics and culture

London Lawrence & Wishart 2015

Lawrence and Wishart Limited
99a Wallis Road
London
E9 5LN

Typesetting: e-type
Cover design: Andrew Corbett

© Soundings 2015
Individual articles © author

The authors have asserted their rights under the Copyright, Design and
Patents Act, 1998 to be identified as the authors of this work.

All rights reserved. Apart from fair dealing for the purpose of private study,
research, criticism or review, no part of this publication may be reproduced,
stored in a retrieval system, or transmitted, in any form or by any means,
electronic, electrical, chemical, mechanical, optical, photocopying, recording
or otherwise, without the prior permission of the copyright owner.

ISBN 9781 910448 106

British Library Cataloguing in Publication Data.
A catalogue record for this book is available from the British Library

Published by Soundings

Soundings
A journal of politics and culture

CONTENTS

PREFACE

The project of the Kilburn Manifesto grew out of work by *Soundings* writers to understand the state of political play in light of the financial crisis of 2007-8. The editorial board decided that the most productive way of thinking about these issues was through Gramsci's idea of conjunctural analysis, and instituted a series of seminars and articles to help address the nature of such a project. (Some of these articles were subsequently brought together in an ebook, *The Neoliberal Crisis*, which is now being published in print by L&W, as a companion to this volume.)

In 2013 we – along with our fellow founding editor of *Soundings*, Stuart Hall – decided to develop this work further and to bring together, in instalments, an online Manifesto. The idea was to form an analysis of the political context that was both unifying and systemic, but was also respectful to the particularities of the issues and areas of society to be discussed; we also wanted to involve different voices and perspectives in discussing them. In 2013 we published the Framing Statement for the Manifesto, which we decided to call the Kilburn Manifesto, as all three editors lived in this area. Following that, eleven further instalments of the Manifesto were published with free online access, in order to make the ideas and the ensuing debate as accessible as possible. Various versions of the instalments were also made available in other formats, including in *Soundings* journal, on Open Democracy and on *The Guardian's* Comment is Free. By popular request, the full versions of all these instalments are now collected together here in one print volume. Each chapter of this book is partly the product of the specific moment of its writing, slightly different for each piece written over the past two years. To emphasise this developmental process over time, we have retained the original temporal markers in the chapters. Newspaper headlines, breaking news items and so on remain the same, to reinforce the different contexts within which the debate around the manifesto unfolded.

As readers will know, Stuart Hall died in February 2014, but he was contributing to the development of the Manifesto, and to its writing, until quite soon before his death. This project could not have taken place without his initial commitment, and without his contribution to the ideas which are developed in these texts.

Throughout the two years of this project, the Kilburn Manifesto has always been a collective and collaborative endeavour. After the publication of each instalment we held a public seminar in the Marx Memorial Library, and the discussion always continued afterwards in the lively space of the upstairs room at the pub around the corner. We found these discussions enormously helpful and engaging – and it's worth pointing out that the liveliness and openness of the manifesto debate has taken place in the kind of public, common spaces (the library, the pub, the web) that are currently so threatened by neoliberalism.

Our thanks go to all the people who were respondents to the instalments at the seminars: Mevan Babakar, Anna Coote, Hilary Cottam, Emma Dowling, Jane Foot, Deborah Grayson, Ewa Jasiewicz, Samuel Kirwan, Shiv Malik, James Meadway, Pragna Patel, Justin Rosenberg, Polly Trenow, Guy Shrubsole, Andrew Simms, David Wearing and Alison Winch – for giving us your time and providing such thought-provoking responses.

Our thanks also go to all the contributors, to members of the editorial board of *Soundings*, and especially to Sally Davison, Lynda Dyson, Katharine Harris and Becky Luff in the Lawrence & Wishart office. Thanks also to Jo Littler for all of her work on the seminars, particularly her excellent chairing. Finally, we would also like to thank the many people who came to and contributed to the meetings and seminars which accompanied this project, and the Marx Memorial Library for providing our venue.

Doreen Massey & Michael Rustin

AFTER NEOLIBERALISM:
ANALYSING THE PRESENT

Stuart Hall, Doreen Massey and Michael Rustin

With the banking crisis and the credit crunch of 2007-8, and their economic repercussions around the globe, the system of neoliberalism, or global free-market capitalism, that has come to dominate the world in the three decades since 1980, has imploded. As the scale of toxic debt became evident, credit and inter-bank lending dried up, spending slowed, output declined and unemployment rose. The system's vastly inflated financial sectors, which speculate in assets largely unrelated to the real economy of goods and services, precipitated an economic crisis whose catastrophic consequences are still unfolding.

We believe that mainstream political debate simply does not recognise the depth of this crisis, nor the consequent need for radical rethinking. The economic model that has underpinned the social and political settlement of the last three decades is unravelling, but the broader political and social consensus apparently remains in place. We therefore offer this analysis as a contribution to the debate, in the hope that it will help people on the left think more about how we can shift the parameters of the debate, from one concerning small palliative and restorative measures, to one which opens the way for moving towards a new political era and new understandings of what constitutes the good society.[1]

For three decades, the neoliberal system has been generating vast profits for multi-nationals, investment institutions and venture capitalists, and huge accumulations of wealth for the new global super-rich, while grossly increasing the gap between rich and poor and deepening inequalities of income, health and life chances within and between countries, on a scale not seen since before the second world war. In North America and Western Europe – hitherto dynamos of the global economic system – rates of growth are now lower than during the early post-war decades, when there was a more even balance of power between the social classes. There has been a steep decline in manufacturing and a hot-house expansion of financial services and the service economy; and a massive shift of power and resources from public to private, from state to market. 'The market' has become the model of social relations, exchange value the only value. Western governments have shown themselves weak and indecisive in responding to the environmental crisis, climate change and the threat to sustainable life on the planet, and have refused to address the issues in other than their own – market – terms.

Likewise, the financial crisis has been used by many Western governments as a means of further entrenching the neoliberal model. They have adopted swingeing 'austerity measures' which, they claim, is the only way of reducing the deficits generated during the bonanza period of the 1980s and 1990s. They have launched an assault on the incomes, living standards and conditions of life of the less well-off members of society. In the UK, the cuts programme has frozen incomes, capped benefits, savaged public sector employment and undermined local government. It has encouraged private capital to hollow-out the welfare state and dismantle the structures of health, welfare and education services. The burden of 'solving' the crisis has been disproportionately off-loaded on to working people, targeting vulnerable, marginalised groups. These include low-income, single-parent families; children in poverty; women juggling part-time employment with multiple domestic responsibilities; pensioners, the disabled and the mentally ill; welfare-benefits and low-cost public housing 'dependants'; the young unemployed (especially black youth); and students. Youth facilities have been closed; and citizens who depend on public amenities for their social well-being find themselves bereft. Apart from its punitive and regressive social effects, this is a strategy destined to fail even in its own terms, since its main consequence will be a serious fall in demand and a collapse of tax revenues, deepening the downward economic spiral, with little fall in the deficit.

In other words, the crisis itself has been used to reinforce the redistribution from poor to rich. Moreover, it has also provided the alibi for a far-reaching further restructuring of state and society along market lines, with a raft of ideologically-driven 'reforms' designed to advance privatisation and marketisation. It has encouraged private, individualised solutions to social problems. This makes it all the more important for the left to make the argument that it is time for a new moral and economic settlement.

find. climate change, e.g. the notion of individualised carbon footprint.

GLOBAL DIMENSIONS OF NEOLIBERALISM

This neoliberal hegemony, both in its pomp and in its crisis, has had global implications. Dynamic, expanding capitalist systems have their own strategic and geopolitical imperatives. Neoliberalism has sought a favourable climate towards business across the globe. It demands low tax regimes, limited state interference, and unimpeded access to markets and vital resources. It calls for internal security, the capacity to contain external enemies, and strong rulers in control of their populations, with whom bargains can be struck and influence exercised. It engenders hostility to more democratic and alternative experiments. These principles have guided the strategies and underpinned the network of alliances, blocs and bases that the West – led by the US – has constructed. The Middle East clearly demonstrates that maintaining generally favourable conditions of operation – securing spheres of influence (the US/Israel alliance), dealing with military challenges (Iran, Pakistan), repressing political instability (the Horn of Africa) and defeating threats (the Taliban, al-Quaida, Afghanistan) – figures as much as do specific resource 'grabs', such as for oil (Iraq, the Gulf States).

The particular global character of neoliberalism was part of its initiating armoury – for instance through the Washington Consensus from the 1980s onwards – and it is also an element of its historical specificity. It is a globalisation in which a new form of financial imperialism is crucial (and London has been central in its invention and dissemination), and in which a key dynamic has been a planetary search for new assets in which to speculate (through, for example, exported programmes of privatisation, spiralling markets in commodity futures, the buying up of vast tracts of land).

London – centric financial imperialism

But neoliberalism never conquered everything. It operated within, and created, a world of great diversity and unevenness. Its early – classic – laboratory was Chile, but the rise of South East Asian tigers was, critically, a state-aided development (by no means the official neoliberal recipe). And in spite of the Western triumphalism of 1989,

Russia also retains its specificities – a hybrid of oligarchic and state capitalism combined with authoritarianism. China, too, struggles to define a different model; it currently combines centralised party control with openness to foreign investment, and acute internal geographical dislocations and widespread social conflict with break-neck rates of growth and the lifting of hundreds of millions out of poverty. Indeed, conflict has erupted in many parts of the world where the neoliberal orthodoxy has been adopted. India, so frequently lauded for its embrace of the market consensus, exhibits both extraordinary rifts between the new elites and the impoverished, and multiple and persistent conflicts over its current economic strategy. Other major sites of conflict have been the water and gas wars in Bolivia, and the struggle of 'the poors' in Thailand. The emerging articulations of progressive governments and grassroots social movements in Latin America are, in varying ways and in varying degrees, responses to the impact of previous neoliberal policies. The alter-globalisation move-ment has been vocal. This has not been a simple victory.

In fact, its very diversity and conflict has been an element in neolib-eralism's current fracturing. The economic (im)balance between China and the USA has been both a central mechanism of comple-mentarity and, increasingly, a source of instability. The crisis in the Eurozone has also been a critical weak link in the global structure. Having failed to design a financial architecture that could address uneven development between constituent countries, the Euro-elite powers (the troika above all) now attempt to blame the inevitable disaster on the constituent countries themselves (or some of them). They thus set peoples against peoples, provoking dangerous national-isms, while the culpability of the elite is effectively obscured. It is a geographical conjuring trick that converts the political frontier from being one between conflicting economic and social interests into one between national peoples, and moulds those peoples' self-identifica-tions along nationalist lines.

Meanwhile, and over the longer term, a tectonic shift of economic power is taking place, to China and the other BRIC countries, bringing with it growing confidence and increasing claims for voice on the world stage. Trade, and indeed conversations and contacts more generally, increasingly bypasses the North Atlantic region altogether. At the same time, while the number of millionaires increases even in the poorest places, in many countries, most obviously in sub-Saharan Africa, there is rising impoverishment, widespread malnutrition (partly a product of the speculation in food prices), ecological devastation and political instability. There are battles over the control of energy and mineral resources. In the face of overwhelmingly unfavourable external pressures and restraints, governments cannot deal with poor schooling, hunger, malnutrition, disease and health pandemics or resist western consumerism, the arms traders and freelance mercenaries.

The 'squeeze' has triggered an increase in local, tribal, inter-ethnic and religious sectarian violence, civil wars, military coups, armed militias, child soldiers, 'ethnic cleansing' and genocidal rape; and these in turn have precipitated cross-border and international migration, as civilians flee war-zones, join refugee camps or seek asylum abroad. The 'failed (or failing) states' which Western strategists proclaim to be a major threat to security are themselves often the perverse consequences of neoliberalism and western intervention. And the very concept of failed state is often used as an ideological weapon.

[margin note: violent consequences of neoliberalism]

Most recently, the response to the crisis by the North Atlantic elites has made matters worse – for instance through its effects on prices and currency levels. The fact of global instability and looming crisis has by no means modified the neoliberal offensive. If Chile was the laboratory for the early phases, Greece has become the laboratory for an even more fierce implementation, while the Arab Spring may yet be recuperated to open up new fields for market forces. And in Latin America the recent US-sanctioned coups in Honduras and Paraguay have been swiftly followed by radical concessions to foreign capital.

IDEOLOGIES AND CONFLICTS

[margin note: crisis = turning point; incubator for societal change]

The present economic crisis is a moment of potential rupture. The welfare-state 'settlement' that preceded the neoliberal era in the North Atlantic world had crumbled in the 1970s, and, with the end of the Cold War, Thatcherite and Reaganite neoliberalism won the contest over which way forward would be taken. This outcome was not inevitable. Conflicts between social settlements and the crafting of hegemonies are the product of contending social forces. During the welfare state era, the working class did make economic gains. Wealth was modestly redistributed, egalitarianism and social rights became more embedded. Capital's share of the surplus was significantly eroded. But this was a shift that could not be tolerated. The expanded globalisation of its operation was partly (among its many determinants, and along with privatisation and financialisation) a means of restoring the declining share of the surplus taken by capital. Resistance to Thatcherism's 'war on society', conflicts over democratic government in London and other cities, struggles in the global South, the rise of new social movements, opposition to the poll tax, and contests over the rights of organised labour everywhere – all these were critical moments in the struggle to determine what would follow. Social forces locked in conflict across different areas of social life have always been at stake.

The current neoliberal settlement has also entailed the re-working of the common-sense assumptions of the earlier, social democratic settlement. Every social settlement, in order to establish itself, is crucially founded on embedding as common sense a whole bundle of beliefs – ideas beyond question, assumptions so deep that the very fact that they *are* assumptions is only rarely brought to light. In the case of neoliberalism this bundle of ideas revolves around the supposed naturalness of 'the market', the primacy of the competitive individual, the superiority of the private over the public. It is as a result of the hegemony of this bundle of ideas – their being the ruling common sense – that the settlement as a whole is commonly called 'neoliberal'. But while commitment to neoliberal economic theory is a key part of the overall consensus, it is also the case that the theory itself plays a crucial role in legitimising the restoration and reinvigoration of a regime of power, profit and privilege.

As we have seen, the rubrics of neoliberalism, embedded in a common sense that has enrolled whole populations materially and imaginatively into a financialised and marketised view of the world, are implemented when they serve those interests and are blithely ignored when they do not (the bail-out of the banks being only the most recent and egregious example). Likewise its attacks on the state and on notions of the public are propelled not just out of a belief in an economic theory but from the hope that they will lead to the reopening of areas for potential profit-making through commodification. This drive to expand the sphere of accumulation has been crucial to the restoration of the old powers.

ORIGINS AND EXPLANATIONS

Neoliberalism has its origins in eighteenth-century liberal political theory and political economy, from where it derives its touchstones. It has been revamped and reworked to be appropriate to these times and geographies, and it is multiple in form in reflection of these expanded geographies. But its core propositions, of the free possessive individual engaging with others through market transactions, remain the touchstone. From the very beginning these propositions were the product of class interests – in the UK in the eighteenth century, of the rising agrarian, commercial, and later manufacturing, bourgeoisies. The attempt has always been to present them as eternal truths – concepts of markets and individuals being merely descriptive of an ideal state of nature. That this was not so has been demonstrated over centuries, as the 'free market' and the free-standing individual have had to be actively produced and imposed. Whether through Acts of Enclosure, impositions of 'structural adjustment', military interventions or attacks on public expenditure, market societies are products of intervention (and often by states).

That market forces are imposed on some but not others has been true since the colonial metropole's 'free-labour' regimes were harnessed by the imperial system to the 'forced-labour' of plantation slavery. This contradiction became more evident when they collided in the slave revolts and the struggles over Abolition. Market forces are never universally imposed. There is no such thing as a fully marketised system. Capitalism relies on monopolies and 'socialised' risk, and on spheres that exist outside the logic of its operations – including that of the reproduction of people, and the natural world. Free wage-labour has always been augmented by unfree forms of exploitation such as serfdom, slavery, bondage, indenture, peonage. These mark the limits of 'the market's' generalisability.

Indeed, much of what has gone on through globalisation over the last thirty years resonates with events in late eighteenth-century and early nineteenth-century England, when industrial and urbanised capitalism was first finding its form. The expulsion from their land of millions in the global South recalls the enclosures of the commons. The vast migrations to the ever-expanding cities are like the migrations of earlier industrialisations (these within-nation migrations being just as socially disruptive and potentially explosive as migrations between nations). There is the creation of a vast new force of 'free labourers' with all the personal and social wrenchings (as well as new freedoms) that that can entail, and the further commodification of land and labour. International migration itself (in part a result of all of these developments and their attendant geographically uneven ramifications) represents the creation of a free global labour force – just as the age of the Swing rioters and of Peterloo saw the creation of a national labour market in Britain.

Meanwhile, looking as it were in the opposite direction, from the UK outwards, while successive governments hang pathetically on to the coat-tails of a USA whose economic hegemony is itself under challenge from China and the other BRIC countries, the City of London – again building on its long assumption of supremacy, but now thoroughly internationalised and one of the fountainheads of neoliberalism – has found itself, at least for a while, a new imperial role.

Neoliberalism's project, then, is a reassertion of capital's historic imperative to profit – through financialisation, globalisation and yet further commodification.

CAUSES AND COMPLEXITIES

It is never easy to define what is cause and what is effect in conjunctures of this kind. There are legitimate differences of view about the causal emphasis that should be allotted to ideological, political and material factors, or the weight that should be given to the conscious actions of social classes versus the dynamic attributes of social structures. The picture is never simple. It is certainly true that class interests have been active in imposing neoliberalism on the world, and now refuse to concede the relative gains of the past three decades; and it is also the case that classes have shared economic interests – both those that are particular to specific sectors (for example, agriculture or manufacture), and those that are general – concerning the maintenance of stability and a favourable climate in which to 'do business'.

However, the shift in economic and social power over the decades since the 1970s was not driven by a single motor. The economic is critical; but it cannot determine everything – even 'in the last instance', as Althusser famously argued. Any given conjuncture represents, rather, the fusion 'into a ruptural unity' of an ensemble of economic, social, political and ideological factors where 'dissimilar currents ... heterogeneous class interests ... contrary political and social strivings' fuse.[2] What has come together in the current neoliberal conjuncture includes class and other social interests, new institutional arrangements, the exercise of excessive influence by private corporations over democratic processes, political developments such as the recruitment of New Labour to the neoliberal consensus, the effects of legitimising ideologies and a quasi-religious belief in the 'hidden hand', and the self-propelling virtues of 'the market'.

Classes are also formations with complex internal compositions that change over historical time. Those among whom neoliberalism became the dominant tendency now constitute a global class that includes – alongside older echelons – the world's leading industrialists and businesspeople, CEOs of the great corporate firms, the new transnational, trans-ethnic speculators, directors of large financial institutions, hedge-fund operators, venture capitalists, as well as the senior executives who manage the system and have a major stake in its success. We must add, too, the key but subaltern archipelago of consultants, marketing experts, public relations people, lawyers, creative accountants and tax-avoidance experts whose fortunes are tied to its success. No doubt the huge privileges and immunities won by this formation explain why they seem so morally denuded, impervious to any sense of a wider community or responsibility for their actions, and completely lacking in any understanding of how ordinary people live. Their resistance to reform has been obdurate, their greed brazen. They reward themselves extravagantly, while insisting that 'we are all in this together', and that their real purpose is 'serving customers' and 'corporate responsibility', not protecting their own interests.

Of course, the term class interests does not imply that classes are monolithic, that they appear on the political stage as unified actors, or are fully conscious of their interests and pursue them rationally. There are important conflicts of interest (for instance in the UK between, say, those of finance capital and those of small businesses, northern manufacturing and small farmers). These real contradictions may offer political opportunities. Furthermore, interests are always open to conflicting ideological interpretations, and their redefinition can have political effects.

Nor is economic class the only salient social division. Gender, racial, ethnic and sexual divisions long predate the birth of capitalism, and still structure social relations in distinctive ways. They have their own binary categories (male/female, masculine/feminine, straight/gay, religious/secular, colonial/metropolitan, civilised/barbarian), and they figure differently from class in the distribution of social and symbolic goods (though they are articulated to class). They 'manage' their own systems of reward and scarcity (paid/unpaid, legitimacy/ illegitimacy, normal/abnormal, saved/damned). They position the bodies of their subjects differently in the Nature/Culture continuum. They 'govern' different moments of the life-cycle and attribute to people different subjective capacities (paternal/maternal, emotional/ cognitive, duty/pleasure).

These social divisions each have privileged sites of operation (for example, home/workplace, private/public) and distinct disciplinary regimes (patriarchal power, property inheritance, unpaid domestic labour, control of sexuality, gendered and racially-differentiated wage rates). They deploy different modes of oppression (religious persecution, social and sexual discrimination, racialisation). They construct their own hierarchies of 'othering' and belonging, via discrimination, stereotyping, prejudicial speech, inferiorisation, marginalisation, abjection, projection, fantasying and fetishisation. When these social divisions operate within a capitalist system, they are, of course, profoundly shaped by it and articulated to it. But they retain their 'relative autonomy'. This requires us to rethink social relations from another perspective (for instance reframing the exploitation of labour in production from the perspective of the reproduction of social labour, which is heavily gendered). These divisions have been reworked through the present settlement, sometimes being reinforced and sometimes refashioned in ambiguous ways.

Thus, a general social and political heterogeneity is evident in the protest movements against the austerity cuts. They have been spearheaded in Britain by professional organisations as well as by the unions. New social movements like UK Uncut, Feminist Fightback or Occupy are characterised by complex class, gender and ethnic composition. The Green Party provides a bridge between environmental movements and mainstream politics. Mobilising resistance thus requires alliances of a sort which only a multi-focused political strategy can hope to construct.

COMMON SENSE, IDENTITY, AND CULTURE

Ideology plays a key role in disseminating, legitimising and re-invigorating a regime of power, profit and privilege. Neoliberal ideas seem to have sedimented into the western imaginary and become embedded in popular 'common sense'. They set the parameters – provide the 'taken-for-granteds' – of public discussion, media debate and popular calculation.

Not all of this, though, is specific to the neoliberal settlement of recent decades. Even during the redistributivist welfare state, the basic tenets of free-market capitalism were not fundamentally challenged. Redistribution transformed the lives of millions, but its project remained ameliorative. The very language of politics revealed this: we 'intervened' (i.e. took conscious social action) into 'markets' (i.e. the naturally pregiven state of affairs).

One key strand in neoliberalism's ideological armoury is neoliberal economic theory itself. So 'naturalised' have its nostrums become that policies can claim to be implemented with popular consent, though they are manifestly partial and limited. Opening public areas for potential profit-making is accepted because it appears to be 'just economic common sense'. The ethos of the 'free market' is taken to licence an increasing disregard for moral standards, and even for the law itself. Commercialisation has cultivated an ethos of corruption and evasiveness. Banks, once beacons of probity, rig interest rates, mis-sell products, launder drug money, flout international embargoes, hide away fortunes in safe havens. They settle their 'misdemeanours' for huge sums that hardly dent their balance sheets. Similarly, when private firms that have been publicly contracted fail to meet targets they are allowed to continue. Graduates stacking supermarket shelves are told they don't need to be paid because they are 'getting work experience'. Commercialisation permeates everywhere, trumps everything. Once the imperatives of a 'market culture' become entrenched, anything goes. Such is the power of the hegemonic common sense.

But it is a common sense that has to be produced and maintained. The capture of political influence by corporate wealth and power serves to maintain their hold over the political process and state institutions (as in the phone-hacking/*News International* scandals). Corporate ownership of dominant sectors of the media gives capital sway over the means and strategies of representation: the retinue of CEOs, public relations people and lobbyists who haunt the TV studios to reassure us that 'things have been put in place to prevent it happening again', have guaranteed access, and function as the primary definers of reality. Contrary views have a more fleeting visibility. A few intrepid journalists do an impressive job of unmasking, but the media more generally seems to find itself thinking within the groove of the prevailing neoliberal orthodoxies. Even where 'balance' is provided, this rarely questions the prevailing terms of debate, and there is usually a reluctance to pursue with any rigour the serious issues involved.

The ideology of competitive individualism has also been imposed via the stigmatisation of the so-called 'undeserving' poor. 'Welfare scroungers', who cannot provide for themselves through their own efforts, are labelled morally deficient – 'idlers who prefer a lie-in to work', 'living on benefits as a "life-style" choice'. Similarly, everyone – parents, students, clients, patients, taxpayers, citizens – is expected to think of themselves as consumers of 'products' that will bring them individual economic advantage, rather than as social beings satisfying a human need, producing something of use, or participating in an experience of learning from which others as well as themselves may benefit. In these ways, neoliberalism has been engaged in constructing new entrepreneurial identities and re-engineering the bourgeois subject.

Looking at the broader cultural picture, we detect similar tendencies: in consumer and celebrity cultures, the drive for instant gratification, the fantasies of success, the fetishisation of technology, the triumph of 'life-style' over substance, the endless refashioning of the 'self', the commercialisation of 'identity' and the utopias of self-sufficiency. These 'soft' forms of power are as effective in changing social attitudes as are 'hard' forms of power such as legislation to restrict strikes.

It is the reassertion of the powers of capital that has produced the neoliberal world as we know it today, as its agents have taken command of the new circuits of global capital. The widening of inequalities is the main launch-pad of this restoration bid. And this has put into question the long-promised transfer of income, power and responsibility from rich to poor, men to women, centre to margin. Countervailing values – equality, democracy and citizenship – have been circumvented, and dissenting social forces fragmented and dispersed. The reinvigorated finance sector has been articulated with a new imperialism. These 'victories' are flaunted in brash material form – each new high-rise a middle finger raised.

THE FUTURE OF THE CRISIS

This phase of free-market capitalism has now entered a serious economic crisis from which it cannot easily engineer an exit. But the shape of the crisis remains 'economic'. There are so far no major political fractures, no unsettlings of ideological hegemony, no ruptures in popular discourse. The disastrous effects of the crisis are clearly evident; but there is little understanding of how everyday troubles connect to wider structures. There is no serious crisis of ideas. Indeed the crisis has been exploited as a further opportunity to reinforce the very neoliberal narrative that has led to the system's implosion, and to push its project even further. Neoliberals dogmatically insist that it was the 'restraints' on, not the excesses of, the market that bear the responsibility for its manifest failure. Extensive work, backed by daunting resources, has gone into securing consent to this version of events. There are forensically targeted attacks on groups like Occupy London, the very unpretentiousness of whose tents, huddled between the monumental edifices of Mammon and God, gave it symbolic power. Its questions resonated. It had to go.

And yet, there is no hegemonic closure – hegemonies, even the neoliberal one, are never totally secure. Materially, the cuts bite deep and hard, and there are more to come. There is growing distress, discontent, de-politicisation, scepticism and loss of confidence in the political class. The distress is palpable. But people feel puzzled about where to go next. Polls suggest that the drive for privatisation has not won the day: but are egalitarianism and social collectivism still alive and well? There is a sense that something is wrong with a system which distributes wealth in a 1% – 99% way. Politicians feel obliged to reassure the public daily that the cuts are 'fair'. There are other such resonances in popular consciousness. But who is nurturing them?

Farther afield, in Europe, there is popular dissent, opposition to austerity strategies and support for 'growth-and-jobs' alternatives. There is the democratic awakening of the 'Arab Spring' and, in Latin America, explicit challenges to neoliberal hegemony. Hegemonies are never completed projects: they are always in contention. There are always cracks and contradictions – and therefore opportunities.

However, in the UK, Labour, the official opposition, is in serious difficulties. It leads in the polls but it is not yet winning hearts and minds. It shuttles between conflicting ways forward. It seems afraid of its own (left) shadow, in hock to the old Blairite rump and a belief in the conservatism of the electorate, trapped in parliamentary rituals, mesmerised by electoral politics. It has been rendered speechless by the charge that it opened the door through which the Coalition is triumphantly marching. It seems unable to draw a clear line in the sand: a political frontier. It makes effective tactical interventions but appears tongue-tied when invited to enunciate an alternative set of principles, to outline a strategic political approach or to sketch out a compelling alternative vision.

A 'MANIFESTO' BY INSTALMENTS

Our purpose is to set out an agenda of ideas for a progressive political project which transcends the limitations of conventional thinking as to what it is 'reasonable' to propose or do. We will try to open a debate which goes beyond matters of electoral feasibility, or of what 'the markets' will tolerate. Electoral change *is* urgent, critical and necessary: but it will not change much if it means a continuation of the existing assumptions under a different name. As to practicality – 'what works affects lives' – yes, but there must be a fundamental break with the pragmatic calculations which disfigure current political thinking. It is the maps, not the facts, which have disintegrated. The neoliberal order itself needs to be called into question, and radical alternatives to its foundational assumptions put forward for discussion. Our analysis suggests that this is a moment for changing the terms of debate, reformulating positions, taking the longer view, making a leap.

For us, this is not a question of restoring the tried remedies of the post-war welfare-state settlement. Of course, that would not be an altogether bad place to start. But that compromise, for all its attempt to achieve a different balance of values and power from that dictated by markets, nevertheless accepted that the market sectors should still be left essentially free to generate profits, while a public system managed by elected governments would merely be allowed to redistribute some of the ensuing resources, and provide for some social needs which markets would otherwise neglect. (And by the 1970s, as the left itself argued, some of the other flaws of the welfare settlement, for example the state's frequent paternalism and lack of responsiveness, were contributing to the ebbing away of support.) The rise and crisis of neoliberalism should have taught us that that historical solution was not radical enough. In any case the political conditions of existence of the previous social democratic settlement are no longer operative. Debating how and why the terms of reference have changed is certainly worth doing. But such debate will only be fruitful if new transitional demands, framed in the light of the analysis of contemporary global realities, point us further ahead.

NOTES

1. Regular *Soundings* readers will recognise that this is a case we have been developing for some time. For more background to these arguments see *The Neoliberal Crisis*, Lawrence & Wishart 2015.
2. Louis Althusser, *For Marx*, Verso 1969, Part 3, 'Contradiction and Overdetermination', p99.

1. VOCABULARIES OF THE ECONOMY

Dorren Massey

A t an art exhibition last summer, I engaged in a very interesting conversation with one of the young people employed by the gallery. As she turned to walk off I saw she had on the back of her t-shirt 'Customer Liaison'. I felt flat. Our whole conversation seemed somehow reduced, my experience of it belittled into one of commercial transaction; my relation to the gallery and to this engaging person had become one of market exchange. The very language positioned us, the gallery, and our relationship, in a very particular way.

We know about this practice, and its potential effects, in many arenas. On trains and buses, and sometimes in hospitals and universities too, we have become customers, not passengers, readers, patients or students. In all these cases a specific activity and relationship is erased by a general relationship of buying and selling that is given precedence over it.

The language we use has effects in moulding identities and characterising social relationships. It is crucial to the formation of the ideological scaffolding of the hegemonic common sense. Discourse matters. Moreover it changes, and it can – through political work – be changed. We have been *enjoined* to become consumers rather than workers, customers where once we were passengers. (And indeed the process is never complete. The young person in the gallery had no choice but to wear this t-shirt, but our conversation was nonetheless authentic and engaged, even to the extent of overflowing our assigned roles – maybe even resisting them.) The point is that attempts to mould our identities through language and naming take political work, and may be contested. In the 1950s the adjective 'public' (worker, sector, sphere) designated something to be respected and relied upon. It had, if only vaguely, something to do with our collectivity. It took a labour of persistent denigration of 'the public' to turn things around. And that labour has been crucial to the ability to pursue the economic strategies we are currently enduring. 'Equality' too was once a term to be used with unquestioned positivity; under New Labour the very word became unsayable. And so on.

The vocabulary we use, to talk about the economy in particular, has been crucial to the establishment of neoliberal hegemony.

There is a whole world view – and economic theory – behind that meeting in the gallery. It is one in which the majority of us are primarily consumers, whose prime duty (and source of power and pleasure) is to make choices.

The so-called truth underpinning this change of descriptions – which has been brought about in everyday life through managerial instruction and the thoroughgoing renaming of institutional practices in their allowed forms of writing, address and speech – is that, in the end, individual interests are the only reality that matters; that those interests are purely monetary; and that so-called values are only a means of pursuing selfish ends by other means. And behind this in turn, the theoretical justification of this now nearly-dominant system is the idea of a world of independent agents whose choices, made for their own advantage, paradoxically benefit all. Moreover, for this to 'work' no individual agent can have sufficient power to determine what happens to the whole.

That the world is not like that is evident. There are monopolies and vastly differential powers. There is far more to life than individual self interest. Markets in practice need vast apparatuses of regulation, propping-up and policing – a 'bureaucracy' indeed. Moreover, this privileging of self interest, market relations and choice in each sphere of economic and social life leads inexorably to increased inequality. And this now glaring inequality (globally as well as intranationally) is protected from political contest by another shift in our vocabulary. Every liberal democratic society needs to negotiate some kind of articulation between the liberal tradition and the democratic tradition. In our present society that articulation is quite specific: 'liberty' has come to be defined simply as self interest and freedom from restraint by the state, and that reduced form of liberty has become so much the dominant term that the resultant inequalities have eviscerated democracy, and the vocabulary of equality has been obscured from view. Much has been written elsewhere about all these things.

Our argument here is that this vocabulary of customer, consumer, choice, markets and self interest moulds both our conception of ourselves and our understanding of and relationship to the world. These 'descriptions' of roles, exchanges and relationships in terms of a presumption that individual choice and self interest does and should prevail are in fact not simply descriptions but a powerful means by which new subjectivities are constructed and enforced. Gramsci's understanding of the significance of 'common sense', Althusser's theory of ideological state apparatuses and the 'interpellation' of subjects, and Foucault's descriptions of discourses as aspects of 'governmentality' are theoretical resources through which these phenomena can be recognised and understood.

The new dominant ideology is inculcated through social practices, as well as through prevailing names and descriptions. The mandatory exercise of 'free choice' – of a GP, of a hospital to which to be referred, of schools for one's children, of a form of treatment – is, whatever its particular value, also a lesson in social identity, affirming on each occasion that one is above all a consumer, functioning in a market.

By such means we are enrolled, such self-identification being just as strong as our material entanglement in debt, pensions, mortgages and the like. It is an internalisation of 'the system' that can potentially corrode our ability to imagine that things could be otherwise.

This question of identity and identification, moreover, goes beyond our individual subjectivities. *Everything* begins to be imagined in this way. The very towns and cities we live in are branded in order to contend against each other, including internationally, in a world in which the only relationships are ones of competition.

So, the vocabularies which have reclassified roles, identities and relationships – of people, places and institutions – and the practices which enact them embody and enforce the ideology of neoliberalism, and thus a new capitalist hegemony. Another set of vocabularies provides the terms through which the system describes itself and its functions. These frame the categories – for example of production, consumption, land, labour, capital, wealth – through which the 'economy' (as a supposedly distinct and autonomous sphere of life) is understood. These definitions constitute another element of 'common sense' – about the way the economic world 'naturally' is and must remain.

THE NAMES OF THE SYSTEM

What are the key terms in this system of definitions, and how do they work? Here it is useful to think about bundles of ideas.

There is, for instance, a bundle around *wealth, output, growth* and *work*. The economic system is assumed to be about what we call wealth-creation, and the achievement of 'growth'. Growth is measured by the increase in 'gross national product', which is an aggregated sum of everything produced in the economy, whether made within the private or public sectors. It is usually cited as a percentage rate of change, often on an annual basis. The dominant conception is that it is the well-being of individuals and society alike (in so far as these are clearly distinguished as values or entities) that is denoted by these terms. Apart from the ongoing debate about anomalies in how these things are measured, there has also been, thanks to the achievements of social democracy, some recognition that increases in aggregate wealth are by themselves an insufficient measure of well-being, given that the fruits of growth are not distributed equally. But social democrats have traditionally confined their ambitions to altering the balance of distributions – between what is called the private and the public, the market and the state systems – while not seriously questioning the dominant architecture of the system.

We argue that this dominant architecture now needs to be called in question. The whole vocabulary we use to talk about the economy, while presented as a description of the natural and the eternal, is in fact a political construction that needs contesting.

Let us focus for a moment on the example of *growth*, currently deemed to be the entire aim of our economy. To produce growth and then (maybe) to redistribute some of it has been a goal shared by neoliberalism and social democracy. But this approach must now be questioned. Why?

In the first place, there is what might be seen as a technical problem – at least for the social democratic argument that growth allows mitigation of inequality through redistribution. In the case of the British economy and probably more widely, there is in the immediate future likely to be insufficient growth to enable the degree of redistribution desired by a progressive agenda (or at least not without major political confrontation). A return to the redistributive model of social democracy of decades past is therefore impossible. This model, in its crudest formulation, entailed providing the conditions for the market sector to produce growth and to accept that this would result in inequality (though it should also be noted that different models of growth produce different degrees of inequality – the model we have in the UK at the moment being acutely inegalitarian). The role of the state was then, through taxation, the provision of public services and so on, to redistribute some portion of this growth in order to help repair the inequality resulting from its production.

This is anyway a bizarre arrangement. It institutes a curious sequentialism – first produce a problem, then try to solve it. (Why produce the problem – inequality – in the first place?) This does nothing to question the inequality-producing mechanisms of market-exchange (though of course some restraints have been introduced). Indeed, this arrangement has meant that the main lines of struggle are focused on distributional issues, rather than the nature of the system. Moreover, the very success of even this restricted distributional struggle was one of the reasons for the breakdown of the arrangement. As we pointed out in the Framing Statement, the gains made by labour under social democracy proved intolerable to capital and a backlash was launched. Even mere redistribution could only be allowed to go so far. And one crucial element in that neoliberal backlash was the dislodging of the common sense which underpinned these aspects of the social democratic approach – in particular the commitment to (a measure of) equality and the important role of the state and public intervention – and indeed the very notion of the public – in achieving this. Changing our economic language was crucial in shifting our world-view.

The fact that the neoliberal successor to this social democratic model has now run into its own crises provides an opportunity for a new imagining. As already said, rates of growth are likely to be insufficient to reinstate the previous arrangements. Moreover the whole ideological and political – and discursive – climate has changed so much that a return to the previous model would be difficult to pull off. It would in fact be no greater a task to argue for a new model altogether – one in which the workings of the economy did not in the first place produce a level of inequality that demanded subsequent correction.[1] Certainly it would involve a more thoroughgoing, and popular, critique of market forces as producers of inequality. It would also mean arguing again for the vocabulary, and politics, of equality. Some new vocabulary is indeed already emerging – though not the most easy on the ear or on popular imaginings – 'predistribution'. The word may be awkward, but if it is pointing to the need to design a system of production which, in its own very workings, is not productive of intolerable levels of inequality, then it is on the right track.

A second reason why our current notion of wealth, and our commitment to its growth, must be questioned – certainly in the global North – is to do with our relation to the planet. The environmental damage – in particular but not only through climate change – brought about by the pursuit of growth threatens to cause a catastrophe of which we are already witnessing intimations. This is a global issue in which relatively rich, though unequal, societies such as the United Kingdom have international responsibilities. The UK on occasions prides itself on its relative greenness. But to the extent that there has been any improvement it has resulted from the closure of coal mines (not pursued for environmental reasons!) and – even more – from the outsourcing of our manufacturing. If, as we argued in the Framing Statement, one stimulus to globalisation was capital's desire to escape the demands of 'First World' labour, then one of its results has been a shift in the geography of the production of pollution to the global South. China, among others, now produces goods that would once have been made in the UK, and which we still need (or anyway want). But the dominant voices criticise China for its pollution; and official statistics do not even count the energy used and the environmental damage done, by the transport across the world to our shores of everything from machinery to pet food to Christmas decorations. Meanwhile there exists an export trade in the toxic wastes that we do produce to countries so impoverished they are prepared to deal with it for us.

Of course much of the change in the global South derives from the increasing industrialisation and wealth of a few of its constituent countries. Yet it is argued that in no foreseeable technology could the planet cope with everyone living at the standards now common in the global North. Who then must change?

Moreover, environmental destruction and the catastrophes consequent upon climate change will not fall evenly across the world. Probably such ills will fall most quickly, and most heavily, on more impoverished places, which in any case have fewer resources with which to offset such damage. The prospect is a nightmare of potential famines, forced migrations, social disorganisation and wars.

Finally, there is perhaps an even deeper question. We now know that increased wealth, when it is measured in the standard monetary terms of today, has few actual consequences for people's feelings of well-being, once there is a sufficiency to meet basic needs. In pursuing 'growth' in these terms, as a means to realise people's life-goals and desires, economies pursue a chimera since, while growth may occur, all the evidence is that our levels of satisfaction with our lives remain obstinately static. Indeed, insofar as the dominant model of growth leads to increased inequalities, as it does, we now know also that it is a prime generator of ill health, crime, and social suffering, compared with what might be the case in a more equal and fair society. There is increasing unease with a concept of wealth, and of gross national product, measured only in monetary terms. It was widely questioned in particular at that moment of the implosion into financial crisis, when all the talk was of disaster brought about by competitive greed. Even David Cameron mused that there was more to life than GDP. That moment has been lost, but deeper dissatisfactions surely rumble on. And they cannot be addressed by adding something warm and cuddly on to the GDP; the problem is structural. Can we redefine wealth to include riches that go beyond the individual and the monetary? Might we not ask the question, in the end, 'What is an economy for?' What do we want it to provide?

We could take this line of questioning, and its provocation to re-imagining, in many directions – and we hope that readers will participate in doing so.

'Work' is another area within this cluster of ideas around wealth-creation and growth that is in need of new words and new imaginations. There are many aspects to this. For instance, and most obviously, there is the question of what counts as work. Where only transactions for money are recognised as belonging to 'the economy', the vast amount of unpaid labour – as conducted for instance in families and local areas – goes uncounted. This is a major gender issue too. Childcare provided in exchange for a wage counts towards the national income, while childcare provided by parents or neighbours or grandparents does not. In its Industrial Strategy of the 1980s the Greater London Council found that a substantial proportion of the labour performed in the capital was unpaid – and this was labour that was necessary for the social reproduction of the city. This is a question of recognition, of the way we think of the economy as a part of society, and of valuing what it takes for a society to be reproduced.

Moreover, beyond even this, we would like to question that familiar instrumental categorisation of the economy as a space in which people reluctantly undertake unwelcome and unpleasing 'work', in return for material rewards which they can then consume. Indeed, this view of 'work', to be traded off against 'leisure', is required by the neoclassical economic theory that currently holds sway (as though paid work and leisure is all of our days, so that the other – unpaid – things that we have, and want, to do in life thus once again disappear from view). But it is a view that misunderstands where pleasure and fulfilment in human lives are in reality found. Work is usually, and certainly should be, not a liability and a sacrifice, but a central source of meaning and fulfilment in human lives. This is widely recognised in the anguish felt when work is absent, for example when, as in many countries today, up to half the population of young people can find no employment. And it is seen in the higher rates of sickness and mortality which are associated statistically with retirement from work. This is in part because it is through work that people develop and express their capabilities as human beings. And also because work is a principal way in which people maintain connections with their worlds, both in immediate ways (through relations with co-workers or those for whose well-being work is done) and in more abstract but nevertheless meaningful terms, such as in making a contribution to the good of others, which then gives moral sense to the benefits which are obtained in return. Work, as earlier generations of socialists once understood, has – or could have – moral and creative (or aesthetic) values at its core. It is misunderstood by the dominant discourse, in which it is assigned merely self-regarding and possessive purposes. A rethinking of this could lead us to address more creatively both the social relations of work and the division of labour (a better sharing of the tedious work, and of the skills) within society.

A second bundle of terms that deserves further attention is that clustered around *investment, expenditure* and *speculation*. It should be noted immediately, for this is crucial to what follows, that these terms carry with them implicit moral connotations. Investment implies an action, even a sacrifice, undertaken for a better future, while speculation (here in the financial rather than intellectual sense) immediately arouses a sense of mistrust. And while investment evokes a future positive outcome, expenditure seems merely an outgoing, a cost, a burden.

Investment and *expenditure* are distinguished from each other according to a strict economic rationale, a distinction required by the way in which the national accounts are set up. But this distinction is cross-cut in popular parlance and ordinary political debate by another understanding. Together they produce rich soil for the construction of political attitudes. Thus, in the national accounts, investment is money laid out for physical things such as buildings and infrastructure, while expenditure is money used to pay – for instance – for the wages of people operating the services for which the investment provides the physical possibility. So building a new school is investment, paying the teachers, the administrators and the dinner ladies is expenditure. (Pause for a moment, and ponder the gender implications of this distinction.)

This distinction, moreover, is often cross-cut with another – that between public and private. On this understanding, money advanced by a private firm to further its profit-making intentions is seen as a worthwhile investment, while money advanced by the state, whether for infrastructure or for employment in schools or the health service, is seen as only increasing the deficit, because it is paid for out of taxation.

The political effect of the combining of these definitions is devastating. Thus, for instance, while building new houses or railways through taxation may be seen as investment by the first distinction, paying for doctors, social-service workers, teachers, nurses, street-cleaners, dinner ladies – when this is done by the public purse – is seen on both definitions as merely a cost. Paying for them through taxation, therefore, emphatically carries the connotation of being simply a burden. But if we return to that question 'what is an economy *for*?', and if we answer that it has something to do with the reproduction of a society, then this vocabulary is misleading (to say the least). Education is equally then an investment, generating the capacities on which a society depends. Likewise, the provision of health and social services more generally is one of the most valuable and essential forms of production and investment there can be.

And crucial to maintaining these things within the public sector (thus taking on the second distinction, between public and private) is challenging the persistent characterisation of taxation as a negative thing. 'Everyone hates paying taxes don't they?' But people lay out money in the market sector seemingly without a second thought, including for things they could perfectly well get through the state, and it seems not to incur such opprobrium. Private transactions – OK; taxation for social investment and services – almost universally resented. What is in contention here is social solidarity; the knee-jerk language reflects – and reinforces – the prioritisation of individual choice over collectivity, over the very notion of (the construction of) a society. Words and oft-repeated phrases carry, and reinforce, understandings that go well beyond them.

These questionings of our vocabularies are perhaps obvious. But we need to *argue* them. The existing vocabulary is one of the roots of the elite's ability to maintain the horrible straitjacket we are in.

Moreover, there is one distinction we should be making a lot more strongly: that between *investment* and *speculation*. Or, perhaps more properly put, between value creation and value extraction. The term 'investment' is widely used in the media for both activities. So when businesses put money into plant and machinery, or research or staff development, it is called investment. And when finance is put into buying something that already exists (an asset) – commodity futures, fine wines, already-existing property … – that is also called, conventionally, investment. But in the first type of case the money goes into a process of value creation; in the second there is no such process – the 'investor' just holds the asset in the hope that the price will rise, and then will sell it at a profit. This is, on other occasions, called speculation. It is not the creation of value but the extraction of value from the pool that already exists. Its effect, therefore, is not the expansion of the pool but its redistribution, towards (if prices rise) those who purchase the assets.

The above is a very rough and ready distinction, and the difference is anyway not absolute, but the broad contrast is important for us to address at this moment because much of what lies behind the recent decades of neoliberalism, in addition to the predation of the public sector by the private, is this buying and selling of already-existing assets, and indeed the creation of new ones in which to speculate – derivatives and various forms of the commodification of risk, carbon futures.

Again we can take this further. For the obfuscation of the difference between value creation and value extraction helps obscure another one: that between *earned* and *unearned income*. As Andrew Sayer wryly observes, 'Interestingly, [this is a distinction that] has fallen out of use just when unearned income has expanded'.[2] Unearned income derives, not from participation in the production of goods and services (value creation) but from controlling an already-existing asset. And it is the latter that has formed the economic basis of the rise, under neoliberalism, of the super-rich. It has not been as a result of participation in production that they have gained their wealth. (The idea that the City is a centre of wealth-creation is thus bizarre – it is more a centre of a system of wealth-extraction that spans the world.) In this sense much of the new economic elite is parasitic, extracting value from the rest of society. They are 'rentiers' – here too we need to reclaim and revitalise our vocabulary. And many in the upper-middle strata of rich societies have been drawn into this as well – through house-price rises (unearned, and in the UK greatly exacerbating not only general inequality but also the North-South divide), and through pensions (invested in secondary share-markets). And so material interest melds with misleading economic vocabulary to further the transformation of common sense, to fortify a financialised ideology, and to pacify many into at least acquiescence if not enthusiasm.

The results of all of this have included a massive redistribution from poor to rich, a significant contribution to a rise in food prices and malnutrition around the world, property booms, the underpinning of a new financial imperialism and, of course, instability and crash, with their repercussions around the world, as the speculative bubbles burst. Moreover this extraction of value has reduced the ability of the rest of the economy to pursue value creation. And we should note that the City of London, seen as the centrepiece of the UK economy, was a prime mover in all of this.

These are important economic, and political, distinctions. The rise in the significance of the trading of assets has been central to the financialisation of national and global economies. It relates too to that erasure of activities other than those of exchange – whether that be creating goods and services, being passengers on a train, or visiting an art gallery. All that is necessary in this (their) world is to buy and to sell. The naturalisation of this, through financialisation, as the essential nature of economic activity, has thus been a crucial element in the establishing of a new common sense. Indeed, as Mariana Mazzucato has argued, 'the battle against the excesses of the financial sector will remain lost without a theory able to distinguish when profits move from being a result of value creation, to [being] ... a result of value extraction'.[3]

THE (SUPPOSED) NATURALNESS OF MARKETS

Underpinning the apparent common sense of these elements of our economic vocabulary (and there are many more) is the understanding that markets are natural: that as either external to society or inherent in 'human nature', they are a pre-given force. The assumption is all around us. There is the language that is used to describe the financial markets as they roam Europe attacking country after country – an external force, a wild beast maybe, certainly not the product of particular social strata and their economic and political interests. There is the understanding of 'human nature' and of the long histories of human societies as 'naturally' – as part of their very nature – given to market trading (and that therefore markets are the best way of organising societies) – an understanding beautifully demolished by Karl Polanyi in *The Great Transformation* as long ago as 1944, but still living on as an effective underpinning of political discourse. There is that shrug of resignation and powerlessness by ordinary folk as something happens that they do not like: 'well, it's the market I suppose, isn't it'. A 'thing' one cannot gainsay. There is the idea that we 'intervene' (social action) into the economy (equated with the market and seen as an external nature). There is, within the academy itself, the pretension on the part of neoclassical economics to be a natural, or physical, science, rather than a social science. The degree to which these ideas, this ideological scaffolding, currently infuse the hegemonic common sense is astonishing. The assumption that markets are natural is so deeply rooted in the structure of thought, certainly here in Europe, that even the fact that it is an assumption seems to have been lost to view. This is real hegemony.

And it has effects. It removes 'the economic' from the sphere of political and ideological contestation. It turns it into a matter for experts and technocrats. It removes the economy from democratic control.

This assumption of the naturalness of markets is crucial to the insistence that There Is No Alternative. It is one of the ghastly ironies of the present neoliberal age that we are told (as we saw at the outset of this argument) that much of our power and our pleasure, and our very self-identification, lies in our ability to choose (and we are indeed bombarded every day by 'choices', many of them meaningless, others we wish we didn't have to make), while at the level that really matters – what kind of society we'd like to live in, what kind of future we'd like to build – we are told, implacably, that, give or take a few minor variations, there is no alternative – no choice at all.

At the international level too the same kind of language is deployed, aiming for the same effects. Thus, that common-sense sequence of 'underdeveloped – developing – developed' places 'developing' countries behind 'developed' ones, in some kind of historical queue, rather than as co-existing in their differences. It thereby – and not coincidentally – obscures the many ways in which the 'developed' countries restrict the potential of the so-called developing (the power-relations within neoliberal globalisation for instance) and implies that there is only one possible historical path, which all must follow.

We are not arguing that there is no place for markets in a reformed economy. What we are challenging is the special status our current imaginings endow them with. We should be thinking of 'the economy' not in terms of natural force and intervention but in terms of a whole variety of social relations that need some kind of coordination. Each form of social relation has its own characteristics and implications, and thus appropriateness to different parts of the economy and society. Above all, we need to bring 'the economic' back into society and into political contention, and not just as debates about economic policy, but questioning also the very way we *think about* the economy in the first place. Without doing this we shall find ourselves always arguing on the political terrain of existing economic policy. For something new to be imagined, let alone to be born, our current economic 'common sense' needs to be challenged root and branch.

Thanks to Sue Himmelweit for talking some of these issues through with me.

NOTES

1. Other chapters of the Manifesto develop thoughts about economic strategy.
2. A. Sayer, 'Facing the challenge of the return of the rich', in W. Atkinson, S. Roberts and M. Savage (eds), *Class inequality in austerity Britain*, Palgrave Macmillan 2012.
3. Mariana Mazzucato, 'From bubble to bubble', *The Guardian*, 16.1.13.

2. A RELATIONAL SOCIETY

Michael Rustin

In the previous Manifesto chapter we described the ways in which vocabularies of the economy – the ways in which it is conceived and described in the dominant discourse of 'free markets' – give rise to misleading and false conceptions of the good. We have argued that the present economic order is in many respects destructive to well-being, and is fast becoming unsustainable in its own terms, because of its propensity to crisis, and because of the burden it places on planetary resources and the physical environment. Thus, the principles of economic life are, in our view, in need of deep and substantial rethinking. This chapter proposes one sphere where such rethinking may begin.

Neoliberalism has as one of its basic presuppositions the idea that the human world is composed essentially of individuals, who should as far as possible be free to make their own choices and to advance their own interests, in pursuit of whatever they may deem their happiness to be. To be sure, individuals are expected to avoid interfering with the freedom of others, and systems of moral and legal regulation exist to ensure that such limits and protections are enforced. But these are seen as applying to what are essentially individuals, acting without reference to a wider social context.

In reality, of course, individuals do not pursue their interests in isolation from or even in negotiated contractual exchanges with one another; they do so within large and complex economic and governmental systems, which generally have far more influence on their opportunities and chances in life than the personal decisions they make. The capacity to formulate desires and aspirations, and the capabilities to advance them, are substantially shaped by individuals' conditions of birth and family origin, even in those societies which are most open to individuals' own strivings. Livelihoods (the essential

37

means of life, and the grounds for being able to make choices and pursue goals) are usually made available to, or withheld from, people, by decisions taken within organisations of many kinds, such that the individual freedoms which the dominant order proclaims as its first principle are in fact mightily constrained by forces over which no individual has control – although of course some have more power than others.

Economic libertarians such as Robert Nozick believe that democratic (and other) governments wrongly interfere with individuals' freedom to dispose of themselves and their property as they wish, for example through taxation. Many socialists and Marxists hold, to the contrary, that the division of powers between those who own capital and those who own only their labour imposes gross inequities on who has access to what kinds of freedom, and makes a mockery of the idea of the equal freedoms of the individual. Gerry Cohen also put forward a telling refutation of Nozick's idea of freedom, by drawing attention to the unjustified assumptions he made about what morally belongs innately and exclusively to an individual, and what does not.[1]

Our argument is that the entire basis of this debate – the idea of the autonomous, self-seeking individual as the foundational 'atom' of the human world – is wrongly conceived. For human beings are essentially *social* beings – and individual freedom and choice, where they emerge and exist, are the outcome of delicate and precarious social arrangements, not primordial facts of nature.[2] A besetting fault – indeed pathology – of contemporary capitalist societies is that in their relentless advocacy of individual freedom, gratification and possessiveness, they undermine the very social conditions which make its exercise, for most people, possible.[3]

This chapter is concerned with the kinds of relationship with others on which individuals depend for their well-being, through various phases of their lives. The quality of social institutions – in the spheres for example of health, education, work, criminal justice or citizenship – depends substantially on what qualities of human relationship they facilitate. In the abridged version of this article published in *Soundings* 54, I go on to discuss human relations with nature. Spatial relations, important in understanding links between the global and the local, are not considered here.[4]

terminology for the welfare state

HUMAN NEEDS AND THE WELFARE STATE

In the long arguments about what in one discourse is called the welfare state, in another social protection, and in another social rights and entitlements, a crucial demand has been for recognition of the realities of unavoidable and universal human dependency.

Human beings come into the world entirely helpless, and are dependent, for many years, on the care of others. Indeed, they are even dependent, as human scientists now tell us, on their loving care, since the capacity of persons to develop minds and emotional resources depends on the quality of attention given to them through their infancy and childhood. Throughout their lives, but in particular in their later years, people are vulnerable to illness, and nearly all will experience a period of time when they are as intensely vulnerable and dependent upon the ministrations of others as they were when they were first born.

In complex, educated, industrial societies, our experiences of dependency and need are not confined to those that are, in a basic sense, given to us by our biology. Societies require individuals to achieve learning and development, take up roles and positions within them, and to survive social transitions (for example to and from school, into the world of work, to parenthood, to disoccupation and retirement) and sudden rupture in the pattern of their lives. These are expectations placed on individuals from their earliest days of life, and where they are not, or cannot, be met, a repertoire of remedies and sanctions are invariably mobilised to bring about some acceptable level of compliance with social norms. (Different societies employ different regimes of compliance for their deviants, and these change with the times, as Michel Foucault among others has shown.) When children first enter the world, they already bring with them complex material and relational needs, whose satisfaction or otherwise by their primary carers will always have lasting consequences for their later development and well-being. A child's entry into the world beyond his or her family, and into the different stages of education and the challenges which this brings, carries with it another cluster of needs, for the provision of which children and their families depend on others, in schools and other supportive social agencies. Later still, comes the transition for young people to being receivers of and participants in education, to the world of work, when individuals are expected to become the makers of goods and the producers of value in their own right. This transition involves its own vulnerabilities, which in present economic circumstances have become particularly acute, since for many young people work of any kind, and especially work which offers the prospects of personal satisfaction and development, are absent. Today, even the transition from university to employment, for the relatively privileged young people who have been to university, is often hazardous and full of anxiety, so defective has society become in its support of such crucial stages in the life-course. Paul Mason has recently argued that the existence of large numbers of unemployed graduates in many parts of the world has been a potent force in 'kicking off' protests, in the Arab Spring and elsewhere.

Nor is the experience of becoming a parent to be understood as a merely 'natural' function, capable of being undertaken outside of a supportive network of social relations, including families, friendships and formal institutions. These include the medical services necessary to support the birth of a child, and the material arrangements which are essential if a family is to have somewhere to live, and resources on which to live – which can no longer to be taken for granted given the deficiencies of contemporary housing and employment opportunities.

And later still, there is an inevitable transition from the world of work into retirement, and the experiences this can bring, which may range from the imposition of an abrupt loss of identity (which may amount to a kind of social death) to entry into a phase of post-retirement life which can have the potential both for new kinds of freedom and satisfaction, and for experiences of loneliness and emptiness.

The modern 'welfare system', for want of a better term, was constructed during the earlier epoch of capitalism that we have called the social democratic settlement, as a set of responses to these various phases of dependency. This settlement recognised – and indeed insisted – that the 'law of the market' could not, for the majority of people, provide sufficiently for such needs.

One means of public intervention then chosen was material support, providing for the redistribution of money and resources to individuals and families at dependent phases of their life-cycle when these could not be adequately provided by individual self-provision (and of course this still, in somewhat attenuated form, continues to function). And although there was usually some element of redistribution between richer and poorer involved in these transactions, a much more important logic was redistribution not between members of different social classes, but between people at different phases of their life-cycle. That is, from those at a phase of life when they *were* able to support their families from their earnings in the labour market, to those who at another phase of life became excluded from it, for reasons of age, sickness, economic circumstances (local or more pervasive unemployment) or misfortune. One of the achievements of Peter Townsend's research on poverty was his demonstration that poverty was a condition which was and is suffered by large numbers of unexceptional individuals, at particular phases of their life-cycle, and was not merely the experience of a particular social class of the disadvantaged and the poor.[5] The idea that poverty is such an exceptional, marginal and indeed blameworthy condition lies behind the current scapegoating of 'scroungers' and those dependent on welfare benefits, as if they were in some way responsible for the crisis and weakness of the British economy, which they plainly are not.

Many forms of intervention in response to human needs are not, however, primarily material or financial in nature, but involve activities of nurturing, caring, educating, advising, nursing, rescuing and protecting. In the myriad of occupations devoted to these services (child care, medicine, teaching, nursing, social care, even policing) the primary work consists of responding in qualitatively specific ways to the needs of people, with the attention, commitments and skills which are appropriate to each particular situation. A diversity of capabilities and sensitivities are involved in all of these activities, each supported at best by distinct occupational cultures, whose moral essence is illuminated by the French sociologist Pierre Bourdieu's concepts of 'habitus' and 'field'.

Today, in the system of neoliberal capitalism, the primary goals of these fields of work – namely to respond to needs arising from different kinds of vulnerability – are at risk of being pushed to the margin by the reframings of organisational and personal tasks in terms of economic gain, market advantage, profit seeking and compliance with instructions and regulations that often have little relevance to the tasks in hand. One of the main reasons why there is such dismay and outrage in the public sector at the changes being imposed on it so ruthlessly at the present time is the belief of its workers that the principal value and meaning of what they do goes unrecognised, disparaged and even abused by policy-makers and the managements that are made to serve as their instruments.

It is of course inevitable that in modern societies the services which provide for human vulnerabilities are organised within formal institutions. These are often highly complex organisations, sometimes involving sophisticated technical resources, as in medical care. For reasons of scale these are necessarily 'impersonal' in some of their operations. Resources are always necessarily limited, and impersonal procedures – for example the use of web-based systems to convey information or make appointments – may be time- and cost-saving to good effect. Good quality human services, even if they depend primarily on face-to-face interactions (such as between teacher and pupil or therapist and client) can neither be created nor maintained without education, training, planning and organisation. Difficult choices have to be made in deciding how to provide complex human services, in regard to which kind of institutions work best in which circumstances. There is no universal solution to be found to the question of what organisational forms can provide the optimal containers for each kind of service. Different arrangements will be appropriate in different circumstances – and may include, for example, uniform forms of provision sanctioned by the central state, services largely shaped by professional expertise, locally-provided services sanctioned by voters, voluntary services, or those provided by competitive providers in a market. What is, however, certain is that many different 'voices' and interests need to be involved in deciding democratically, and through public discussion, which institutional forms are best in what conditions.

Yet a single imposed 'universal model' for the provision of services is exactly what is now being propagated and enforced under the regime of neoliberalism. This is based on the doctrine that services will be provided effectively and efficiently only where providers are motivated primarily by financial incentives. One aspect of this is the belief that the transfer of a hitherto public service to a private provider is *ipso facto* likely to lead to its improvement and to greater efficiency. This programme of privatisation was first introduced in the previous period of Conservative government (with denationalisations and the compulsory contracting of services by local government), was slowed down under New Labour though remaining very much part of its agenda, and has now been accelerated under the Coalition government. Indeed the urgency of this process, for example in the National Health Service, suggests that the government intends to entrench such transfers from the public to the private sector before the next general election, through binding contracts, so that they have become 'facts on the ground' in the event of their defeat.

The assumption that the introduction of a profit incentive will of itself improve provision is, however, a false one. It seems often to lead to a displacement of attention from the provision of the service, and the complex systems and cultures required to achieve this, to the short-term aims of financial return. The gross scandals of A4E, the firm to whom the lion's share of the Preparation for Work programme was handed over, and of G4S, the company entrusted with providing security for the London Olympics, are examples of the risks. Similarly, the assumption that scrapping 'regulations' defining standards will on its own deliver sufficient incentive to companies to invest where formerly they did not appears to make the most simplistic assumptions about what determines investment decisions in a complex economy. (This agenda of deregulation now encompasses the spheres of health and safety, employment protection, building standards regulation, planning controls, energy saving requirements and even fire regulations and disability access requirements.) The corporate sector has itself rejected a number of deregulatory proposals of this kind as simply irrelevant to its decision-making; these include, for example, the proposal to reduce the period within which employees will have protection from unfair dismissal, and the offer of employee shareholdings in return for the surrender of employment rights.

It is this same logic which now demands that provider organisations and their sub-units operate as businesses or quasi-businesses, with the state of their balance-sheets given priority over all other indicators of their performance and value. Such 'market disciplines' have been widely imposed on institutions which are still formally 'public' in their ownership, ostensibly as means to improve their efficiency. But it is clear that the 'public' character of these institutions can be made into a mere external shell, which allows their internal remodelling into structures and cultures very close to those of corporate businesses.

Once this remodelling has taken place, it becomes only a further step to allow 'fully private' providers entry into what have been redefined as 'markets', and for the wholesale privatisation of public services to take place. This is a programme of privatisation in effect by stealth and misrepresentation, since even as these organisational changes are enforced, public denials continue that this direction has anything to do with privatisation. This is also the logic which has legitimated increasing inequalities of rewards to individuals, with differentials between those in more and less senior positions increasing by multiples over recent years, even in so-called public institutions. One hardly has to be cynical to recognise that the tacit purpose of creating a stratum of super-managers (e.g. university vice-chancellors, NHS and local authority executives, and their phalanxes of lieutenants) paid at something approaching the level of private sector managers is to weaken their identifications with the professional cultures and values in which they often began their careers, and to recruit them as accomplices to the new order of the rich.

The problem is that if organisations and their managers and employees are incentivised chiefly to do what is in their own economic interests, the consequence is liable to be the invasion and corruption of their primary tasks and commitments. The 'economic' logic of maximising financial (or reputational) returns for an institution often runs counter to the 'needs-based' logic of fulfilling their professional and human goals. And what may well begin, for a senior public manager, as an external pressure on him or her to meet demands to achieve greater efficiency or solvency, over time may become an internalised commitment to financial goals. These now come to be perceived as the only reality that matters, in contradistinction to what they may now see as a merely sentimental or reactionary loyalty of more junior organisational members to professional client-oriented goals and methods. The seduction of high salaries comes to be not merely the material satisfactions they bring (and financial insurance against the omnipresent risk of failure and dismissal) but also the satisfactions of competing for status, prestige and power with other 'high earners', clearly a major motivation among the elites of the private sector.

The excessively stratified reward system of the Football Premier League, astonishingly tolerated by supporters of the game, now serves as a mirror for the entire society, as it symbolises and legitimises the displacement of spheres of intrinsic value by the esteem accorded to money alone (linked in that instance to the larger financial circuits of Russian – and American – corporate oligarchy and to Gulf oil). Those who try to establish the principle and practice of supporter-owned clubs further a democratic cause whose symbolic significance goes well beyond football.

In many fields of practice, it is people in the most difficult (and often most 'disadvantaged') 'cases' who are both those most in need of services, and the most demanding of their resources. How does an institution, or its practitioners, decide between the priority it gives to the perceived needs of its clients, and its own financial or reputational interest? Marketised systems provide strong incentives to cherry-pick and to cheat, to find ways of maximising economic returns while minimising the commitment of resources to the most needy. How much easier it is to demonstrate strong educational performance if one excludes weak pupils; or to achieve high returns in health care if one avoids taking on the most chronically vulnerable patients. Or to be a 'world class university' if only the most talented and privileged students are enrolled. This is not to mention the grosser forms of cheating which are sometimes revealed, as when payment is claimed (as in the finding of jobs for young people in a recent case) for services which are not even delivered. The principles of responsiveness to the needs of others, and of pursuit of individual and institutional self-interest, are frequently in conflict with one another. A different set of assumptions and values is needed if this contradiction is to be resolved, and a proper priority accorded to human well-being.

The separation of norms and powers through a system in which 'welfare institutions' looked after dependency needs, while the private sector economy gave scope to the pursuit of individual interests, was an earlier attempted institutional resolution of this dilemma. But the marketisation of the entire society, including its provisions for needs and welfare, is unravelling this compromise. Even the commitments of individual practitioners become confused and disorganised when the systems around them insist that what matters most is not the needs of their patients, pupils or other service users, but more self-centred imperatives bearing on the competitive success of their organisation. Sometimes conformity to an organisation's principles of self-interest is enforced by placing employees' own futures in jeopardy, for example through competitive redundancy and re-employment procedures. Regulatory systems – which have become an increasingly pervasive aspect of modern forms of governance – often merely incentivise self-interested behaviour by institutions or their workers, even when their ostensible object is to ensure that they respond appropriately to people's needs. This is because compliance can become an overriding preoccupation within organisations, distracting practitioners from responsiveness to their primary task, rather than assisting them in it.

RELATIONSHIPS AND WELL-BEING

The development of human potentialities and capabilities, and thus the potential both for individuals' fulfilment and for the production of social goods, depends essentially on the quality of relationships within which they are nurtured. This is a proposition to which we think a redesign of our economy and social system needs to give deep attention.

It is obvious, from everyday experience, that this proposition is true. We know that children do better, in terms of physical and emotional health, and educational development, the better the quality of early care that they receive. A measure of governmental acknowledgement of this truth is accorded by the provision of services in early years – it was the rationale for the now-diminishing Sure-Start programme. We know that children learn more in school if they have more attention from teachers. This is why one of the benefits sought in the purchase of private education is smaller classes and more favourable pupil-teacher ratios. (Another benefit, of course, not much related to this, is the achievement of social segregation from the less fortunate, and closer association with the more privileged.) The universities of highest standing have more resources to spend, per student, than lower-ranked universities. The principal resource in question is the time of their academic staff, although whether universities always choose to devote this to the education of their students, as against other reputational priorities, is another issue.

In entering paid work for the first time (or perhaps at any time) the finest gift any new entrant can receive is a supervisor, manager or mentor who has an interest in and a commitment to his or her well-being and development. It is a good fortune when someone's early occupational experience is of this kind, and it often makes a lasting difference to later career development and fulfilment. Furthermore, such qualities of concern, once experienced, are often internalised, and become part of a 'habitus' which is lived out in later practice, to the good of later entrants into a field or institution who benefit from a 'passing on' of the attention earlier given.[6] (Thus, gifts may not merely be given in reciprocal exchange, but may also later be passed on to strangers.) Such good occupational practices, based on recognition of the importance of relationships for personal development, are not merely the attributes of individuals. They can be embodied in institutions and occupational cultures, over long periods, and may contribute a great deal to the reputation and success of a particular organisation or enterprise. Someone once told me, apropos of a particular young person entering her first permanent job, 'She is fortunate – that organisation (which my informant knew well) has a reputation for nurturing those who join it.' And so it proved.

We know, further, that the quality of attention which doctors or nurses give to their patients makes a great deal of difference to an individual's experience of illness, and the anxiety and emotional (indeed physical) pain to which this gives rise. There is a substantial scientific literature on the emotional dimensions of health care, from the different research perspectives of information-sharing, emotional labour, and unconscious defences against anxiety. But there is no room for doubt about the central relational issue. Furthermore, although the developments which have taken place in regard to care of the dying, through the hospice movement and its broader extensions, owe a great deal to the pharmaceutical management of pain, its achievements are also due to the recognition of the emotional and relational ambience surrounding patients. Indeed one is inseparably linked to the other, since lack of attention to physical pain is sometimes an effect of an environment in which the patient cannot be seen as a whole person. Such inattention is often a self-distancing defence against the recognition of pain and suffering.

Of course one could also cite countless more 'exceptional' cases, of the many prominent individuals, for example writers and artists, sometimes from obscure and difficult backgrounds, who have attributed the beginning of their creative life and its opportunities to a particular friend or teacher, whose interest in them was the key to their discovering or recognising their potential. Or one could point to the common experience of young people learning to do music, or to act, or to swim, and how much difference the quality of attention from a teacher can make.

A MEASURE OF VALUE

This perspective suggests that a significant measure of value, and indeed of the well-being of a society, should lie in the qualities of relationship which are available to individuals at each stage of their life-course. It is not, as we argued in Chapter 1 of this Manifesto, economic growth as it is counted in money terms by which we should measure the progress or improvement in our society, but by the attention given to people and their development. It is surely obvious, furthermore, that as the investment in human labour that is required to produce material goods diminishes, thanks to modern technologies, so the potential availability of human resources for the development and care of persons should increase. There is no conceivable material or technological excuse for unemployment, when there is abundant work which could and should be done, in nurturing, developing and expressing human capabilities.

Nor should this be thought of simply as the substitution of one kind of 'consumption' for another, or a change in the balance between them. Labour invested in human relationships is a form of 'production', as much as labour invested in the manufacture of commodities. Since it shapes future capacities, it is even more an investment in the future. This is the case for the 'human work' which takes place in schools or day-nurseries, or in training and developing employees, or in looking after the ill, or indeed in the appropriate punishment and care of offenders. It is also the case in the work of looking after customers – think of the difference this makes, comparing good and bad experiences on holiday or even while shopping.

In the post-capitalist future which we would like to see, a different priority given to the cultivation of human needs and capabilities would be a significant indicator of progress. A different economic and institutional architecture from that which we now have will be needed if we are to bring these objectives into the centre of public policy, and as indicators of progress.

QUESTIONS OF POLICY

It may reasonably be asked what the implications of this argument might be for policy. Changing a climate of basic assumptions may be a good thing, but how do such changed ways of thinking become embedded in social action? And furthermore, how can such changes be made real – as opposed to, in effect, being stolen by management personnel and customer relations departments, to make it seem as if their organisations have become more sensitive to human needs, while in reality little has been altered but appearances? (And governments too have proved adept at seeking legitimacy by changing the appearance of what they do, rather than its reality.)

Below are some brief pointers to means by which development in the directions proposed can be considered:

1. There is the apparently mundane but in fact crucial issue of numbers. The number and ratio of staff members assigned to look after people – especially dependent people, whether they be infants, children, students, patients or the very old – is always a crucial indicator of the quality of care and attention that will be available. They are in a sense its 'material base', whose limitations cannot be overcome by mere will or good intentions. This obvious reality is routinely denied – even lied about – by those wishing to 'economise' on the costs of services, even though the smallest inspection of what is provided through the market for 'private' customers makes it clear that human attention is nearly always the principal 'extra' that is being paid for by the privileged. We need both to argue the material case for sufficient staffing, and to contest the notion that 'efficiencies' can make cuts bearable.

2. There are the norms and practices of inspection and audit, now routine in all public services and no doubt in private corporations too. Audit and inspection are commonly seen as engines of standardisation and one-dimensionality, and indeed they have for the most part been of this kind. But need they be? Could forms of public accountability not be developed which are inclusive and democratic, and which were attentive to the human qualities of services, rather than to their conformity to rules, procedures and 'outputs'?

   The questions need to be posed of what it is that is to be inspected for, and who is to do the inspecting. How open and dialogic are the relations between the auditors and the audited, the watchers and the watched? What qualities of relationship are desired to exist between providers and clients, in for example a day nursery, a care home, a hospital, a school, a university or even a prison? The recent disaster of the Mid Staffordshire Hospital Trust shows the extent to which current regimes of inspection may neglect such basic dimensions of quality. Systems of inspection which gave a high emphasis to the relational qualities of institutions, and which involved communities of practice in thinking about these issues, would be a potential means of change.

3. There are also questions of the initiation, training, support and leadership of work-forces, in all of these sectors. This is not simply a question of making institutions more democratic in their governance, or more equal in their distribution of payments and rewards, though this is nearly always desirable. Relationships of dependence are, almost by definition, not equal, and inequalities are also inherent in most environments which facilitate learning. The functions of leadership and authority can be benign and responsible, rather than exploitative and repressive, and such roles are essential to a good society, in many of its spheres of activity. Enabling individuals to learn, over a life-time, to acquire the capabilities to be good citizens, attentive to the development and needs of others as well as to their own interests, is more relevant to human well-being than the pursuit of the chimera of 'economic growth' as the measure of human happiness.

NOTES

1. G.A. Cohen, *History, Labour and Freedom*, Oxford University Press 1988.

2. This idea that individuals are the outcome of complex social arrangements and relationships was the starting point of the field of sociology, for example in the work of Emile Durkheim in the second half of the nineteenth century. It was the grounds for sociology's critique of the 'individualist' disciplines of economics and psychology as descriptions of the ontological foundations of human existence. The rise of sociology to prominence during the decades of the post-war welfare settlement, and the antipathy to it by neoliberals from the 1980s onwards, reflects these differences in world-view, refracted in academic as well as in many other spheres of life.

3. Another dimension of the debate about relationality concerns the functions of the government and the state. IPPR's recent short book *The Relational State* (G. Cooke and R. Muir (eds), IPPR 2012) argues for a reconceptualisation of the role of the state, its principal author Geoff Mulgan arguing that just as the state previously changed from being a coercive to a delivery state, now is the time to move towards the relational state. This argument seems to be a self-critique of New Labour's approach to government when it was in office, and as such is welcome. Mark Stears and others in this symposium suggest that it is mistaken to suppose that

the state can be relational, but propose instead that it can facilitate relationships, through supporting structures in which the commitments of people to one another can flourish. I am closer to Stears's position than to Mulgan's in this argument. But this focus on the functions of the state only addresses some of the issues we are raising here. A top-down, centralising and bureaucratic state is certainly one enemy of a relational society. But, in our time, its greater one is the ethos of an unfettered corporate capitalism, insisting on individual choice and the virtues of competition as its principal values. On this crucial subject *The Relational State* is silent.

4. On spatial relations see David Featherstone and Joe Painter (eds), *Spatial Politics: Essays for Doreen Massey*, Wiley 2013.

5. See P. Townsend, *Poverty in the United Kingdom*, Penguin 1979.

6. This concept of the 'internal' denotes the idea that relationships have unconscious as well as conscious dimensions. The 'object relations' perspective in British psychoanalysis has relevance to the perspective put forward here, as I have proposed elsewhere.

3. COMMON-SENSE NEOLIBERALISM

Stuart Hall and Alan O'Shea

And let this be our message – common sense for the common good.

David Cameron, 24.4.11

When politicians try to win consent or mobilise support for their policies, they frequently assert that these are endorsed by 'hard-working families up and down the country'. Their policies cannot be impractical, unreasonable or extreme, they imply, because they are solidly in the groove of popular thinking – 'what everybody knows', takes-for-granted and agrees with – the folk wisdom of the age. This claim by the politicians, if correct, confers on their policies popular legitimacy.

In fact, what they are really doing is not just invoking popular opinion but *shaping and influencing* it so they can harness it in their favour. By asserting that popular opinion *already agrees*, they hope to produce agreement *as an effect*. This is the circular strategy of the self-fulfilling prophecy.

But what exactly is common sense? It is a form of 'everyday thinking' which offers us frameworks of meaning with which to make sense of the world. It is a form of popular, easily-available knowledge which contains no complicated ideas, requires no sophisticated argument and does not depend on deep thought or wide reading. It works intuitively, without forethought or reflection. It is pragmatic and empirical, giving the illusion of arising directly from experience, reflecting only the realities of daily life and answering the needs of 'the common people' for practical guidance and advice.

It is not the property of the rich, the well-educated or the powerful, but is shared to some extent by everybody, regardless of class, status, creed, income or wealth. Typically, it expresses itself in the vernacular, the familiar language of the street, the home, the pub, the workplace

simplification:
'common sense' language + the tabloid press

and the terraces. The popularity and influence of the tabloid press – one of its main repositories – depends on how well it imitates, or better, ventriloquises the language and gnomic speech patterns of 'ordinary folk'. In the now-famous example, it must say not 'British Navy Sinks Argentinean Cruiser' but, simply, 'Gotcha'.

According to Antonio Gramsci, the Italian political philosopher who has written perceptively on this subject, common sense 'is not critical and coherent but disjointed and episodic'.[1] However, it *does* have a 'logic' and a history. It is always, Gramsci argues, 'a response to certain problems posed by reality which are quite specific and "original" in their relevance'. It draws on past ideas and traditions; but it also keeps evolving to give meaning to new developments, solve new problems, unravel new dilemmas. 'Common sense', as Gramsci argued, 'is not something rigid and immobile, but is continually transforming itself'.

It also has a content. It is a compendium of well-tried knowledge, customary beliefs, wise sayings, popular nostrums and prejudices, some of which – like 'a little of what you fancy does you good' – seem eminently sensible, others wildly inaccurate. Its virtue is that it is obvious. Its watchword is, 'Of course!'. It seems to be outside time. Indeed it may be persuasive precisely because we think of it as a product of Nature rather than of history.

Common sense tends to be socially conservative, leaning towards tradition (even if, as Eric Hobsbawm argued, much tradition was only 'invented' yesterday!). Its pace of change seems glacial. In fact, it is constantly being reconstructed and refashioned by external pressures and influences.

Common sense feels coherent. But Gramsci argues that, like the personality, it is 'strangely composite'. 'It contains Stone Age elements and principles of a more advanced science, prejudices from all past phases of history ... and intuitions of a future philosophy'. For these and other reasons, it is fundamentally contradictory. It tells not one narrative, but several conflicting 'stories' stitched together – while failing to resolve the differences between them. Bits and pieces of ideas from many sources – what Gramsci calls 'stratified deposits' – have slowly settled or sedimented, in truncated and simplified forms, into 'popular philosophy', without leaving behind an inventory of their sources. The Framing Statement argues that, for example, contemporary neoliberal ideas about 'free markets' derive from and are consistent

with the eighteenth-century theories of Adam Smith and the early
political economists, though most people have never heard of, let
alone read them. Many common-sense moral judgements – for
example about sexuality – have a Judeo-Christian lineage, though we
do not know where in the Bible they are to be found.

Many people intuitively favour 'an eye for an eye, a tooth for a
tooth' conception of justice – while at the same time believing that
Muslim Sharia Law is a barbarous form of law. Some who depend on
benefits to survive believe all the other claimants are 'scroungers'.
Some who hold that unbridled competition driven by self-interest is
the only way to succeed also believe 'we should love our neighbours as
ourselves'. Margaret Thatcher, the mistress of common-sense language,
and of squaring circles, supported both the 'free market' (i.e. one
without much state regulation) and a 'strong state'.

However, as well as being conservative in outlook, common sense
also contains critical or utopian elements, which Gramsci calls 'the
healthy nucleus … which deserves to be made more unitary and
coherent'. He is referring to the apparently obvious taken-for granted
understandings that express a sense of unfairness and injustice about
'how the world works': landlords tend to exploit tenants, banks responsible for the 'credit crunch' expect to be bailed out by taxpayers rather
than take the crunch themselves. CEOs receive immense bonuses
even when their companies perform badly; profitable businesses will
avoid paying tax if they can; and companies profiting from a fall in
commodity prices will not pass the gains on to consumers.

Gramsci called these apparently 'natural' insights into the wicked
ways of the world 'good sense'. And good sense provides a basis on
which the left could develop a popular strategy for radical change – if
it takes on board the idea that common sense is a site of political
struggle. Common sense and 'good sense' co-exist. Our ability to live
with this incoherent structure may be due to the fact that the 'stratified
deposits' of common sense represent the outlook and interests of very
different social groups: 'Every philosophical current leaves behind a
sedimentation of "common sense": this is the document of its historical
effectiveness'. It is this that allows us to hold contradictory opinions
simultaneously, and to take up contradictory subject-positions.

As citizens, we expect public services in return for paying taxes. But
as 'taxpayers' we are invited to think that we should pay as few taxes
as possible, whatever the social consequences. Margaret Thatcher

exploited such contradictions, arguing that, as workers, we have sectional interests, 'but we are all consumers and as consumers we want a choice. We want the best value for money'. Hence: 'the same trade unionists, as consumers, want an open market'. The difficulty is that most of us are simultaneously citizens, taxpayers and workers. So discourses which try to win us over must privilege one way of positioning ourselves over others. Common sense thus becomes a contested arena. As Doreen Massey argued in Chapter 1, we know that doctor/patient, teacher/student, citizen/state, client/provider, shopper/supermarket relationships all have specific, and very different, social contents. However, if we can be persuaded to see ourselves simply as 'customers', then all the other relationships are reduced to one common denominator: the fact that we are consuming a product [sic] in a market [sic] which only has value because we pay for it [sic]. Everything becomes a commodity, and this aspect of our activities over-rides everything. In this way a whole new way of seeing society (as a market) is coming into play. If developed, it could provide the cornerstone for a new kind of (neoliberal) common sense. *neoliberalisation of common sense*

The Framing Statement argues that this is indeed what is happening. Slowly but surely, neoliberal ideas have permeated society and are transforming what passes as common sense. The broadly egalitarian and collectivist attitudes that underpinned the welfare state era are giving way to a more competitive, individualistic market-driven, entrepreneurial, profit-oriented outlook. There is no proof as to how far this process has gone: the evidence is hard to 'read', and the trend is certainly not one-way. However, after forty years of a concerted neoliberal ideological assault, this new version of common sense is fast becoming the dominant one.

One common-sense assertion that has become widely acceptable is: 'You can't solve a problem just by throwing money at it' – often aimed at Labour's 'tax and spend' policies. True, perhaps. But there are very few problems which would not be considerably alleviated by being better funded rather than having their budgets savagely cut. The right's use of this slogan is of course highly selective: they have no qualms about money being 'thrown' at the banks or at the economy via quantitative easing.

Taxpayers, it is said, want 'value for money' and 'greater efficiency'. Citizens certainly have a right to see their money well spent. But are the fire service, the police, ambulance crews, youth and community workers, mental health staff, or child-minders *necessarily* more efficient because there are fewer of them? Can their benefit to society be measured exclusively in terms of their exchange value? If policing is more efficient when information-led, how come the 'backroom' staff who provide the information are seen as dispensable, on the grounds that they are 'not front-line staff'? More and more, these common-sense 'truths' serve as a cover-up for savaging the public sector in line with the dominant neoliberal, anti-state ideology.

These days, we are told, we all want greater freedom and personal choice. Indeed, not only are we given 'freedom to choose', we are *required* to choose: which hospital to be ill in, which life-style to adopt, which identity to fashion, which celebrity role-model to imitate. Certainly, there is no reason why only the well-off should exercise choice. However, there is also strong evidence that the responsibility which comes with so much choice can create unfulfillable expectations, anxiety and a sense of the precariousness of life.[2] This sense of insecurity is then further exacerbated by the increasing introduction in the workplace of personal targets, appraisals and performance-related pay, to keep staff up to the mark. Michael Gove now plans to introduce the latter into the teaching profession. But 'it's all down to us' – apart from being untrue – is a hard 'truth' to live with. What if we make the wrong choice?

The *structural* consequences of neoliberalism – the individualisation of everyone, the privatisation of public troubles and the requirement to make competitive choices at every turn – has been paralleled by an upsurge in feelings of insecurity, anxiety, stress and depression. These are now responsible for one in every three days sick leave from work.[3] We need to acknowledge these *affective* dimensions that are in play, and which underpin common sense.

How then does common sense make sense of these changes in lived experience? Have most people accepted that it is inevitable and natural to understand most of our life as consumers and market competitors?

There are in fact many signs of resistance to be found. These include older forms of political protest, such as the trade unions, and newer, emerging, forms such as Occupy, UK Uncut or 38 Degrees. However these do not in any way constitute a single social force, as happened to some extent with the GLC in the 1980s, when, although the traditional left and the new social movements did not always agree – and certainly were not unified – they did occupy the same space, and struggle over the same budget, and together offered a broader and more effective political force than we have seen since then.

There is also much individualised disaffection. To fall ill with anxiety is itself a symptom that some people are finding it difficult to live with neoliberal culture. Another is a marked retreat, in popular culture, to an isolated self-sufficiency. There is unfocused anger, a grudging, grumbling resentment at one's lot, and a troubled uncertainty about what to do next. There is a sense of being abandoned by the political class and widespread cynicism, disaffiliation and de-politicisation.

Many groups, of course, do have cultural resources to resist these trends – and these include historic working-class solidarities, defensive organisations, strong local loyalties and a culture of mutual support. Others have insight into new processes, such as digital technologies and communication, which are changing the shape of society. But these have not resulted in any coming together in a vigorous, effective response.

FAIRNESS

The resistance which lies in the 'good sense' components of common sense is more elusive, but still possible to illustrate. To attempt this, and to demonstrate why this understanding of common sense is valuable for fighting the spread of neoliberal discourse, we will now focus on one pivotal element – the idea of 'fairness' and its role in popular discourse during the winter of 2012/13. We have selected 'fairness' as our instance because no one is *against* it. It is a term that the whole political spectrum struggles to inflect to their own project.

First we outline the role of fairness in recent political history; then we look at material from readers' comments attached to one news report in the *Sun*. We draw on this, first, to give an indication of the range of appropriations which are in play in popular discourse at any one moment, and, second, to take a more detailed look at the ways in which one particular commenter 'cuts and pastes' various beliefs, terms and political positions into what Gramsci called a 'strangely composite' common sense – one which combines its elements differently and flexibly to address different contexts and topics. In the course of this we point up the danger of politicians getting too fixated on the 'public opinion' provided by polls.

What counts as fair has been pivotal to our political history. The welfare state was set up in the 1940s as a collective contract between all members of the society to guarantee a fairer distribution of wealth, and a chance for everyone to flourish and make a useful contribution. These aspirations were supported by a broad consensus across the population.

The neoliberal right has been working hard to undermine and trans-code this inclusive meaning of 'fairness' since the 1970s. Margaret Thatcher made it her project to break up the consensus and substitute a market approach. But she also validated this by a common sense appeal to 'what we all already think':

> A great number of people in Britain are becoming increasingly alarmed about a society which depends on the state's help – on entitlement. What has happened is that so many of the people who have done everything right and saved for their old age and put a bit by, seem to have had a raw deal. Some of those who have done only too little and have not done it very well have been on the beneficial end of what has been going ... You can't have welfare before someone else has created national wealth.
>
> Speech to party workers, Berwick, 30.8.78

Two decades later, David Cameron echoed the same sentiment:

> For too long we've lived in an upside down world where people who do the right thing, the responsible thing, are taxed and punished, whereas those who do the wrong thing are rewarded ... And for that person intent on ripping off the system, we are saying – we will not let you live off the hard work of others. Tough sanctions. Tougher limits. In short we're building a system that matches effort with reward ... instead of a system that rewards those who make no effort.
>
> Speech, 23.05.11[4]

Here 'fairness' is a quasi-market relation, a reward for personal effort – a long way from the collectivism of the 1940s.

Recent attitude surveys (from the Joseph Rowntree and Resolution Foundations) suggest that the decades of playing off 'hard-working families' against those who for one reason or another are unable to find work have achieved the intended result. The surveys found a *neoliberalism re-shaping notions of fairness from an inalienable right to an individualised lens of 'you get out what you put in,' etc.*

decline in sympathy for the poor and those on benefits. The concept of fairness was generally disconnected from any notion of rights ('No-one is owed a living'), and seen simply in terms of fair rewards for effort.

The 2012-13 fairness debate focused on George Osborne's decision to cap benefit payments below the rate of inflation, and Duncan Smith's welfare reforms, which were accompanied by the launch of a large-scale 'moral panic' demonising claimants, which was amplified enthusiastically by the press, and not strongly resisted by broadcasters (including the BBC).

In his now notorious contribution, Osborne asked:

> Where is the fairness, we ask, for the shift-worker, leaving home in the dark hours of the early morning, who looks up at the closed blinds of their next door neighbour sleeping off a life on benefits? When we say we're all in this together, we speak for that worker. We speak for all those who want to work hard and get on.
>
> Conservative Party Conference, 8.10.12

This vivid image has been amplified by personal stories, and profiles of specific out-of-work families on benefits greater than the average wage (with no reference to the fact that a very large chunk of this is housing benefit paid directly to profiteering landlords). A YouGov poll found that people on average thought that 41 per cent of the welfare budget went on benefits to the unemployed, while the true figure is 3 per cent; and that 27 per cent of the welfare budget was claimed fraudulently, while the government's own figure is 0.7 per cent.[5] This suggests that the 'folk devil' figure of the 'scrounger'/'skiver'/'shirker'/'fraudster' living a life of idle luxury has resonated with many people's concerns, resentments and insecurities.

This is the ideological climate in which both polling and online responses have to be understood. The debate has been conducted within a neoliberal framing of the agenda across most of the political spectrum and media output. This frame takes for granted that the market relation is central (you can only have what you pay for), the deficit is the problem, and cutting public expenditure is the only solution; and, within this, cutting welfare benefits is the priority – and it's all a result of 'Labour's mess'. (The Labour Party itself hasn't strongly challenged this!) In the context of this closing down of the debate, along with the onslaught of propaganda and misinformation, it is not surprising that polls show that support for capping benefits below the rate of inflation can be rallied.

But we have to beware taking poll findings as the unquestionable truth, or as reflecting deeply held political positions. The YouGov poll also showed that when respondents were given the correct figures, their views changed and they became more sympathetic towards benefit claimants. This demonstrates that the earlier responses were a result of an effective misinformation campaign by the government and the press, and not of some 'uncontaminated' opinion of those polled. As David Stuckler has recently pointed out:

> People's support for welfare depends greatly on how the question is framed. When the question links taxes to specific programmes and recipients, the young tend to express stronger support. For example, only 20 per cent of British youth agree with the very broad idea of giving more money to the poor, but when asked about support for specific vulnerable groups, such as the disabled or working parents, more than 90 per cent would like to increase or maintain existing levels of support.[6]

Opinion polls are taken – especially by the media – as objective fixities, as an indisputable tide against which politicians turn at their peril – rather than as yes/no answers to questions framed from within the dominant agenda of the moment. They are a tool in the struggle over common sense, rather than an objective reflection of it.

People are less decided about issues than polls suggest. To get a better sense of the way discourse works, and of how people are engaging with neoliberal frames and agendas and reworking their common sense in response, we need to do more than work with simple answers to questions commissioned by vested interests. We have to capture discourse which is volunteered, which arises from the writer's own set of concerns, and is as spontaneous and unfettered by what others may think as possible. Online comments are rather like this, especially as everyone contributes under a pseudonym.

Online responses to newspaper articles are often very thin, and dominated by egotists and spoilers, but the *Sun*'s blogs are voluminous and richly varied, with an energy that comes from genuine anger, irony, moving accounts of people's own difficulties, unashamed prejudice, etc. This is why we've chosen to use material from the 158 comments in response to the *Sun's* report (8.1.13) of Iain Duncan Smith's introduction of the bill to cap benefits below the rate of inflation as an indication of how notions of 'fairness' are currently being contested. The contributors are, of course, in no way 'representative' of any social group. The analysis of 'common sense' isn't about representativeness; it is about how the field of discourse is constituted at any particular moment in time. Each contribution is unique to the speaker – their own specific inflection of elements from within that field. As Gramsci said, there are as many Catholicisms as there are Catholics – each one appropriates, inflects and deploys their Catholicism differently.

It should also be noted that some of the contributors are fairly obviously not even regular readers of the *Sun*, and are intervening from 'outside'. This includes those who are consciously trying to shift the discourse for political reasons, and even the newspaper proprietors themselves. But they all have to address the benefits issue on the terrain of 'common sense' and in everyday language. By looking at the discursive strategies each contribution uses, we can see in greater detail how they establish a field of debate, contend with each other, and privilege particular common-sense framings of an issue.

The following quotations give an indication of some of the different inflections of 'fairness' in play. A good number joined enthusiastically in the demonisation of benefit claimants:

About time these lazy dole lovers got a taste of what everyone else has.

In the coming days we'll hear all the benefit scroungers moaning that it's not fair, blah, blah, blah. The ones I know of can afford 2 holidays a year, a new top of the range phone every year, new TV etc and say it's their right!!! No it's not their right, the benefit system is there for you to get by, not live the life of two holidays a year, out on the razz every weekend etc. Time to wake up and smell the coffee, about time too.

But one contributor vehemently and wittily challenged these stereotypes:

Thank you to some of the commenters here. With all of your 'scroungers', 'iPhones/iPads', 'Sky subscriptions', 'widescreen TV's', 'backsides', 'lazies', 'work shies', 'immigrants', 'expensive holidays' and 'Jeremy Kyles' I managed to complete my internet idiot bingo card for the day, despite the absence of 'booze and fags'. Seriously, I actually wonder if some of you are even human beings or just a bunch of spambots. lol.

Others openly directed their scorn against the rich – not so surprisingly, since outrage against the bankers' bonuses has become widespread. Iain Duncan Smith was often seen as an agent of the 'toffs' attacking the weak and vulnerable. George Osborne was almost universally condemned as an enemy of the poor. Also many saw MPs in general as a greedy, self-serving section of the wealthy:

> The only scroungers are in the GOVERNMENT, they have high wages and claim large amounts in expenses. We are all in this together, Ha Ha Ha.

> Could we have 1 per cent cap on MPs expenses too. After all, we're all in this together.

Others, however, echo the distinction between the 'deserving' and 'undeserving' unemployed, based on the nineteenth-century Poor Law, which Iain Duncan Smith regularly borrows. Some also used this distinction to attack immigration; and, as is common when immigration is being debated, race and animosity towards foreigners is often implied, though they may not be mentioned explicitly:

> While I am of the opinion that no-one who is too lazy to work should be better off on welfare than some working families, I do not think it fair that someone who has worked for many years and then finds themself out of work through no fault of their own and has contributed tax and national insurance, should be getting the same paltry benefit as someone who has never worked a day in their life. I also object to immigrants who have never contributed to our economy being given handouts and for those with large families, being put up in mansions that the general working public could never afford but are expected to subsidise. It is high time that we closed our borders to those who are not able or willing to contribute to our economy.

This contribution accepts Cameron's definition of 'fairness' as a 'system that matches reward with effort', a right to get out only what you put in. The reasonable-sounding nature of this position serves to deflect the criticism one might expect toward the xenophobic undercurrents it relies on. It represents a success for neoliberalism – a dismantling of any collective social responsibility and a reduction of citizens to barterers – 'something for something': worlds away from the collective social model. However the next example reintroduces this into the debate, and also recognises that the attempt to equate benefits with the workshy is deceitful, given that most recipients are in work:

> There is a reason for benefits: quite literally no-one knows when they might need the welfare state. This government cannot claim to be on the side of strivers while also taking their benefits away. Every time Iain Duncan Smith portrays benefit cuts as targeted on the workshy, remember: three-quarters of the families getting tax credits are in work. If you tell a lie big enough and keep repeating it, people will eventually come to believe it.

A few others have an even starker political analysis – a deliberate refusal of the neoliberal frame:

> These benefit changes will hit the poor and lowest paid the hardest. But that is what the greed driven and morally corrupt Tories do. They target the weakest in society, to deflect from their own ineptitude and thievery. They have given the rich tax cuts, allowed tax avoidance to continue to the tune of £60+ billion a year, and given £4 billion in bonuses to publicly owned banks since 2010. This is a very horrible Government, led by people who only know the world of public schools.

We also find an incipient critique of competitive individualism:

> The vast majority of people on disability benefits are … disabled. Many of those go through life suffering and struggling with their afflictions. Making it so they have to struggle to survive financially on top of that is nothing short of cruelty and is the sign of a broken society where people are only out for themselves.

instability of common sense + definitions

These are just a few of the range of 'fairnesses' currently in play contesting the issue of welfare benefits. We will discuss in the final section how political movements could engage with this material. But first we want to illustrate the 'strangely composite' nature of common sense at the level of the individual – how most (all?) of us articulate together ideological elements from very disparate sources, such that there is an unresolved struggle over common sense *within* the individual as well as between individuals and groups – an instability that can be addressed by the left.

The next contributor demonstrates just this: we find a cluster of very disparate 'common senses' inhabited and held together by the same individual. In her three contributions to the discussion, she draws upon a hotchpotch of different discourses – including the radical insight that the decline in wages is a major cause of rising benefit payments:

> Instead of Labour banging on about people losing their tax credits whilst working (their core voters), they should be asking themselves WHY 9 out of 10 people needed tax credits to work for a living in the first place. Minimum wages should have been increased under their watch, but it was more profitable election wise to throw money at people to bribe them to vote for them. Always the party of the gutless, Labour always take the road of least resistance no matter what the cost to the public and the cost now is being born by their grass roots voters – disgraceful performance.

However, in other comments, the same contributor uses the 'shirkers' discourse of the Tory right, echoing the harsh moralism of Margaret Thatcher:

> People moaning about benefit cuts must be benefit claimants. Every time someone moans on here about the amount they receive not being enough according to them it is always to pay for store cards/ credit cards, phone bills etc. Benefits are for food and rent – fullstop! If you have anything else you normally pay for whilst working that is your fault, especially items on subscription or contracts or loans, anyone with a brain does not spend money they know they do not have coming in to pay in cash! That is the problem with this country, the people have been living well beyond their means for years.

In yet another contribution she combines her call for a living wage with hostility to immigration:

> There are going to be riots in the street before long because even though the benefit system needs reforming, wages are far too low and people IN work cannot survive on what they are being paid, so they will be marching for an increase in the minimum wage and so they should, also for a complete halt in immigration. How can you even begin to consider creating extra jobs when Romanians and Bulgarians in their thousands are panting at the bit to get here for either jobs or benefits. It is a disgrace, something has to be done.

In this sequence, then, on the one hand declining wages are identified as the underlying cause of the rise in benefit bills: everyone, she implies, needs enough to live on and wages should be high enough to deliver this. But on the other hand she makes the argument that benefit claimants should not be able to afford telephones, etc, but only food and rent, and again identifies immigration as a major cause of the present crisis. It's a patchwork of received ideas not yet reconciled into a coherent perspective, and applied selectively and to different effect in different contexts – though it clearly includes elements of 'good sense' alongside the 'othering' of immigrants and benefit claimants.

What can we learn from this material? Firstly that while neoliberal discourse is increasingly hegemonic and setting the agendas for debate, there are other currents in play – empathy for others, a liking for co-operation rather than competition, or a sense of injustice, for example.

We can also learn how people connect together contradictory aspects of their understanding of society – how, for example, they marry class anger with the politics of UKIP or the BNP; what anxieties underpin these links; and how scapegoats are deployed to simultaneously address and disavow underlying social problems.

The left and the Labour Party must take the struggle over common sense seriously. Politics, as Gramsci insisted, is always 'educative'. We must acknowledge the insecurities which underlie common sense's confusions and contradictions, and harness the intensity and anger which comes through in many of the readers' comments. Labour must use every policy issue as an opportunity, not only to examine the pragmatics, but to highlight the underlying principle, slowly building an alternative consensus or 'popular philosophy'. It must harness to this the already strongly existing sense of unfairness and injustice. In other words, it must engage in a two-way learning process, leading to what Gramsci called 'an organic cohesion in which feeling-passion becomes understanding'. This may be complicated in the context of a popular cynicism toward the political class in general, but there is no alternative.

The Labour Party may be busy developing alternative policies, but there's no sign that it is breaking with the neoliberal framing of debates, of challenging the taken-for-granted assumptions listed earlier. Rather, it is nervously responding to polls which frame their questions within this neoliberal agenda, fearful to go against the 'public opinion' derived from it which suggests that the public want benefits to be cut further.

A recent instance of this is Ed Miliband's speech (6.6.13) on his policy for social security reform. He could have begun with a searing critique of the Coalition project and its neoliberal principles, and then marked out a qualitatively different set of values which will inform Labour's project, and the policies which follow from those principles. As it was, he began by stressing how little money there will be to spend, and saying that he'd handle it with 'decent values at the heart of the system' (but only very loosely indicating what these are – 'One Nation' values of greater fairness and co-operation and inclusiveness rather than conflict), before going on to work through the policy areas, arguing for his alternatives. There was no critique of the austerity agenda as a whole.

The policy which made the headlines in most of the media was that Labour, if elected, will match the Coalition's cap on welfare spending, for the first year at least. This came towards the end of the speech, although it was hinted at earlier. The detail of the speech proposes that the plan is to achieve this limit through alternative strategies – such as pushing the minimum wage upwards towards a living wage; controlling the housing budget by supporting councils to get a better deal from private landlords; subsidising youth employment; and urgent infrastructure spending to create more jobs and build more houses. Such measures would reduce the need for benefits, rather than reducing actual payments. But while many people became aware of the headlines, only a few managed to take in these details. And even if they did, at best the speech reads as a more humane way of realising the austerity agenda. Those policies could have been framed within a radical critique of the whole Coalition project, but they weren't. Our local canvassing experience is of traditional Labour voters having taken in the headlines and in response asking 'why bother?' – no-one is offering an alternative to 'austerity'.

This headline must have been expected and indeed intended. It was a push for the middle ground (and Blairites responded favourably). But it is such a short-term tactic, and one that makes no impact on the neoliberal hegemony. The speech repeatedly stresses that the strategy is long-termist, but ultimately it reads as a series of alternative policies to the same end, when it could have been framed as a campaign for a different kind of society. Far better to recognise the widespread 'good sense' of the anger towards the banks, and at the widespread social injustice in contemporary Britain, the growing support for the living wage, the widespread sense of insecurity, and to reject boldly the inequalities produced by a laissez-faire market; to frame Labour policies as a crusade for a society which harnesses the market to the needs of its people, rather than letting it dictate how we have to live. If this were to become the framing agenda, we might find polls asking 'Should someone who does a full-time job be paid enough to live on?'. Or 'If someone is made redundant, should the state provide support while he/she is finding a new job?' As David Stuckler argues above, if we did so we would find a public opinion of a different order.

Labour can only win the battle of ideas if it takes its role as a 'popular educator' seriously. Each crisis provides an opportunity to shift the direction of popular thinking, instead of simply mirroring the right's populist touch or pursuing short-term opportunism. The left, and Labour in particular, must adopt a more courageous, innovative, 'educative' and path-breaking strategic approach if they are to gain ground.

NOTES

1. All quotations from Gramsci are from *Selections from the Prison Notebooks*, Lawrence and Wishart 1972.
2. Renata Salecl, *Choice*, Profile Books 2010.
3. The Young Foundation, *Sinking and Swimming*, online report, 2011.

4. www.conservatives.com/News/Speeches/2011/05/David_Cameron_
Building_a_bigger_stronger_society.aspx.
5. www.tuc.org.uk/social/tuc-21796-f0.cfm.
6. www.theguardian.com/commentisfree/2013/jul/30/generation-
y-halfhearted-its-a-lie?INTCMP=SRCH.

4. AFTER NEOLIBERALISM: THE NEED FOR A GENDER REVOLUTION

Beatrix Campbell

In 2013, a time when capitalism ruled the world, the former British Library precinct within the British Museum – where Karl Marx once spent many productive years calculating this outcome – hosted an exhibition of the earliest evidence of human imagination. 'Ice Age Art' assembled a cornucopia of figurative objets d'art created up to 40,000 years ago (or more), depicting humans and the other animals with whom they shared space.

The audience was greeted by voluptuous fecundity: ripe, round female figures, with reindeers in flight, fish, birds, mammoths, lions, flutes, fish hooks, needles, and an occasional male. I trust that Marx would have been awed.

T.J. Clark, a distinguished art critic, was not so much awed as affronted by the sheer, surprising woman-ness of this universe. Writing in the *London Review of Books* he catches himself out for assuming that the image-makers were men, and concedes the prevailing inference that it is 'more likely' that the creators were women. He speculates on pregnancy not as the moment when women's bodies are home to another, but as a kind of alienation, 'a body becoming other to itself'. It is all so 'fearful, astonishing, ominous', he mutters, and the figurines 'fat, fat, fat'. He acknowledges what many of his readers, no doubt, will have already guessed: 'I know I am lost'. No willies, few weapons, no bodies whose raison d'être is to be desired.

But during my three visits there, I sensed not estrangement but wonder, whispered joy, the intoxicated rustle of spectators fascinated by imagination that appeared to be – as the children's illustrator Maurice Sendak said of himself before he died in 2012 – 'in love with the world'. But who knows? Who knows what or how they were thinking, these Ice Age humans? Who knows what they intended their audience to see and feel, and what they wanted their creations to mean?

That said, this art does seems to enunciate a challenge to an Enlightenment notion – recently reiterated by Steven Pinker in his grand theoretical work of 2012, *The Better Angels of Our Nature: Why Violence Has Declined* – that our ancestors were brutal and brutalised (and blokes), making their way in the world savagely; that they are strangers to us because we, their refined descendents, are uniquely rational, prosperous, democratic and pacific.

From three (yes, three) corpses of men who lived a mere 5000 years ago, Pinker is able to deduce the existence of general homicidal tendencies that, through evolution and enlightenment, have now been tamed. I would be much more cautious about inferring anything so definite about life in the era of Ice Age, whether from their art or indeed their cadavers. We surely cannot claim that it was either peaceful or violent: we don't know. But whatever else it is, Ice Age art is a forensic riposte to fantasies of liberal, capitalist modernity as progress to prosperity, democracy, peace and love.

Ice Age imagination reminds us that war and peace have histories, they are social practices; that violence between humans is not universal, eternal, inevitable and valorised. And what's more, violence and crime are specialisms – almost exclusively associated with specific cultures that create masculinity-as-domination. Feminism insists that violence is not biological or hormonal, but social; that crime, violence and war are productive of power; that they are – as theorists in second-wave feminism ventured – 'resources' in the 'achievement' or 'doing' or 'performance' of masculinities.

Drilled to kill, doomed to die: mastery and martyrdom is the heart-breaking dialectic of the manufacture of militarised, violent masculinity. Pinker's evolutionism cannot help us understand either the astounding, industrialised violence of the twentieth century or the contagious armed conflicts of the twenty-first.

In the post-cold-war era the world is not at peace, it is plagued by what Mary Kaldor calls 'new wars' – and in this context gender hierarchy and oppression is renewed. The making and maintaining of militarised masculinities is vital to these new modes of armed conflict that are proliferating across the flexible frontiers of globalised capitalism, between and within states. Violence is franchised out to auxiliary militias, security corporations and freelancing warlords:

gangs, guerrillas, police, death squads and vigilantes prosper; their networks of criminal free trade and spatial domination overpower the best efforts of 'new democracies' from Soweto to Sao Paulo. As Kaldor insists, rape and pillage are the modus operandi of 'new wars': they should not be seen as collateral damage. Neoliberal capitalism radiates violence. The richest society on the planet is armed. And it invests in one of the largest prison systems in the world. Violence circulates between state and citizen. In 2011, the US locked up one in every 107 people, and one in 50 were on probation.[1] Half a million people are 'correctional' officers, not to mention the many thousands of others who service and supply the system of incarceration.[2]

Violence is not unthinking, visceral, primitive; it is produced by, and is productive of, power and control over land, riches and people. Violent hyper-masculinities and concomitant gender polarisation are, therefore, not residual: they are remade in civil society and in state apparatuses. Indeed the violence that neoliberal capital and its accomplices generate is an integral part of its evolving gender settlement – which I call neo-patriarchy.

THE END OF THE EQUALITY PARADIGM

In spite of this increased violence, and the inequality that is inherent in neoliberalism, in the last quarter of the twentieth century the world's institutions reached a consensus: they joined together in hailing the goal of gender equality. Ironically, this was at the very moment when we were witnessing the limits, the exhaustion, of the equality paradigm.

The notion of equal opportunity was, in any case, incapable of withstanding the structures of gender: the sexual division of labour, and violence as a resource in the making and doing of masculinity. But with the collapse of the postwar consensus on welfare states and the mixed economy, the equality paradigm is now being defeated by the counter-revolutionary, neoliberal priorities of the world's financial institutions. They preach equal opportunity, but in practice produce a 'regressive modernisation' that reshapes but continues the patriarchal division of labour, and of traditional masculinities and femininities.

So, beware the liberation language of global capitalism: it rules the world, and it deploys the language of freedom, choice and competition to oust solidarity, co-operative creativity and equality.

Capitalism co-option of (any freedom)

After the deluge of state communisms, the world is quivering with
resistance but struggles to find new ideological and institutional
forms for those great values of solidarity, co-operation, creativity and
equality – values that are crucial for gender equality. In this moment
of capitalism's hegemony – its apparent inevitability, invincibility
and normality – the language of the marketplace appears not only to
govern the economy, but life itself.

It is a lie, of course. Capitalism does not do life. And that lie is never
more exposed in the twenty-first century than when we bring to it the
light of gender and the unsaid – the silences and secrets that are
knotted in the articulation of capitalism and patriarchy.

'Woman' as commodity, as carer, as producer and reproducer
(though rarely hailed, it appears, as taxpayer and never as citizen) is
positioned anew as Other; the sovereignty of ideologies of masculinity
is simultaneously rattled and reinstated. Gender, uniquely, exposes the
limits of this articulation, its contradictions and – most important –
its unsustainability. The old sexual contract is recognised as
unsustainable but retained in modernised form. Neoliberal neo-patriarchy is the new articulation of male domination.

But gender, uniquely, exposes the limits of neoliberal hegemony, its
contradictions and – most important – its unsustainability. Though
neoliberal neo-patriarchy is hegemonic, it is an unstable site of torrid
angst, complaint and trouble – and radical alternatives. As Leonard
Cohen saw:

> There is a crack in everything
> There's a crack in everything
> That's how the light gets in (_Anthem_).

Although gender remains an often invisible, or at best marginal, theme
in radical and party political discourses, it takes us to the fissures and
fault-lines, to the unsustainabilities, of the new, global capitalist settlement. For gender, like nature, is omni-relevant: it is everywhere, in
everything. The new global settlement is nothing if not a new sexual
settlement. Global capitalism works with patriarchal principles, institutions, cultures and psyches. So, our liberation from this tragedy is
inconceivable – it is, literally, unthinkable – without feminism.

Before returning to the theme of patriarchy's violence, I want to
turn now to talk about the continuing sexual division of labour within

Britain. I then look at the ways in which the global reach of neoliberalism is undermining equality and reconfiguring gender in Asia and South America.

EXPLOITATION AND THE GENDERED DIVISION OF LABOUR

A key problem for the concepts of equal pay and equal opportunity in both socialist and capitalist societies is that they never envisaged the transformation of men and masculinities. And understanding this – including understanding that this was an effect of the historical defeat of women in the nineteenth century – helps make sense of the gender inequality problem as not as a problem of evolution or choice (women choosing to have babies!) but of politics.

Historically, labourism participated in the settlement that created men as breadwinners, cared for by the sequestered and unpaid domestic labour of women. That division of labour was cemented in the 1880s by the compromise between capital and labour that was expressed in the concept of men's wages as the 'family wage.' And that principle prevailed in collective bargaining for almost a century. Of course, there have always been women and men for whom equality was the heroic ethic of their union or their party. But that principle was not the practice, either in wage bargaining or, later, in incomes policies.

In the 1970s and 1980s, the impact of women's liberation and other movements on trade unions and labourism began the process of transforming what could be perceived of as a men's movement (a form of class politics engaged at the expense of anyone who was not male and white). For a couple of decades, the impact of European directives and of the women's liberation movement was palpable in trade unions; and the effects of a new politics could be seen in the rise of the radical municipalism that was promoted by a new generation of metropolitan labourism; and, a little later, it was evident in the great wave of devolution.

Women's political representation improved during this period, though Britain's mother of Parliaments, the House of Commons, ranks only 65th in the world league: despite more women than ever having been elected, they still constitute a meagre 23 per cent in the unreconstructed Commons. But in the devolved institutions women's representation has increased more substantially: in the Welsh Assembly it is 40 per cent, and in the Scottish Parliament 35 per cent.

The notion of equal opportunities was always skewed by the domestic division of labour: women's relative poverty always provided the alibi for men's relative absence from the unpaid labours of love and care. But there was huge change in the last quarter of the twentieth century. However, these new movements toward equality were scarcely seeded in Britain before, at the end of the twentieth century, equalities legislation – most of it barely a quarter of a century old – began to be routinely and institutionally disparaged and sabotaged.

And by the 2000s progress on equal pay had stalled. Four decades of activism had dragged women's relative pay upwards, but only up to a point. In the twenty-first century, despite some heroic equal pay activism in the tribunals, the disabling of unions in the private sector, the consolidation of gendered segregation and divisions of labour, resistance to any reduction in men's 'working day' by companies, governments and men generally – all these contributed to the renewal, rather than the decline, of inequalities.

In the 1970s the gender contradictions of the labour movement had been dramatised by a number of events. At the beginning of the decade, following the recommendations of the Prices and Incomes Board, government and unions agreed to the introduction of another patriarchal perk in the public sector: the bonus, which was mainly available to men. This bonus system became a vector of secrecy and sexism for the following thirty years. Meanwhile, as if in a parallel universe, the 1969 Equal Pay Act was to be implemented. Then in 1974-75 there was a major battle over the Social Contract between the Labour government and trade unions, many elements of which would potentially redistribute resources to women.[3] In exchange for restraints on industrial action, a flat rate pay rise was proposed – that is an equal £6 pay rise for all, (£3 for part-timers); this was designed to boost the relative earnings of the low paid – the majority of whom were women – in a period of inflation-led wage increases that were increasing the pay gap. And the Social Contract also included a provision – again especially important to women – for the enhancement of the social wage, particularly through investment in education and health. But multiple pressures yielded an ugly tangle between egalitarian tactics and patriarchal hierarchies. Under the unbearable weight of the oil crisis, and prime minister Jim Callaghan's endorsement of monetarism, the Social Contract collapsed. 'Free collective bargaining' was restored, and with it 'time honoured and, therefore, conservative conventions'.[3] This was the last time that an egalitarian pay policy, linked to the expansion of the social wage and the redistribution of social power, was contemplated in Britain.

The battles of 1970s Britain – and what followed after the left's defeat – represent a case study of the effects of a shrinking down of the socialist project to the individual wage (rather men's wages), alongside the valorisation of 'free collective bargaining' as the detonator of capitalism.

By the time that Labour returned to government in 1997, its social contract, insofar as there was one, operated informally between New Labour and the City: in return for relative autonomy for the financial industry and the City, Labour's social programme was to be funded from the tax harvest yielded from the unleashed and soaring finance sector. Despite the best efforts of feminism in the Labour Party (one of whose most significant achievements was the exponential increase in the number of women MPs in the House of Commons), parliamentary culture remained masculinist, and New Labour 'overly so', as Joni Lovenduski has argued. Where women's interests converged with other agendas – law and order, for example – feminists were able to find room to reform. Where women's interests demanded redistribution between women, men and capital, they attracted indifference or opposition. No new legislation addressed the problem of equal pay, and little attention or resources were allocated to it; while New Labour's adherence to the now diminished powers of trade unionism had the effect of restricting women's access to the means of making a difference.

A glance at the statistics vindicates a pessimistic prognosis. The crawl to economic equality between men and women is over in the OECD countries. The Equality and Human Rights Commission warns that progress toward equal pay is 'grinding to a halt'. The European gender pay gap is stable at around 25 per cent. It begins at the beginning of working life and – irrespective of generation – it grows over the life cycle. The gender pay gap declined by an average 1 per cent per year after the most egalitarian moment – the mid-1970s, when the Social Contract converged with implementation of the Equal Pay Act. But this flattened out in the 2000s. The annual pay gap between men and women is about 26 per cent, but it is 65 per cent between part-time women (mainly mothers) and full-time men. Men's pensions are 50 per cent higher than women's.

These figures do not represent the lag between a patriarchal past and an emerging, egalitarian future. They are probably as good as it is going to get. The gap is structural. In the twenty-first century, a relative life-time gender gap confronts young women just as it constrained their mothers. That is the story of equal pay in 'old' European capitalism.

Time and care

The old sexual contract based on the family wage and women's domestic labour – which itself only episodically represented reality – is dead. By the twenty-first century the male breadwinner was almost extinct. Most women for most of their adult lives now participate in the labour market. But the patriarchal structure of paid work is virtually untroubled by this seismic change. Now, as ever, women's 'public life' and labour force participation is contingent on taking care of men, children and elders.

Whilst women en masse reclaimed the realm from which they had been excluded, waged work in every political system remains contingent on the work of care that, though often unseen, unpaid and unaudited, contributes massively to wealth and wellbeing. In the postwar period welfare states took on some of the work of care: they mediated it, paid it and professionalised it. Indeed, during the 1970s, second-wave feminism's tendency towards anti-capitalism and anti-statism came to be modified by the recognition that welfare states are the necessary (if not sufficient) context for gender equality – state welfare has been a decisive context in which to mandate public investment in the work of care that falls to women. As Land and Himmelweit have shown, public investment in care involves redistribution from men/taxpayers towards women and children.

But when neoliberal politics and the world's financial institutions marginalise state welfare, as well as depriving women of support in their role as carers, they reconstitute women care workers as the precariat – it is estimated that 300,000 care workers are on zero-hours contracts; and they also reinstate patriarchal divisions of labour and redistribute incomes towards men.

The prevailing common sense has been that when it comes to gender things are getting better; that women are now equal to men; and that, if not now then soon, they will be recognised and rewarded equally (unless, that is, they compromise their equal opportunities by exercising the choice to have babies or take care of people). It has become 'common sense' that men are sharing housework and child care, that the sexual division of labour is in decline. Not so. It is not dying, it is changing.

For employers, command and control over time is a priority. Yet nowhere in the world has neoliberalism been answered by movements over working time equivalent to the great nineteenth-century campaigns for the ten-hour day and later the eight-hour day. And the new pressure on time for care is overwhelmingly experienced by women. Time use studies of the minutiae of everyday life reveal that, though men do more, they don't do much more. Progress toward domestic democracy is also stalled.

British men's contribution to domestic work increased at the rate of about one minute a day, per year – that is, by about 30 minutes – over the three decades from the 1970s to the 2000s. This is not nothing, but it's not much. Men's contribution to the work of care during the same period increased by about 30 seconds a day per year. Meanwhile, women's housework has reduced slightly, whilst employed women's commitment to childcare has actually risen more than men's. It is the same story in the US, and even in Norway – the most supportive country in the world to fathers. Change has been palpable, but pitiful.

VIOLENCE

As we have seen, men's violence is not – as Pinker would have it – an epiphenomenon of primitive, uncivilised or under-developed cultures. It is a resource in the quest for dominion that always menaces women and the sustainability of social space; and it is also currently assailing the 'new democracies' that are struggling to transform societies brutalised by institutional (and avowedly capitalist) tyranny, from South Africa to Brazil.[4]

These new zones of armed conflict attract what we can call The Impunity: victims cannot expect justice or redress, and neither states nor citizens expect to be called to account. And, away from the war zones, the violation of women's bodies – a crime of sexual dominion – remains perhaps the most tolerated crime in the world.

Sex and violence in Britain

In 1970, the very year that the Women's Liberation Movement was born in Britain, Rupert Murdoch's media empire – arguably the most successful late twentieth-century invasion of British culture – was sponsor of a re-invigoration of popular sexism. The jewel in the crown of Murdoch's empire, the *Sun*, exactly synchronises with the rise of feminism, and its riposte was Page 3: daily pictures of nude women. Murdoch didn't merely reflect 'public taste', he helped to create it. No government dared confront his empire, and none were prepared to challenge the politics of sexism that was the point of articulation between the empire's trademark sensationalism, cruelty and criminal corruption. That is, until the empire went too far: bugging the royal family laid it open to the risk of investigation. The phone hacking scandal slowly, slowly gathered momentum until calls for public and parliamentary scrutiny became irresistible. What emerged was an alarming matrix of illegality at the core of which was sexism and a trade in sexual scandal.

You can witness the correlation between sex and violence when you go into any institution that warehouses extreme masculinities: prisons are packed with young men who see their violence as the manifestation of their manliness. They are clear: they are soldiers. Their walls are adorned with the sexism. Enter any young offenders' prison in Britain and you will be greeted by pledges, in many languages, to equality. I once stood on a prison wing when the young men's magazines arrived: alongside the *Sun*, read by the prison staff, sat a teetering pile of sexist lads' mags of the kind that were launched by the 'blokelash' in the 1990s.

By the 2000s, however, the lads' mags were in terminal decline, displaced by the wide availability of pornography on the internet. Sexism – like its nemesis, feminism – captures new contexts and technologies; old stuff in new spaces.

Sexist abuse of women on the web reached a crisis point in 2013, when feminist bloggers exposed sexualised abuse, reported death threats to the police and demanded that companies try to take more responsibility for the violence of virtual harassment. Journalist Toby Young, one of the middle-class metro men who like to lower the tone, has recently introduced a fresh alibi for sexism: it was a 'sophomore thing', he replied, when accused by feminist Labour MP Stella Creasy, on BBC's *Newsnight*, of tweeting about a fellow 'MP's tits'.

The web frees up social space for both women and men to improvise, to find their voice, create new popular cultures: for feminism to protest, and for sexism to stalk women, spread its pleasures and invent new templates of insult – all fortified by anonymity. Violation of women's bodies, whether in the virtual or real world, carries little risk of punishment. Despite radical consciousness-raising among the police, judiciary and law-makers about the meaning of rape and abuse, sexual assault is a crime that by and large escapes justice.

Ninety per cent of rape is not reported. Eighty per cent of rapes that are reported are not acted upon. Of the 14 per cent that go to trial in Britain, only half result in conviction. In 2013, the police referral of reported rapes to the Crown Prosecution Service declined. And these figures are more or less replicated throughout the world. This universal 'procedural injustice' is a virtual guarantee of impunity for men who rape women.

Since we know that rape is shrouded in humiliation – that reluctance, rather than enthusiasm, drives levels of reporting – it is clear: impunity does not come from confusion but collusion. In no society in the world does the criminal justice system take the side of women (or indeed the majority of men who don't rape women). This is the routine, everyday manifestation of The Impunity. It is a catastrophe for women and a crisis for democracy because it vindicates pessimism about the possibility of making a difference. What can democracy mean to women who have no expectation that the law will be enforced and their persons protected?

Post-colonial violence

Force is the accomplice of neoliberalism across the world. Kaldor argues that the new forms mark the end of the Clausewitzian theatres of war: mayhem and predation are designed to terrify populations and lay waste to territory by the commission of 'conspicuous atrocity'. At the beginning of the twentieth century around 85 per cent of casualties of war were military (almost all men) rather than civilian (often women and children), but by the end of the century that ratio had 'almost exactly reversed'.[5] Looting, pillage, population displacement and rape are not so much occupational hazards as central to their modus operandi.

In Latin America, from Brazil to Mexico, Columbia and Venezuela, organised crime and violence plague these societies emerging from dictatorship and struggling to survive the impact of neoliberal economic policies. Millions of people live in toxic, unplanned, unprotected urban landscapes, where emaciated local states have little or no jurisdiction or powers of intervention; where the violence of dictatorships or civil wars continues to discipline relationships between political and police apparatuses enfeebled by neoliberal policies; where boundaries between politics and legal and illegal 'free trade' are fluid and patrolled by hyper-masculinities.

Their experience confirms what is well established in South Africa (see below) – not to mention Europe – that poverty alone does not generate violence. The poorest people on earth are women. But they are not the perpetrators of violence, they are the victims. (So, too, of course, are boys and men who become 'the killables', whose life expectancy is foreshortened by their peers in gangs, criminal networks, police, militias and vigilante death squads.)

Latin America's 'new democracies' are ill-equipped to confront, let alone control, the drugs and guns 'industrialists' who migrate more or less unhindered across borders, whose local foot soldiers service global operations. Brazil's profound inequalities have been seriously mitigated by the government's efforts to address poverty. But men's violence undermines public peace and sustainability.[6] Homicide rates (per 100,000) soar in Brazil (21), Columbia (31), Venezuela (45), El Salvador (69), Honduras (91). The most unprotected neighbourhoods live in a state of 'endless war', where murder rates are multiplied by 'muertes legales' – extra-judicial executions. In the Dominican Republic, for example, according to Lilian Bobea, the murder rate quadrupled from 6 per 100,000 in the 1980s to 26 per 100,000 in the 2000s, overpowering community organisations and local and national state apparatuses. The penetration of public institutions by criminal networks sometimes means that violence indicates not so much a failure on the part of democratic institutions, more the basis on which they function.[7] Despite the best intentions of the new democracies, men's violence is 'fragmenting social space, fostering fear and creating distrust in institutions'.

The articulation of apartheid and patriarchy produced South Africa as one of the most violent societies on earth: it had the highest homicide and rape rates in the world. Its remarkably peaceful liberation from apartheid was then swiftly captured by neoliberal neo-patriarchy: fiscal austerity, privatisation, export-oriented production – and violence. Twenty years after liberation there are more police and security guards than nurses: 400,000 private security guards and 190,000 police officers to 212,000 nurses. Every month the security industry registers 20,000 new members – men patrolling other men are stationed everywhere – whilst over 40 per cent of nursing posts remain unfilled.

Stephen Pinker, who likes to position societies in relation to notions of European enlightenment, evolution and civilisation, categorises South Africa as a society undergoing 'de-civilising processes'. But it would be more accurate to conclude that the violence of the apartheid era has been modified and enhanced by the violence of its neoliberal present.

There is undoubtedly a strongly gendered element within the general levels of violence. Rachel Jewkes's research for the Medical Research Institute found that a third of men admitted to raping a girl or woman. Two cases in particular opened a window on South African society in 2013.

Guns and a bloodied cricket bat were discovered in the fortified home of South Africa's great white paralympian Oscar Pistorius after he shot his lover Reeva Steenkamp (white) through the bathroom door one February night. 'Afrikaaner men are very patriarchal, and within that, gun ownership is seen as part of masculinity', commented Jewkes. In another shocking incident, seventeen-year-old Anene Booysen (black) was found dumped and dying on a construction site in a small town in Western Cape on 2 February 2013. Her intestines were discarded beside her raped and sliced body – mutilated not by strangers but by a group of friends with whom she had enjoyed a drink the night before. 'It was her vagina and her breasts they wanted to destroy. It was her walk and her talk. It was her girl-ness …', wrote the feminist activist Sisonke Msimang.

Nowhere exposes more eloquently than these societies that there is that no necessary correlation between industrial sophistication, democracy, peace and socio-sexual equality.

GENDER IN ASIAN CAPITALISM

Asian capitalisms tend to be prototypes of strong states, weak welfare provision, and modernised male domination. Home to almost half of the human population they (as much, if not more than, Europe or North America) are defining the twenty-first century's sexual settlement.

In the post-socialist society of China, the chasm between men and women's time and money represents a counter-revolutionary reprise of a patriarchal division of labour. The state-sponsored Confucian capitalism of China is creating inequalities faster than in any other transitional society; traditional masculinities and femininities are being reinstated as if the revolution was a transgressive anomaly.

Before the turn to economic liberalism, China's workers were poor, but they were equally poor. The transition to capitalism released 200 million people from poverty, but accelerating inequalities and the demolition of the welfare system also sponsored the 'mother of all redistributions'. Unprecedented migration to the cities located millions of workers in urban dormitories – so that, while producing commodities that find their way into homes everywhere in the world, they themselves have neither homes nor money nor time for children. Millions of their children are raised thousands of miles away by relatives in the countryside.

After capitalism was introduced at the end of the 1970s, the gender pay gap grew: in 1988 women's pay was 86 per cent of men's; by 2011 it was only 67 per cent. Before capitalism, parenthood had little impact on pay. After capitalism, the parenthood penalty rose to 40 per cent. Privatisation and cuts scythed public child care provision – a massive redistribution away from children and women. China's transition can thus be seen as a transition to state-sponsored neo-patriarchy. In China, most women, like men, do paid work full-time. But most men, unlike women, do little domestic labour: women work 86 hours a week, but men only 58. That time differential explains almost a third of China's stout gender pay gap.[8] This is China's bequest to the new gender settlement.

In India, the rush to urban industrialisation, following the government's embrace of neoliberal fiscal reform in 1991, has modernised the patriarchal values that had already fatally defeated the egalitarian proclamation of its 1947 constitution. As Jayati Ghosh has shown, far from feminising the paid labour force, neoliberalism has generated a form of 'jobless growth': a rise in GDP without expanding employment – and a defeminised labour force. Women's share of the labour market has plunged from around half to a quarter, and the gender pay gap has increased in every category of work.

Technology has also been enlisted to further intensify the masculinisation of the population: the introduction of ultra-sound technology to determinate the sex of embryos in the early 1980s has facilitated foeticide. This is an entirely new refinement of the boy preference (and femicide) that has been apparent in India since the first census in 1901. It will shape gender, generation, social welfare, migration and violence for this century.

In South Korea, a paragon Asian tiger, and perhaps the most techno-savvy society on the planet, men do least housework, and women's labour force participation is the lowest in the OECD countries. The gender pay gap is the highest: 38 per cent. Among employed women it has one of the highest levels of 'precariousness' – 70 per cent (precarity is spreading fast).

CONCLUSION

The future will be shaped by the 'new' capitalisms of Asia, Latin America and the post-socialist societies. They are defining – as much, if not more than Europe and North America – the twenty-first century sexual settlement.

Whether in its Asian forms, or the Anglo-American model, or the post-dictatorship democracies of Latin America, capital may employ women but it does not emancipate them. If the world's proletariat is growing, so too is the precariat – capital's favoured form of labour market, in which all the risks and responsibilities of life are transferred to the worker – the part of the labour market where women predominate.

Since the 1970s we have learned that social solidarity through the medium of welfare states is the minimum necessary condition for society to take the side of women. This is not to say that social-democratic or socialist states were feminist – their tragedy is that they weren't. But the economic regimes forced on states by the World Bank and the IMF have waged war on the public good; and their neoliberal imperative is also the articulation of neo-patriarchy in global governance. This is a historic defeat. For the moment, 'the long march through the institutions' – a vision of non-violent radical transformation – struggles for breath.

It is not surprising, therefore, that, with few exceptions, the response to the economic havoc wrought by the banking system has been becalmed – or that some of the most spectacular challenges to sexism appear in do-able improvisations within popular culture.

In no society or system are women paid the same as men for a day, a week, or a lifetime's work. In no society do men share equally the work of care with women. Sexism finds new cultures and contexts; violence and sexual aggression attract impunity.

And in a world dominated by neoliberal neo-patriarchy there is little indication that this will change in favour of women – without a gender revolution.

NOTES

1. US Bureau of Justice, 2011: www.bjs.gov/index.cfm?ty=pbdetail&iid=4537.
2. US Bureau of Labor Statistics, 2010: www.bls.gov/ooh/Protective-Service/Correctional-officers.htm.
3. For an excellent account of the Social Contract, written from the point of view of a union representing low-paid women workers, see Bob Fryer and Steve Williams, *Leadership and Democracy: The History of the National Union of Public Employees*, Volume 2, 1928-1993, L&W 2011.
4. David Purdy, 'The Social Contract and Socialist Policy', in Michael Prior (ed), *The Popular and the Political*, Routledge 1981. See also Beatrix Campbell and Valerie Charlton, 'Work to Rule', in the same book; and *International Socialism*, 'Tearing up the Social Contract', March 1977. Available at: www.marxists.org/history/etol/newspape/isj/1977/no096/notm1.htm.
5. See Alba Zaluar, 'Crimes and Violence trends in Rio de Janeiro, Brazil: Case Study prepared for Enhancing Urban Safety and Security: Global Report on Human Settlements', UN-HABITAT 2007; Available from www.unhabitat.org/grhs/2007.
6. Mary Kaldor, *New and Old Wars: Organised Violence in a Global Era*, Stanford University Press 2007 (second edition), p107.
7. Zaluar, 'Crimes and Violence trends ....'.
8. Lilian Bobea, 'Organised violence, disorganized state', in Arias and Goldstein (eds), *Violent Democracies*, Duke University Press 2010.
9. Liangshu Qi and Xiao-Yuan Dong, 'Housework Burdens, Quality of Market Work Time, and Men's and Women's Earnings in China', Departmental Working Papers 2013-01, Department of Economics, University of Winnipeg.

5. Class and generation under neoliberalism

Ben Little

THREE STORIES

Angry – but at what?

thump, thump … thump, thump, THUD

It's 1 am, and that's the noise of my upstairs neighbour in Mile End, Jack, banging on my ceiling with an unidentified heavy object. He thinks he's being kept awake by the sound of the extractor fan in our bathroom that's linked to the light switch, but we've brushed our teeth in the dark for some six months now. This time, I'm fairly certain the noise is from the spin cycle on the new neighbour's washing machine. They work unsocial hours and haven't cottoned on to the fact that their appliance shakes the entire building.

In my encounters with Jack, a professional in his late twenties and from a relatively wealthy background, it's slowly dawned on me that his anger is representative of a broad social trend. His territoriality is an expression of lost privilege. He compares the noise our fan makes to that of an audience member at the proms jingling coins in his pocket or people talking through an opera he went to on holiday ('I just listen to Radio 3 now, I can't bear it', he says). He is cultured, and he expects to sleep blissfully ignorant of his neighbours' night-time sorties to the loo.

Jack's sleep-deprived rage may be directed at me, but what he's really angry about is beginning his adult life, making a home and starting a family in material conditions that are unacceptable given the standards he's been acculturated to expect. Specifically, his class-based expectations of privacy are not being met. It's a rage I admit I've

85

felt myself at times, although I've tended to direct it at landlords and profiteering estate agents.

In the 1970s and 1980s, middle-class, young parents in London could mostly afford to buy whole houses or live closer to the centre, and if they were renting would expect their money to go a long way. Probably around half of Jack and his partner's salaries will go on rent and bills, making saving to buy a house difficult, and currently that's money spent on a flat in which he can't even get a good night's sleep. The five-apartment building we both live in was a house converted shortly before the 1997 laws on soundproofing were introduced at the start of what has become the long house price boom since the recession of the early 1990s. The whole building is probably only slightly larger in size than the house Jack was brought up in.

Jack's frustration is shared by many young, normatively successful people across the country. It is an expression of collapsing middle-class 'entitlements' – that you can do everything right, work hard, get good grades, land the right job and still not get the disposable income, job security, pension or, yes, housing that you benchmark against your parents' experience as 'doing ok'.

Much has been written about the decline in prosperity and security of the global North's young middle class, in Europe known as the 1000€ generation. In places like Italy, Spain, Portugal and above all Greece, the crisis hitting young people, and increasingly not so young people (this is a problem that was already emerging before the economic crisis of 2008), is unprecedented. Across the western world, there is a collective double-take happening for those born since roughly 1980, as the comforts of life once taken for granted in a 'developed' nation become difficult to obtain and competitively rationed. On current socio-economic trajectories, it seems likely that this is increasingly going to become the reality in most places in the world.[1]

So Jack's complaint is of an increasingly common kind, and signals something in the wider shifts that are going on in our society under neoliberalism. The middle class – which grew rapidly in the second half of the last century – are now seeing living standards fall rapidly in significant ways. In the UK, many of us may have iPhones to tuck us up in bed, but the use of house price increases to buy the votes of our parents' generation through inflating their paper wealth has hidden a political shift in favour of the richest that is sucking economic life from the middle class. And because this new political and economic order is partly disguised by being played out in generational terms, many people in Jack's situation are confused about who to blame for their financial insecurity and declining social status.

Fear and loathing in Tottenham

> Yeah, I went to the EMA protests. That was hippy shit, fun and all, but the riots … Now that was political! Everyone gets hung up on the looting, but the real reason for the riots was taking back the spaces we've been pushed out of by the cops and society.

This is one of my first-year students talking about her experience of political activism. Every year at the North London university where I teach, I run a session for first-years in campaigning on participatory democracy – in which we simulate the democratic process through a large group structure. (It doesn't always go as planned. Usually they come up with something suitably well-meaning, but a couple of years ago, students decided through respectably democratic means that the biggest issue facing the planet was poverty and the best way to solve it was to cut taxes for the rich as that would incentivise people to work harder. Neoliberal values sometimes run deep.)

This year, one group began a quite remarkable conversation – a very intense debate about the nature of political activism in their peer group. There was a back and forth going on, with students from non-traditional higher education backgrounds for once challenging those who were more comfortable in a university environment. This first group saw the student protests over tuition fees and EMA as a waste of time: they hadn't really achieved anything and had left the protestors vulnerable to the police. On the other hand – while the more middle-class students were condemning them – the more working-class students insisted that the wave of summer riots of 2011 that started in Tottenham had been a form of protest connected to where the participants actually lived. They saw the riots as challenging the police, who were seen as the key source of their oppression (largely through 'stop and search' and other racist and age discriminatory practices); the police were seen as making it clear that young (usually black) people were not welcome in public spaces.

Not all agreed on these points, but the conversation then became broader. Students discussed how as young people generally they were treated with suspicion and fear in shops and on street corners; how the places they used to go for leisure as teenagers had been closed down; and how many felt alienated, not from politics as such, but from society as a whole. What was also interesting about this discussion was that it resonated not just with the students from British backgrounds but throughout the group, gaining nods of agreement from the international students.

Talk quickly turned to uncertain job prospects and an intense anxiety about their future. From that conversation it would seem that our society has increasingly little to offer young people apart from disdain and fear. We are not investing enough in their futures or easing their transitions into adulthood. Instead we are heaping them with debt and telling them that any failure is their own fault. These young people are at the sharp end of neoliberalism. (This is, of course, in interesting contradiction to a media culture that still retains a certain fascination with youth as a commodifiable cultural goal – as promoted, for example, by makeover TV and both women's and men's magazines.)

Working-class young people like my students and their friends are at the sharp end of neoliberalism. Unlike Jack, many of my students don't have high expectations in terms of housing and quietude, although some do fantasise about a secure middle-class life. They are the first year-cohort to have had their EMA withdrawn, and the second to pay £9000 fees; and it is possible that they will soon be ineligible for housing benefit until they reach the age of 25, and so will be forced to stay with parents until they get a stable job good enough to pass a landlord's credit check (there were 85 applicants for every graduate job last summer). And for those who leave home there will be no going back if their family relies on housing benefit – it will be sink or swim, as the bedroom tax ensures that holding a spare room in a family home is no longer an option. Meanwhile my students' friends who had not made it to university were in the main having an even tougher time, with fewer prospects.

What these young people need is support, clear pathways into adulthood and jobs – or, at the very least, a change in the way in which we structure their expectations, if those life transitions are no longer to happen in the way in which they used to. The move from education into employment, regardless of the age or qualification level at which it is made, must be as central to our politics as schooling or retirement, and given as much support and attention. Instead our culture treats young adults as social pariahs and tells them it's their fault that they can't get jobs or off benefits, focusing on the examples of the successful few to suggest the inadequacy of the rest.

Weightless millionaires

> Between 2:31 pm and 2:51 pm on 6 May 2010, the DOW Jones Industrial Average of major US stock prices fell by an astonishing 998 points (approximately 9 per cent), its largest every same-day point decline. This drop, subsequently known as the Flash Crash, caused a temporary loss of more than US$1 trillion in market value, with some major stocks falling briefly to $.01 per share. Prices rebounded quickly, and the loss in market value was regained in the following days. One of the causes behind the Flash Crash is now believed to be high-frequency trading (HFT): automated trading by computer programmes that buy and sell stocks in trades that often last only seconds.[2]

Every second, millions of market trades are made across the world by HFT operators. With competency measured in microseconds, virtual brokers and traders exchange commodities, currencies and stocks with the barest of oversight or approval from human beings. Of course, were something to go seriously wrong a frazzled financial services worker could pull the plug on the machines that make them millions, a few pennies at time, but by the time the programmes wound down the consequences could be severe for any individual trading company or stock, or – as happened on 6 May 2010 – for the financial markets as a whole.

The microsecond trade has become the timescape of neoliberal capitalism. Time, like any other measure, is a variable that can be used more efficiently in the pursuit of profit, while faith is placed in markets to sort out the social outcome through pricing and competition. To describe neoliberalism as an inhuman system of capital accumulation and conjoint social control may by now be a cliché, but in the context of the new technologies of the financial services, there can be little doubt that humans appear to be increasingly surplus to requirement in the promulgation of capitalism. For the market fundamentalist, the needs and wants of the vast mass of people have become a problem to

[handwritten margin note: wealth accumulation + responsibility + closes gaps.]

be resolved by technocratic means. And given that markets are increasingly regulated by algorithms and a relatively small number of operators, and that it is markets that provide us with economic stability and growth, the function of neoliberal government becomes simply that of providing bread and circuses – with a full belly and distracted mind, we are less likely to rebel.

Meanwhile, the 'weightless millionaires' float away from the rest of society.[3] These are not the bourgeoisie or colonials of previous eras. No longer tied to factory or plantations, they live on exclusive cruise ships such as *The World*, or do circuits from Tax Haven to Tax Haven, in the meantime fiercely protecting their prodigious wealth through modern technology. As the regulation of and extraction of profit from markets becomes automated, they do not need to stand over their wealth in situ, as they used to do when it was bound to productive forces. All this permits the infrastructure of elite financial governance to lift away from the mass; and where it does need physical space it is concentrated in increasingly exclusive geographic centres – New York, London, Shanghai.

For the neoliberal elites for whom there is no threat of poverty, no fear of hunger, just the relentless drive towards further accumulation, life carries on in an endless present of parties, board meetings and acquisitions. The mega-rich will carry on as usual, finding faster and faster ways to get even richer and ensure that society falls in line to facilitate their ascent – higher and higher, further and further away from the rest of us, less and less responsible for and dutiful to the real economy that their ancestors' wealth once represented. And it becomes apparent that what is going to be left once the elites have floated away, and the pay-offs that once bought mass consent are spent, is drudgery and subsistence for the rest of us.

GENERATIONAL CHANGE AND POLITICS

These three sketches give a snapshot of some of the different locations in which a new class settlement is emerging in our society. They indicate the location of some of the keener edges of the social changes that are coming. The working and middle classes will condense, and there will be a sharp drop-off at the bottom – from relative precarity to deep poverty; and there will be increasing social mistrust, with lines being drawn along racial and geographic lines as well through social class. My argument is that this new settlement is manifest in an emerging

neo lib ideology in short →
"a continual present"
CLASS AND GENERATION UNDER NEOLIBERALISM 91

generational politics produced by the material effects of neoliberalism on the lives of young people.

Seismic shifts

While neoliberal ideology remains resolutely focused on the short term, forcing our society to occupy a continual present, transnational capital in the material world plans in the long term to ensure that our economies and institutions are shaped according to their interests: among other means through lobbying cartels, media ownership, the purchasing of mass consent through asset giveaways (privatisations of e.g. council housing) and the discipline of defeatist rhetoric (There Is No Alternative). Over the last thirty years there has been a whole set of fundamental changes that have reshaped society in the long-term interests of capital, as we have argued elsewhere in this Manifesto.[4] Indeed this process has accelerated since the 2008 economic crash: what has happened subsequently has deepened the settlement of affairs in favour of the wealthiest. As Neal Curtis argues:

> In effect the crisis in private speculation was dealt with by transferring the problem to the public sector and creating a crisis of government spending. The tightening of the public purse strings, justified as necessary 'austerity', is the chief mechanism for protecting the private wealth that has functioned under these circumstances, while the increased need to involve the private sector in works the state can no longer afford to carry out offers new opportunities for that private wealth to increase and a means for temporarily solving problems caused by the current 'spatiotemporal dynamics of capital accumulation'.[5]

The social democratic settlement is being undone, and the results of its undoing are frequently experienced in generational terms. It is mostly preserved for those grew up within it and would not countenance the withdrawal of benefits – such as pensions or free health and education – that they see as a right; but it is being dismantled for those who are too young to have understood their dependence on it, and who are consistently told that the welfare state permits freeloading and endorses laziness. The longer term shifts are reflected in the life experiences of generations.[6]

Ken Roberts (after Karl Mannheim) argues that a truly 'new' generation is not something that happens automatically over time. A new generation only emerges when there is a major social, cultural or economic shift. For Roberts the last forty years have been dominated by the post-war 'baby-boomer' generation, who have had a common set of values and life experiences. Although these were contested within that generation, the broader terrain of debate was agreed, with a widely accepted assumption that there would be increasing plenty and a greater liberalisation of society, and the key question being how to divide the spoils. Those assumptions no longer hold. As Roberts argues, if socio-economic and cultural changes take place through developmental or evolutionary processes, young people's life-stage problems will be basically similar to – and can be addressed in the same basic ways – as those of the previous generation: 'Governments need simply to update and refresh their youth policies'. But:

> Transformative changes, in contrast, require wholly new thinking by the vanguard members of new generations themselves, and also by governments. Wholly new minds, and maybe new political movements and parties may be required.[7]

What sort of generational politics?

  ↳ Current politics doesn't serve the current generation or current crisis.

Generational politics as I originally saw it was about mobilising young people to engage and participate in politics, both electoral and otherwise.[8] I wanted to demonstrate that their disengagement in political processes had an impact on their lives: the baby-boomer generations and those older than them (and particularly those in the middle classes), as the biggest age-based voting blocks in the country, had been largely cushioned from the worst impacts of austerity and its concurrent structural changes. This can still be seen clearly in the UK where the coalition government have pledged to increase pensions while threatening to withdraw most benefits from young people under the age of 25.

As originally formulated, this was certainly not a 'hate your parents' rhetoric (although that rhetoric has been used by others to divide and distract from the real issues); it was a recognition that an unequal social order is being constructed along generational lines by paying off baby-boomers and exposing young people to the hard realities of a re-organised economy. This is not a wealth transfer from young to old, or a neglect of the interests of the young simply because they don't vote: it is part of a strategic restructuring of how our economy and society work in favour of capital, focusing its efforts on the weakest points of resistance – which include the economy's newest and most vulnerable entrants.

This is the context in which the idea of generation has emerged as a political space in the UK. It is often presented as a straightforward battle between the generations for resources. George Osborne and Nick Clegg have deployed the idea to justify austerity, while Ed Miliband has conjured a 'British promise' of generational progress. On all sides there is a clear sense that generation has emerged as an idea. But too often these complex socio-political changes are rehearsed through the reductive narrative that young people's parents are robbing them of their future, and are coupled with already existing policy positions. Tory politicians frequently draw on this rhetoric to justify a programme that deepens inequality and retrenches the state. Osborne stated in 2011 that: 'we have always understood that the greatest unfairness was loading debts onto our children that our generation didn't have the courage to tackle ourselves'; and in January 2014, once more asserting the need for deepening austerity, he asked: 'Do we say "the worst is over, back we go to our bad habits of borrowing and spending and living beyond our means and let the next generation pay the bill?"'.

Just as Thatcher famously asserted that the family is the only recognisable collective beyond the individual, so this narrative also domesticates broad social problems to the sphere of intra-family conflict, and thereby reduces the political to individual dynastic struggle.

The family metaphor, used often and indiscriminately by politicians just like the personal anecdote – plays better for reactionary politics than progressive ones. It limits politics to the immediate experience, and to the concept of the individual, assuming no broader structuring forces, and no richer imaginary. Such a view arrests solidarity before it begins and judges complex social phenomena through the sphere of the white British nuclear family. It also masks the withdrawal of state aid through a renewed emphasis on young people depending on family resources to get started on adult life.

To put it another way, once the family metaphor is deployed, responsibility for the political failure of young people is shifted back into families: where the state withdraws, parents can be blamed. Generational politics is here deeply entwined with class: families that have the resources to ensure their children have an expensive education, internships at prestigious firms and decent housing can look on the relationship they have with their children as decent, moral and, importantly, loving and nurturing. Those who can't are encouraged to internalise the results of the failure of an economic system, the ideological withdrawal of state support for their kids, and a deeply unjust educational system and labour market, as being their own responsibility.[9]

Nevertheless, relationships across generations are important to my argument – but not in a way that can be reduced to a rhetorically idealised set of family relations. Families will organise their affairs in a wide variety of different ways; and there is no correct set of behaviours or models of support. It is the breakdown of dialogue between different generations *outside of the family* that is revealing about our current neoliberal settlement. A generational politics is a significant socio-political space precisely because it opens up a conflict over the future, but one that is very much rooted in the present: it asks what responsibilities we have to one other and what we can expect at different stages of our lives. It is a political discussion that asks fundamental questions about our commitments to each other, and how the formal political sphere responds to those commitments.

Stuart Hall and Alan O'Shea argued in Chapter 3 that commonsense political discourses often seek to hold together contradictory positions.[10] This is true of current debate about the young. Young people, who have suffered disproportionately from the effects of the recession and subsequent cuts, have been simultaneously demonised. This is sometimes indirect: for example they have suffered in the rhetorical assault on welfare payment recipients, given that over a million of them are unemployed. Chavs in popular media are rarely out of their teens. And, as Danny Dorling argued in the *New Statesman* recently, it is young single mothers who will be hit the worst by looming welfare changes.[11] So politicians want to be seen as calling for something to be done for the young, 'to whom we have a responsibility', while in the next sentence they condemn a 'something for nothing' culture, and divide us into skivers and strivers. Very often the unemployed 'skivers' are the same people they were moments before earnestly trying to save.

Moreover, Dorling argues that it's not just young working-class people, benefit recipients or students who have been hit by this assault on the young. Middle-class and even highly-paid professional people – like my neighbour Jack – are also witnessing a radical, generalised shift in their life expectations. And as young people start to join up the dots that what has been promised is not the same as what's on offer, common stories cohere into a common cause. This has been an incomplete process in the UK, where young people have not cohered across classes. But in the actions of the Indignados in Europe, and in the Arab Spring, we can see international manifestations of the power of such mobilisations against the new status quo. In short, there is a starting to emerge a generational identity that has not been seen since the rebellions and revolutions of 1968. The struggle is now to help this emergent identity coalesce into effective political agency.

Many are suspicious however. John Denham, for instance, indicated his wariness about generational politics at a 2013 Labour Party seminar, on the grounds that it could be seen as an attempt to stop people talking about class. He was right, to an extent. For some advocates of a generational politics this is what their claims of a new politics amounts to: 'stop worrying about the poor, it's the young who are getting shafted'. Of course the young are getting far less support from society than they previously were – as seen for example in the imposition of ever increasing student tuition fees, the loss of EMA, the withdrawal of housing benefit, workfare, rising pension ages. But the key thing to remember here is that the impact of these changes, impoverishing and unfair as they are, is substantially more serious if you're young *and* poor; and that middle- and working-class young people are getting poorer. These things are not about intergenerational conflict; they are indicators of a new socio-economic settlement. Class is just as important as it ever was. My argument is that these shifts both justify the formation of, and constitute the bedrock for, a new politics. Or at the very least a new political discussion.

Making connections

Because it articulates something material, and because it is also about class (and clearly also race and gender), this idea of a generational politics is an important tool for understanding the current political moment. That is partly why it has been so contested. But this is not a politics that can work in isolation. When the hard times of today's young people are deployed as some kind of trump card of oppression, it erases a long history of struggle, of people against elites, and ignores the current iniquities suffered by people of all ages. We risk finding ourselves trapped in the 'continuous present' of modernisation, trying always to be new, and so not allowing the formation of the bonds between classes, generations and peoples that will be necessary if we are to argue that, at this moment of turning, we want a new class settlement, and a new set of relations between generations – one that is not couched in the terms that are presently on offer to us. To do this we need to turn the emerging generational politics into a truly inter-generational one.

Neoliberalism has no future as a democratic formation – because as a political project it lacks an imaginary space beyond a blind faith in markets and individuals. This failing, as Wolfgang Streeck points out, means that capitalism will never be able to meet the requirements of democratic governance. It cannot respond to the ordinary needs of different sections of society.

The three stories with which I started this piece give a flavour of where we are now: a society riven by inequality, based on broken promises, and burdened with a reckless and irresponsible elite, who present themselves as technocrats but behave like parasites. But there is hope here too.

If we could bring together a new generational alliance – between the entrepreneurial attitudes that have been so assiduously inculcated in the young, the valorisation of innovation and instinctive anti-authoritarianism of networked individualism and the remaining old left bulwarks against capital accumulation – we could see some very interesting possibilities emerging. Imagine a movement of unions, co-ops and resurgent state agencies taking a co-ordinated stand against capital while also being effective and innovative, and competing with the capitalist economy on its own terms, distributing surpluses in an egalitarian, democratic manner. Instead of sinking into the jaws of vulture funds, as happened with the co-op bank, such a movement could create new investment models based on seeking outcomes that share wealth rather than concentrating it.

After Bit Coin, we could have new financial instruments and currencies that are explicitly designed to enforce ethical practices while enabling expansion of an alternative economy and providing investment opportunities for alternative pensions and insurance. Under a new socio-economic settlement of the left, there would not be a false trade-off between tuition fees and pensions. There would be no need to seek endless growth to ensure continuous profit extraction; nor would governments play off parent against child. Instead, we could build a social order that understands the needs of every life-stage; and that our collective memory is not disposable or commodifiable nostalgia, but a fundamental defence against exploitation – one that shows that we can flourish in a sustainable economy that looks after the future of the planet, and the young people who will inherit it.

NOTES

1. See Phillip Brown and Hugh Lauder, 'The great transformation in the global labour market', *Soundings* 51, summer 2012.
2. R. Savani, 'High-Frequency Trading: The Faster, the Better?', *Intelligent Systems, IEEE*, vol 27, no 4, July-Aug 2012.
3. As Deborah Grayson and I described them in 'The National in the Network Society: UK Uncut, the English Defence League and the challenge for social democracy', in Henning Meyer and Jonathan Rutherford (eds), *Building the Good Society: The future of social democracy in Europe*, Palgrave-Macmillan, London 2011.
4. See the Framing Statement, for example. In the Manifesto we have used the notion of conjunctural change to characterise these shifts, and it is clear that conjunctural change will also connect to generational experience.
5. Neal Curtis, 'Thought Bubble: Neoliberalism and the Politics of Knowledge', *New Formations* 80-1, p76.
6. Although there are still, and always have been, shocking examples of pensioner poverty – the post-war settlement was far from perfect.
7. Ken Roberts, 'The end of the long baby-boomer generation', *Journal of Youth Studies*, Vol 15, no 4, 2012.
8. See Ben Little, 'Introduction', in Ben Little (ed), *Radical Future: Politics for the next generation*, Lawrence and Wishart 2010: www.lwbooks.co.uk/ebooks/radicalfuture.html.
9. For more on parenting in an age of austerity see Tracey Jensen, 'Austerity Parenting, *Soundings* 55, winter 2013.
10. Stuart Hall and Alan O'Shea, 'Common-sense neoliberalism', Chapter 3.
11. Danny Dorling, 'If you are young in Britain today, you are being taken for a ride', *New Statesman*, October 2013: www.newstatesman.com/2013/10/defrauding-young-britain. Tellingly this is perhaps where

my argument intersects with Beatrix Campbell's Manifesto chapter in mapping how our neoliberal culture puts the squeeze on the most vulnerable, the most in need of support (Chapter 4).

6. STATES OF IMAGINATION[1]

Janet Newman and John Clarke

Does everybody hate the state? It often appears so. Neoliberals detest the state and aim to downsize it or even make it wither away. And defending it certainly raises problems. Many people disenchanted by formal politics no longer look to the state, despairing of its associations with bureaucracy, hierarchy, corruption, secrecy and lies. Others view it as an outdated institution, a left-over legacy of nineteenth-century nation-building and twentieth-century power politics that has little relevance to those seeking to create new responses to contemporary challenges. This has given rise to a search for new forms of social and political engagement – the Indignados movement, new feminist and anti-racist movements, and a proliferation of community mobilisations – that flow across national borders and have little truck with old-style political parties.

However, a politics of the state still matters. And how we imagine the state, how we feel about it, will shape the kinds of politics that are possible. Popular disenchantment with the state reflects the experiences of the kind of state we currently have to live with, at least in Britain – a state that has been commodified, marketised and managerialised, and seems to ignore the human relationships at stake in its encounters with citizens. But the 'rolling back' of the state also creates a strong sense of loss: the loss of state funded institutions (voluntary organisations, advice centres, arts and cultural provision), public services (the local library, hospital, youth centres), public welfare (elder care, childcare), and, not least, the capacity for public governance. In our current conditions of austerity and deepening inequality, many people are looking to the state to regulate financial interests, curb corruption and abuse, and prevent social harm. In such moments, we hear a different view of the state – it is seen as a bulwark against the market's destructive powers; as the guarantor of rights; as 'the equaliser'.

This is the puzzle – the paradox of the state – that we must address: that the state is both despised and desired. Yet this is not a simple paradox, and should not treated as an 'on the one hand ... on the other' kind of argument. The problem facing us in seeking to understand 'the state' is that it is many things, and works through a series of different relationships with those whom it claims to represent, serve, scrutinise, improve or coerce.

This makes a singular politics of the state elusive. What's more, a focus on analysing the defects or merits of the contemporary state tends to overlook the affective dimensions of our relationships with state institutions and practices. This echoes some of the words we have already used – disenchantment, hate, loss, desired, despised. States are the focus of both paradoxical politics and ambivalent affects: complex feelings of attachment/detachment, hostility/closeness, refusal/engagement, and nostalgia/paranoia – for example – suffuse experiences of the state, relationships with the state and political debates about the state. Such feelings mean that would-be rational discussions about the politics of the state often founder in mutual antagonisms, silencings and mis-hearings.

Our own view is centred on the state both as an expression of publicness – as something more than the sum of individual interests or choices – and, paradoxically, as an instrument for the destruction and evacuation of public attachments and identifications. Our primary focus in this chapter, then, is on the renewal and reassertion of notions of public governance, public dialogue and public solidarity. And as an aid to understanding how this might be brought about we draw on a series of newspaper headlines that show something of current contradictory responses to the changing role of the state, and the affective dimensions of those responses.

THE STATE WE ARE IN

The health services could keel over in 2016
The Guardian, 7.8.13

Fat profits: how the food industry cashed in on obesity
The Guardian G2, 8.8.13

When did we give our consent to a secret state?

The Guardian, 4.10.13

The current British state, like many others in the global North, is thoroughly implicated in the neoliberal project; it acts as the agent of global capital, and seeks to restructure society, economy and public culture along market lines. And this project has fundamentally changed the state itself, hollowing it out, shrinking it and changing its purpose. For example, the privatisation of public goods has blurred the distinctions between public and private sectors to the extent that it is no longer clear for what, exactly, the state retains accountability and responsibility. Is obesity a public issue or is it just a consequence of individual greed or 'lifestyle choice'? Or, as argued in the G2 piece above, is it perhaps a direct consequence of profit-seeking by the food industry, and, if so, should the industry be regulated more closely?

The state has also been opened up to powerful interests: the reference above to the health service potentially 'keeling over', for example, was made by the head of the Foundation Trust Network, when calling for the pace of privatising reforms to be accelerated and for political interference to be curtailed. Furthermore, the state is actively seeking to protect the interests of capital by attacking workers' rights, equality legislation and the regulation of wages and working conditions. But, even more than this, it is deeply implicated in the economisation of the social realm, turning citizens into consumers, enmeshing civic and not-for-profit organisations in a web of contractual relationships, and establishing economic calculations as the ultimate measure of value. All of this could be seen as contributing to a view of the state as being in decline as a result of the overwhelming power of markets.

But such a view is challenged by the state's role as an intrusive power, concerned with national security and carrying unprecedented powers of surveillance and control. Revelations about the extent of mass surveillance by security agencies in Britain and the US (our third headline above) have attracted huge public concern. Responses by the liberal media have supported 'whistleblowers' and attempted to disclose and publicise infringements of personal freedoms. But here too divisions within the state have come into view, raising questions about how far the part of the state that is concerned with parliamentary enquiries and committees can exert control over its security arms.[2]

The state is, then, both retreating and expanding; it is plural in the forms of power and authority it exerts. The state that is being undone, securitised and marketised is also the one that inscribed – however partially and conditionally – the rights which previous generations of campaigners and activists fought for: gender and racial equality, the protection of workers from forms of abuse that threaten their health and safety, legislation against rape and domestic violence, rights to pensions and other forms of social protection, and the right to receive education and healthcare and other public services. Are such rights merely residual – left-over traces that have become unsustainable in the face of would-be dominant conceptions of choice and responsibility? We think not – our own research, and that of others, has shown how attached people remain to their identities as members of a wider public. They continue to look to the state to guarantee rights and to ameliorate inequality, hardship and insecurity. Part of our concern here is to see how these continuing attachments might connect to emergent elements.

SOMETHING MUST BE DONE!

Summer of hunger: huge rise in food bank use as demand linked to welfare reform

Independent, 10.8.13

Child poverty in Britain causing 'social apartheid'

Observer, 25.8.13

Such headlines invoke a recurrent feeling that 'something must be done' – and that feeling usually implicates the state in the doing because of its capacity to make and enforce laws, collect taxes, distribute (and redistribute) income and other benefits, and to use a variety of means to get people (and companies) to act in desired ways. The first headline here suggests that the state can have a positive role to play in protecting low paid workers from exploitation by employers through mechanisms such as the minimum wage; the second looks to the state to change its policies so as to avoid a worsening of poverty, social division and the (gendered) social relations of care.

Of course, many of the problems the state is being asked to address are themselves the consequences of its own actions – privatising water provision, creating greater inequalities between rich and poor, and engendering what the second headline terms 'social apartheid'. Indeed, the state continues to be viewed as the only actor who can ameliorate inequality through processes of redistribution. This includes redistribution within families and households to address gendered inequality, and between generations in order to provide for the needs and rights of the growing elderly population as well as to invest in the life chances of future generations. It also involves addressing the deepening inequalities between regions and nations within the UK.

All of these divisions point to the urgency of redistribution through a progressive programme of benefits and taxes. But both benefits and taxes have been stigmatised in the neoliberal climate:

> Stay-at-home mums are making a lifestyle choice and can expect no help with childcare costs, says Osborne
>
> *Daily Mail*, 5.8.13

This headline expresses the contemporary neoliberal view of the state's limits, articulated through the idea that households sink or swim according to their own choices and lifestyles. This, together with the demonisation of those on benefits, represents a profound ideological turn. There is a need, then, for a politics that might rebuild popular support for equality, inclusion, solidarity and social justice as principles for a public realm. For such principles – which are the underpinning of support for redistribution – are under increasing threat, not only through cuts to benefits and services, but through cultural processes of stigmatising benefit claimants.

NO MORE GUILTY PLEASURES

- Council becomes first in the UK to block housing hardship payment to people who spend too much on smoking, drinking and TV
- Edinburgh says lifestyle clampdown is necessary to ration poverty funds

> *Independent*, 24.8.13

This *Independent* front page summons up an image of a dour and censorious state, which places 'lifestyle' conditions on the meagre benefits it offers. But it also reveals something of the strain experienced by councils and others at the 'front line', charged with making hard decisions about how scarce resources should be used. There is a sense of crisis about the state's capacity to function effectively as it is slimmed down, rolled back and hollowed out, and as new expectations are placed on state workers to both control and change the behaviour of those they serve.

But while people certainly fear some extensions of the state's power (intervention into lifestyle choices, the criminalisation of dissent), they do also want the state to act as a powerful guarantor of public interests against private ones: challenging excessive executive bonuses in the financial sector, controlling profit-taking from privatised public utilities, acting against tax avoidance by companies moving key functions to nations with more favourable tax regimes. Conventional mechanisms of state regulation seem inadequate to meet such challenges, not least because of the transnational structures and flows of capital. Indeed, the attack on 'red tape' has helped to build a culture in which corporate interests prevail, enabling moves by employers to circumvent employment rights, the weakening of equality legislation, the failure to punish environmental degradation and so on. These have been the focus of much public criticism and there is clearly a public interest at stake here. Such failures of the state to act as a 'bulwark', we think, exacerbate public disenchantment with the state and withdrawal from political participation.

RE-IMAGINING THE STATE

For all these reasons, there is a current search on the left for alternative imaginaries of the state – from the 'relational state' to a state capable of fostering 'progressive capitalism'.[3] There is also a desire to look beyond the neoliberal project, for example to experiments in the global south which offer alternatives to privatisation, or show how privatised goods can be brought back into public, municipal or cooperative forms of ownership.[4] These remind us that states can be more than a bulwark against the powerful; they can also be a source of emergent rationalities, and provide resources for experiment and innovation. Both these elements are critical for any project of remaking states – the imaginative needs to be combined with material resources to explore new possibilities. States are in the unusual position of being able to provide the resources to support their own remaking.

Our own contribution to the debate revolves around the renewal of public relationships. The idea of the state as representing or embodying a unified idea of the public and public interest is of course no longer viable. The social and political settlements on which earlier forms of the state rested have unravelled, and the idea of a singular public, unadulterated by the transformations of diversity and difference, is now unsustainable. There can, then, be no going back to a mythical golden age of the state. Nor do we envisage a return to the idea that the state can somehow be 'captured' by progressive social forces. Rather, we propose an approach to the state that enhances notions of the commons, that reasserts collective (public) interests and enables collective (public) action. Public-making does not reside wholly in the state but is enacted through a proliferating array of groups and organisations working beyond the state to build new communities, networks and forms of mobilization within and beyond the nation. But here we propose three dimensions of public-making that we think offer scope for a progressive politics reinventing the state and enabling a popular structure of feeling centred on collective identifications and attachments.

The first dimension involves a stronger approach to public governance. Processes of marketisation and the dispersal of state power to a wide range of agencies – individual schools and hospitals, quangos, devolved bodies, voluntary agencies and corporations – have fundamentally shifted the relationship between public and private authority. We are left with thin forms of public authority and regulation that are getting progressively weaker with the recurrent attacks on 'red tape'. While there can be no going back to the monolithic state bureaucracies in which public governance was invested in the past, we want to stimulate discussion of how public authority and democratic legitimacy can be enhanced.

The second line of development is cultural and ideological, and concerns the language through which the politics of the state is conducted. In Chapter 1, Doreen Massey traced the shifts in language that have transformed us from citizens to consumers, from social subjects to individualised market actors. She argued that 'discourse matters', and also proposed that it can be changed. We take this discussion forward here, addressing the need to renew and remake public discourse in order to constitute new forms of public solidarity. This is not only a matter for the state, but the state has a crucial role to play in shaping public opinion and public action (rather than simply treating citizens as solely motivated by individual interests).

This takes us to the third line of development, in which we propose reimagining the state as a dialogic entity. This is not a matter of the success or failure of so-called 'big conversations' initiated by governments seeking to restore their legitimacy by spurious 'listening exercises'. Nor are we merely concerned with inter and intra political party dialogues, or even the official dialogue between states and citizens. Rather we think it is vital to attend to, and nourish, the dialogues in the complex of public and political relationships that inform state action. We said earlier that the state is not a single entity, which implies the dialogic relationships that might connect different facets of the state, linking those shaping and those enacting policy, the regions and nations, policy-makers and publics, and, above all, the different publics who understand and imagine the state and its possibilities in diverse and sometimes conflicting ways.

Thinking of the state in such public terms means going beyond an interest in relationships between states and citizens to considering the complex clusters of relationships through which the state (that strange abstract idea) is brought to life. Each cluster of relationships – whether in the coercive institutions of the state, its security complex, the management of the social order, the shifting alignments of civil society organisations and government, or the infrastructure of support for private capital (corporate, rather than social welfare) – is highly political. Each cluster also informs popular understandings of, and feelings about, the state. But such relationships are fragmented and often competing, making states contradictory and thoroughly unstable institutions. It is this instability and incompleteness, rooted in unresolved contradictions, that creates the spaces of possibility for alternative imaginaries of the state to emerge.

PUBLIC MAKING AS PUBLIC GOVERNANCE

In a recent *Big Issue*, under the headline 'We have the power to make a difference', John Bird offered a non state-centred response to the scandal of 'payday loans' – loans that charge exorbitant interest rates and which are most used by those in dire poverty. It includes the comment:

> Credit at such extreme rates should be outlawed. But can you imagine any government making that happen?
>
> *Big Issue*, 5.8.13

There is clearly a loss of belief in the power of the state to curtail the excesses of capitalism. But does this mean giving up on the idea of the state as a guarantor of rights and a bulwark against inequality? We think not. The idea of active state intervention into the economy has been in retreat over the last forty years, partly as a result of the unhappy turn to Hayekian theory and monetarist policies in the Thatcher/ Reagan years. The banking crisis challenged the hegemony of such economic policies, but did not displace them: indeed the state-sponsored buyouts of parts of the financial sector can be viewed as interventions to prop up failing capital. Any notion that the crisis would open up space for emergent rationalities – expanded public spending to deal with the social consequences of crisis, a less consumerist society more concerned with the sustainability of resources and the quality of life, a renewed trust in public institutions rather than private profit – was quickly deflected by governments anxious to restore the pre-crisis status quo and even exploit the crisis to enable further profit-taking. These are not just questions of economic policy: rather, they raise the possibility of thinking again about power. How might the relationships between the public authority of the state and the private authority of corporations, media organisations and the public be arranged differently?

Royal charter sealed after legal action fails

The Guardian, 31.10.13

Four admit to hacking plots

The Guardian, 31.10.13

These headlines are part of a prolonged media storm over the shift in relationships between parliament and the press following the Leveson Report, and the progress of criminal action against journalists and editors charged with 'hacking' offences, collusion and corruption. The Royal Charter is a state instrument for public regulation, which appears likely to stand alongside a rival regulatory body being set up by the press itself, opening out a significant tension between different regulatory relationships across the line between public and private.

Other headlines reflect a concern with limiting the expansive power of private capital to colonise and appropriate public goods that constitute core elements of basic human well-being.

Employers who flout the national minimum wage to be actively
named and shamed

The Guardian, 23.8.13

The Water Companies and the foul stench of exploitation

The Observer, 4.8.13

The first headline here hints at a possible positive role of the state in
protecting workers – and other citizens – from exploitation, while the
second points to the state's ambivalent role in regulating services that
had once been public, and that, as in the case of water, relate to fundamental resources on which life depends. These suggest the possibilities
of restoring and reworking what might be thought of as the 'residual'
role of the state in public regulation and public ownership. There are
now a number of calls for the re-publicisation of core public services
– water, transport, health and so on. Where services that have been
put to the market fail to live up to the social and political goals they
were designed to meet, arguments have increased for them to be
brought back into public control. Restoring forms of public control
(including user involvement) is not a guarantee of perfect services, but
it is a precondition for achieving the range of qualities that services to
the public should be striving for.

However, while there are good examples of taking privatised
services back into public control in the global south, prospects have
seemed more limited in Britain and some other European nations
because of the tainted memories of past forms of state ownership and
the complex entanglements of public and private authority in the
present. Emerging experiments in cooperative ownership, new forms
of local control, and democratic forms of governance offer promising
alternatives to outright state ownership, given adequate safeguards for
workforce conditions and equality criteria. What matters is that the
state ensures the provision of services, rather than simply making
them ripe for corporate expropriation and profit taking.

The headlines we have so far drawn on in this chapter reflect the
continuing desires of citizens for 'something to be done' where private
interests threaten public interests. The state's role in public regulation,
then, cannot be residual, based on the assumption that self-regulation
can be effective.

But it is important that any expanded role for the state is driven by a more expansive concept of a good society (health, sustainability, care); it should not be concerned only with creating a bigger economy. State agencies must seek out and promote alternatives to the current culture of 'growth'; and invest in a range of forms of social value, rather than pursuing the narrow interest of shareholder value. State intervention must try to reverse the subordination of social and political life to the economy, and instead pose the question of how the economy might serve collective well-being, now and in the future. We also envisage a more coercive national response to questions of corruption and abuse, perhaps through the criminal justice discourse of 'zero tolerance' being reworked to crack down on things that are overtly anti-public, from tax avoidance to the failure of organisations and agencies (whether private or public) to meet their public obligations.

PUBLIC MAKING AS PUBLIC DISCOURSE

In today's political culture the idea that we share a 'commons' – involving mutual interdependence and responsibility – has been increasingly residualised by processes of individuation and consumerism. But these are not automatic processes that flow directly from anonymous forces such as 'globalisation' or 'neoliberalism'. The state has played a crucial role in spreading this orientation as a way of thinking and behaving. And it can play an equally crucial potential role in remaking and renewing public culture. It can, for example, summon public action (not just individual responsibility) around issues of common concern:

> Stop trolls killing our kids, Mr Cameron
>> (father of Hannah Smith, who committed suicide
>> after online bullying) *Mirror*, 8.8.13

> E-crime officers investigating Twitter threats make third arrest
> (report on police action after online threats against high-profile
> women, including Stella Creasey and Caroline Criado-Perez)
>> *The Guardian*, 8.8.13

These headlines summon up an emergent sense of concern about the need for new forms of public regulation. Yet the state often appears to be ineffective in relation to global media, and seemingly unable to respond to racist, sexist and homophobic attacks in social media and internet sites, despite such attacks being nominally illegal. There is, we think, a need for an expansive public leadership role on the part of the state, shaping a public culture that confronts such forms of abuse and intolerance. Instead the state itself has contributed to the making of a culture of intolerance and abuse, as in the notorious 'go home' campaign that targeted migrant populations in London:

Go home campaign denounced by human rights groups
The Guardian, 9.8.13

Liberty target 'illegal' Home Office racist van – with another van
www.Huffingtonpost.co.uk

Critics challenged the 'go home' discourse as contributing to a climate of fear and fostering hostility towards migrants. The 'anti-public' actions of the Home Office served to summon up new forms of public action on the part of oppositional groups such as Amnesty, Refugee Action, 38 Degrees and Freedom from Torture, including the imaginative appropriation and reversal of the government's own language, with mobile hoardings proclaiming the illegality of the Home Office message. Such reversals are exceptional; oppositional groups rarely have the capacities and resources to confront state action head on. But the example shows how a commitment to publicness can inform a contemporary politics of contestation acting in the name of solidarity and social justice around the state.

Such emergent orientations inform our interest in promoting a sense of publicness as a resource for public action – within and beyond the state – through a concern with public discourse. Issues of redistribution, regulation and taxation are not simply matters of policy. They are rooted in culture and ideology, and are subject to slippery discursive shifts that subtly change their meaning. For example in recent years both redistribution and public service provision have been regarded as matters of public finance rather than public culture. There is a need, we think, to shift the debate from how welfare is consumed (with its focus on ever greater conditionality, centred on the demonisation of 'scroungers' and the associated 'culture of entitlement') to a debate about how a good society can be imagined and brought into being. This would require a state that intervenes to promote the public good, that invests in producing social value, and that promotes sustainable futures – economic, environmental and social, both domestically and internationally.

Only by shifting the terms of debate by promoting public discourse – internationally as well as nationally and locally – will states be able to deal with the current crises of austerity, environmental degradation and rising care needs. Such ideological work is difficult in a climate of mediatised adversarial politics, in which political parties jostle for short-term electoral advantage. It would require strong public institutions that embody and enact public values, democratised political parties and a renewed civil service that could look beyond departmental and ministerial interests. But the state is not the only, nor even the dominant, actor here. We have seen in recent years how emergent political movements, new social struggles, innovative forms of public protest and civic action, have changed the terms of debate. Issues from the living wage to female genital mutilation have entered public discourse, opening out new agendas for state action. And the political climate itself has shifted as a result of claims such as 'we are the 99%' – forms of discourse remembered even where the movements themselves fade from view. Each of these creates new forms of public discourse, and generates emergent publics willing and able to act on the public stage, and to be part of a wider dialogue.

PUBLIC MAKING AS PUBLIC DIALOGUE

Talk of public culture and public governance opens up another source of ambivalence. It is now not enough to speak of a singular public, unmarked by the struggles around race, class and gender that demonstrated the exclusions deeply inscribed into state bureaucracy and other forms of institutional power. This is why we argue that a critical function for the state is that of creating the space for public dialogue and debate. We think this points to the need for a fundamentally dialogic state – one which is constantly encouraging, and simultaneously being shaped by, public dialogue.

Thinking of the state in such terms opens out questions about how to enhance dialogic relationships between state and citizen: to open up dialogues that offer alternatives to the dominant cultures of mediatised 'spin' on the one hand (in which the public has little voice) or the quick opinion poll on the other. There is a wealth of experience about how to establish dialogue through public participation and engagement exercises, citizens' juries and new democratic channels (see for example the activities of Open Democracy). There is always the risk of such developments being incorporated and depoliticised; but they nevertheless offer emergent possibilities for re-imagining the state. We want to argue for a shift towards enabling and resourcing civic actors to participate in political and civic life, including material support – especially where civic actors have to compete with powerful corporate interests in public forums. Inequalities of resources and power have limited the effectiveness of experiments to bring public and professional voices into governing bodies. But there is nevertheless a need to open up key institutions that claim to represent the public interest – audit and inspection bodies, industry regulators and others – by rendering them more dialogic.

A dialogical state is one that promotes public dialogue rather than consumer feedback; that fosters political participation rather than consensual passivity; and that engages with a diversity of publics and movements rather than attempting to police dissent. Conflict is an intrinsic part of social and political life, and different political views have to be rehearsed and debated: only by fostering and extending dialogue might the current shift towards consumerist or authoritarian populist versions of politics be challenged. Such dialogues need to be horizontal – among the many publics that make up society – as well as vertical between the citizens and the state.

This means that a dialogic state is also necessarily a dispersed state. The dispersal of state power to other agents over the last fifty years or so has weakened formal democratic accountability, but it has simultaneously generated new spaces of participation. We do not, then, advocate the reconsolidation of power to a unified state machinery. Rather, we support a shift in the balance of power and resources away from the centre and towards the nations and regions of the UK, and towards local governments and a proliferating array of not-for-profit and civic agencies. The state is not the only site of democratic practice, nor does party political democracy offer the only model of engagement. Civic, not-for-profit and community based organisations all offer forums for political participation, while contemporary movements, from Occupy to Open Democracy, from new feminisms to environmental activism, offer alternative models of democratic engagement and political renewal. These can, of course, become stripped of their progressive potential as they become routinised in the machinery of the state; but it is only by dispersing power that new experiments can flourish. The mainstream must, we think, learn from the margins rather than rejecting new movements for their failure to present coherent manifestos or demands.

To set up such a dialogue would need state agencies to actively support the emergence of new publics – and conversations among them. This approach can be captured in the idea of a commitment to a dialogic model of the state – as not only embodying a public interest but as itself being a public-making entity. But here we return to paradox and ambivalence. Many progressive positions, we fear, fail to fully engage with issues of power, or over-romanticise the power of 'ordinary people' or 'local communities'. And the local is not always a fertile ground for progressive alternatives and a vibrant political culture: it can summon up defensive, often racist or homophobic reactions, and can be a space for exclusionary communitarian or narrow faith-based politics to flourish. There is, then, a necessary tension between, on the one hand, liberating local innovation and participation to create a state whose edges are both widely dispersed and porous, and, on the other, retaining a centralised capacity to guarantee rights, to enforce equality and to engage in establishing national and international standards (of legality, for the environment and more).

This tension cannot be wished away – but it needs to be seen as a dynamic tension, built into the fabric of the state. This points to the need for a dialogic state to foster a vibrant public realm at the local, national and international level, and concern itself with the reassertion of public values. History teaches us that states do not renew themselves from within, but only as a result of political movements and social action. States are not the only public-making entity, nor can states be the only form of power or source of leadership in play. Today we are witnessing a resurgence of new social movements, new styles of politics, new mobilisations and new creative interventions that imagine and enact alternative ways of living and working together. These are able to flourish precisely because they choose not to engage with the state or other forms of institutional power. And yet ... if we reject the state as a focus of political and public action, there is no possibility of its renewal.

CONCLUSION

In this chapter we have imagined different directions for the remaking of the state, linked to notions of public governance, public discourse and public dialogue. This is not, however, a call for moving from one form of state to another: from neoliberal to post-neoliberal, from hierarchical to relational, from coercive to enabling. Rather, we have imagined different directions for the remaking of the state, all linked to the reinvention and expansion of public culture. It will be evident that the different ideas of the state we have explored are somewhat contradictory, reflecting our understanding of the state as multi-faceted. We make no apologies for this: there is nothing to be gained from treating states as singular and coherent entities. They are the product of conflict and compromise – not only the shifting compromises between classes, but also a series of other compromises. New forces and interests, emerged as the social and political settlements that gave rise to the post-war democratic state unravelled – and they still make their presence felt on different aspects of the state. But other forces are now at work, giving rise to new compromises – and new possibilities. This view of the state as one crucial site of possibility reflects our view of politics as always unfinished.

This unfinished conception of politics is reflected in our focus on the different kinds of attachments to the state, which persist despite ideological forces dedicated to its undoing. But it is also attentive to emergent ideas and forces that might help construct more dialogical and relational state forms. Our analysis here is grounded in what Raymond Williams called the residual and emergent cultural forms that always coexist with the currently dominant.[5] So, for us, the possibility of remaking the state lies partly in the residual attachments to collectivity and solidarity in insecure times. As Williams argued, the residual is marked by the continuation of questions that cannot be answered in the terms of the dominant, and we certainly see the desires for a bulwark against exploitation, a sense of security in the face of uncertainty, and an attachment to collective institutions that transcend the individualising drive of neoliberal capitalism as residual in just that sense. Such orientations are joined in the present by emergent desires to live better – to put social value before economic; to realise the promises of equality and solidarity; to find sustainable ways of working and living; to inhabit an ethically ordered society; to acknowledge and respond to internationalised obligations. A state in the making might respond to such residual and emergent desires – both embodying them and making them more possible. States are contradictory in part because they are always confronting the challenge of managing the contradictions in, and crises of, contemporary capitalism. Yet – paradoxically – such contradictions create the cracks and spaces of possibility out of which alternatives recurrently emerge.

NOTES

1. We have borrowed this title from a collection of ethnographic studies of the postcolonial state, edited by Thomas Blom Hansen and Finn Stepputat, Duke University Press, 2001.
2. 'Spy agencies face inquiry by parliament', *The Guardian* 17.10.13.
3. G. Cook and R. Muir (eds), *The Relational State*, IPPR 2012; D. Sainsbury, *Progressive capitalism: how to achieve economic growth, liberty and social justice*, Biteback 2013.
4. D.A. McDonald and G. Ruiters (eds), *Alternative to privatization: public options for essential services in the Global South*, HSRC Press 2012, South Africa; M. Pigeon et al, (eds), *Remunicipalisation: putting water back into public hands*, Transnational Institute 2012.
5. Raymond Williams, *Marxism and Literature*, Oxford University Press 1977.

7. Whose economy? Reframing the debate

Doreen Massey and Michael Rustin

It is often argued that the United Kingdom economy is in a mess, a mess from which it must be rescued. We agree.

However, in the Kilburn Manifesto we want to take issue with the way in which, in most political debate, this situation is usually understood.

First of all, the woes of the UK economy do not result from the recent crisis (which was more of a symptom), nor from the austerity-driven response to that crisis (which is a political means of furthering a longer-term dynamic). Neither – and this is more rarely said – do they result solely from the decades of neoliberalism immediately preceding the crisis. Rather, as we argued in the Manifesto Framing Statement, those decades themselves can be seen as a particular, and particularly acute, expression of underlying characteristics and deeper causes that have been with us for a long period of Britain's economic history as a former imperial power.

The Framing Statement sketched out the longer historical and geographically globalising trajectory of capitalism within which the current moment in the UK might be understood. In this chapter of the Manifesto, while bearing this bigger history in mind, we want to focus in on peculiarly British characteristics. There are, of course, many of these, and they are much debated. But here, in an effort to understand the current moment, we pull out two.

First there is the long dominance, changing its form over the centuries but remaining remarkably persistent, of financial interests. These are interests which, from the very beginnings of Empire through to the financially-dominated globalisation of today, have been thoroughly international, with a shifting but often semi-detached relation to the economy situated within the shores of the UK itself.

Second there is the significance of landed property. At least since 'the enclosures' and the clearances, the elite ownership of vast parts of the country, and the associated power of the landed interest, has been a notable feature of British political economy.

Both these sets of interests are utterly embedded in the British class structure and the shape of the British economy. They constitute an elite class power related to finance/circulation and to land and property that has waxed and waned, sometimes been challenged, and over time has changed its form. (One thinks of the long dominance of the Treasury, and of the quick suppression of Wilson's Department of Economic Affairs; the period of manufacturing pre-eminence now 'hollowed out', and the manual working class that went with it, now on the wane and subject to systematic attack.) But it has persisted.

Neither of these interests is centrally about production. They are about money and land, neither of them a product of human labour. They are about the holding of assets and the relations of exchange. The victory of neoliberalism (here as an economic philosophy) out of the ashes of the post-war social-democratic settlement thus fitted perfectly with their interests and their modes of calculation.

The current particular articulation of those interests has bequeathed to us today an economy, and a broader polity, with a very particular shape. Most evidently, it is dominated by the City and the array of sectors surrounding finance; by a more widespread financialised way of thinking; and by the incorporation of much of the population, both materially and imaginatively, into those structures and discourses. The City seized its moment in the 1980s. With the decline of the old social settlement, and the deregulation of currencies and the movement of capital, alongside the transformative possibilities of new technologies, the City reinvented itself, internationalised itself internally, and asserted its presence as a global financial hub. It became a leading initiator, protagonist and disseminator of neoliberalism (privatisation, deregulation, financialisation); and put itself forward as the centre of a new financial imperialism. Its implication in the often highly regressive effects of this system around the world should be a major concern for the left within the UK (see Chapter 8). Here, however, we shall focus on the effects within the UK.

Closely linked to this dominance of financial interests, and the wider speculative and rent-seeking nature of the current system, trading in land and property (including home-ownership) has become a central motor of the economy, which is now running along without a sufficient basis in production, often fuelled by excessive credit. In spite of the famed immobility of land, this trade too is now bound into globalised structures. It is not xenophobic to point out that the urban and rural landscape that is so often at the heart of the iconography of national identity – and which ordinary Brits have for long owned very little of – is now increasingly owned from abroad. Foreign investors buy up farmland, further fuelling house-price rises through encouraging the unproductive behaviour of 'house builders' (see below); and they buy up residential properties in London, thus exacerbating a process, already initiated by bankers in the City, whereby the capital city has become unliveable for people on ordinary incomes. It is in this guise that the long problem of land-ownership in Britain is articulated in the current moment.

The 'mess' we are said to be in is thus deeper, and of longer duration, than is usually assumed.

But we also have a second reservation about the popular formulation. In what sense is this a mess? For whom is it dysfunctional? There are clearly violent instabilities and looming imbalances, both in the UK and globally, but certain groups are doing very well indeed out of this arrangement, as the ever-more yawning inequalities, and the growth of super-rich strata, both here and around the world, clearly demonstrate. As we argued in the Framing Statement, the *aim* of the rise of neoliberalism was an active undermining of the economic and political gains made by ordinary people during the post-war social-democratic settlement. Its whole point was to engineer a class rebalancing. From this point of view it has succeeded. And the predictable crisis of its model has now become grist to its mill: it is being used as a pretext for further restructuring and redistribution.

(For those of us who grew up during that social-democratic period, the effect on our implicit if not explicit historical imaginations is shattering. Those social-democratic decades, now – as the present-day, market-driven common sense closes around them to form them as 'the past' – begin to seem like an exceptional interlude. Most of us imagined them at the time to be part of a longer progress towards a more egalitarian and democratic future.)

WHAT IS 'THE ECONOMY' AND WHAT IS IT FOR?

Given the above analysis, further questions and reconceptualisations are put on the table. We need to air, politically, some basic – and rarely asked – questions, like: 'what *is* the economy?'; 'what is it for?'.

Neoliberalism represents the market economy as virtually coterminous with society itself, as determining its entire system of values. We challenge this conception. We see the economy as only one element in a wider process of social reproduction; it is merely one of the means through which society takes its shape. The economy should be seen as a means to the fulfilment of broader human ends, not as an end in itself. This does not mean that that there are not technical questions about how best to organise the economy, but there are a number of broader questions that are hardly ever addressed.

As the Manifesto argues, the economic elements of society are intimately bound up with its prevailing common sense and political discourse. 'Economics' is not simply a technical matter, beyond politics. And for the same reason economic policy must be about more than economics. Thus 'economic policy' is – and should be explicitly – more than just a set of individual policies addressing disparate issues. Each 'policy' is an expression of a wider narrative, an underlying political philosophy – and the interests and values which they implicitly articulate.

The underlying politics of existing – neoliberal – economic policies have been widely analysed, here in the Kilburn Manifesto, in *Soundings* and elsewhere. We need also to set out an alternative. What would 'our' economy be *for*? What do we want it to provide? And how would it relate to the wider reproduction of society?

We might perhaps start with the idea that the economy should contribute to the enabling of decent lives, and the flourishing of human potential for all, and in a way that is sustainable. We might add that there needs to be a commitment to a measure of equality, to the idea that all should share in social well-being and be entitled to equal dignity and respect. Even something as general as this might provoke debate among us. That is fine. The point is to generate discussion on the economy at a more political and social level.

It is certainly evident that the currently dominant economic philosophy, and the economic model and policies that the Coalition Conservatives and Liberal Democrats have drawn from it, utterly fail even in these more general aims – they are indeed *not* its aims. But we want to stress that, while this is especially the case for the post-crisis politics of austerity, and whatever 'recovery' from it may now be taking place, this failure to align the economy with broader human purposes long precedes the present moment. As we have argued throughout the Kilburn Manifesto, neoliberalism has been seeking for a long time to subvert the commitments to social entitlements and social justice that were embodied, however imperfectly, in the post-war settlement, and which had been had the goal of several preceding generations.

Indeed the nature of the current 'recovery' (consumption-led, asset-based, in housing especially, and confined to the already comfortably-off in London and the South East of England) makes one thing abundantly clear: that our current way of judging economic success, including both the idea of growth and our current ways of measuring it, is correlated to only a very limited degree with general well-being; and that 'growth' itself may have many perverse consequences – intended or otherwise –that undermine and damage well-being. Even given equivalent rates of macro-economic growth, different approaches to its gestation and regulation will lead to very different outcomes for society, as we can see by comparing different national and historical instances. 'The economic' is thus utterly political.[1] But we have to ask: where is the political courage now even to raise these questions, or to call into question the reduction of political debate to the single dimension of the annual rate of economic growth?

THE CURRENT CONJUNCTURE: LIVING WITH FINANCIALISATION

Costas Lapavitsas has described three main ways in which financialisation has manifested itself in the neoliberal economy.[2] Firstly, banks themselves have switched to seeking profit through financial trading rather than through outright borrowing and lending. Secondly, non-financial enterprises have become increasingly involved in financial processes. And thirdly, financial institutions are making increasing levels of profit from individuals and households. People are now relying on the financial system for access to vital goods and services, including housing, education, health and transport; while their savings are also increasingly mobilised by the formal financial system.

All this means that finance and financialisation are at the crux of the present neoliberal settlement. It is not simply that the sector is central to the UK economy; there has been a wider financialisation of economy and society. We argue that these structural transformations within the economic sphere have been embedded in a sea-change in the nature of dominant class-relations; and the financial way of thinking and mode of calculation has been naturalised within society more widely, and within political discourse. In short, we are living with a financialised hegemonic common sense. Addressing this must be at the core of any alternative approach to the economy.

This powerful constellation of forces has a number of adverse effects, which we outline below.

There has been a burgeoning of the sphere of circulation at the expense of that of production, and a dominance of trading in already-existing assets rather than the production of new ones. This can be understood as a dominance of value-extraction over value-creation.[3] And, as Andrew Sayer points out, not only is this a source of income that is primarily unearned, but, as it has grown, the very term (and the distinction between earned and unearned) has mysteriously dropped from view![4]

There has been regressive redistribution, leading to increased inequality between rich and poor. As we have argued, this was, of course, the class project behind neoliberalism. But the implications of the current settlement are far more than simply redistributive. The transformation in dominant sources of wealth away from the production of goods and services and emphatically towards rent, interest, dividends and speculation entails a transformation in the nature of economic (class) social relations (as is also argued by Sayer). On the one hand far more people are drawn into these sources of wealth (through home-ownership, pensions, and so forth). On the other, this increased involvement has the effect of feeding the income divide between the majority and the very rich, whose income bears very little relation to the activities of production. All of these shifts significantly change the terrain of economic struggle, complicating it through the growth of compromised middle strata, and distancing and multiplying the prime source of the divide between rich and poor away from the place of work (the 'factory floor' and its many post-industrial equivalents).

A further effect of the dominance of finance has been the ever-more yawning disparity between London-and-the-South-East and the

North and West. Given the geographical propensities of finance, the North-South divide cannot be seriously addressed without challenging the dominance of the sector in its current form. Moreover, this widening divide is not solely a result of the concentrated location of finance in a small corner of the country; it also results from the active undermining of the possibilities of growth in other regions *by* that geographical concentration (for instance through the sucking in of professional labour to London and the south-east). The City is not the golden goose for the whole of the country that it claims to be; it's more a cuckoo's egg.[5] This overwhelming concentration of economic growth into one corner also distorts macro-economic policy. And it disrupts the functioning of London itself. City centres around the world have been reoccupied by the victorious elites, but in London this process is especially marked. The fact that the poor cannot live there, indeed that under current policies councils are forced to ship them out, not only traduces all notions of place and belonging – supposedly at the core of conservative values – but makes ever more difficult the social reproduction of the city. Likewise, rising land-prices force out the remains of small manufacturing production (profitable in production terms but unable now to pay for the location), thus denuding the old multifariousness of the capital's economy.[6] The spatial contradictions of this neoliberal regime are tearing the country apart.

The rise of financial capital has also had deleterious effects on the political system. Colin Crouch has shown that democratic institutions have been subverted in recent decades by the corporate exercise of power through party funding, lobbying and control of the media and mass communications.[7] The power of invisible bond-holders has displaced that of democratic electorates in many countries of the world as the main arbiters of economic policy, in a process whose worst effects in Europe can be seen in the south, but whose logic also justifies the commitment to austerity of the British government. What is needed is a major reassertion of the role of democratic institutions and practices in the organisation of the economy.

A further consequence of financialisation has been to exacerbate rampant consumerism, fuelled by, among other things, the comparison-inducing effects of inequality, and the desire of finance to lend to the household sector.[8] Much of this is financed by debt (Crouch's privatised Keynesianism), with its attendant instabilities.

Finally, daily life and discourse is being transformed, including our sense of personal identity and imagination. Our very social relations are being financialised. All the rich particularities of real social relations are being lost beneath their general characterisation in terms of market exchange. This is the modern culmination of a much longer story about the increasing role of money in economy and society, and the conversion of use value into exchange value. Both socialist and traditionalist conservative critiques of capitalism in the last few years have focused on the destruction of values rooted in the particularities of relationships to things and people.

Financialisation has taken this process to a further extreme, as it has overrun previous institutional and cultural barriers to the sway of money-values – those established for example in the post-war welfare settlement, but also in more traditional resistances. This is the other side of its huge enabling potential in the stretching of limited and localised relationships over space and time.[9] 'Finance' chimes with the times – its apparent immateriality, its apparent lightness and disembeddedness, its ease of global flow, its character of pure exchange – and it both draws on and powerfully informs the current common sense.

All this, then, is at the heart of British economy and society at the moment. It is this we are up against.

A case in point: homes and properties

Property and homes are a field in which the linking together of finance, landed property, geography and the production of common sense can clearly be seen.

In Chapter 1, we examined the way neoliberalism has transformed our language. We can add in the present context a further example: the way in which houses and homes are now almost universally referred to as 'properties'. This transformation of the notion of a home – together with the dysfunctional nature of the UK housing sector – is both central to, and emblematic of, the reactionary and conflictive nature of the current neoliberal mode.

This can be seen in a number of ways.

Firstly, (differential) rises in house prices are a major contributor to inequality, between owners and non-owners and, among owners, between North and South. Many owner-occupiers in London gain more wealth each year from the (unearned) rise in their house prices than they earn from their employment.

Furthermore, the pressurised race to home-ownership entails both indebtedness and the material involvement of households with the finance sector; and this in turn feeds households' incorporation into financial ways of thinking. And it also further swells the asset-based nature of the UK economy, rather than contributing to its productive base. Moreover properties may be allowed to remain empty for years, in the knowledge that their market value will in any case increase.

The problem is that buildings are seen not as resources which make possible life and activity, but instead as assets which facilitate speculation and accumulation. This kind of logic applies even to housing *production*. This is at a low level, further fuelling price rises. Rather than producing houses, the major 'house builders' have become dealers in land.[10] As James Meek has argued, the focus on making money from land banking and speculating on housing bubbles, rather than building houses, feeds into the preference of banks for property loans:

> An incredible 76 per cent of all bank loans in Britain go to property, and 64 per cent of that to residential mortgages. That is money that could be spent on lending to other, more productive businesses (p16).

This is the current conjuncture in a nutshell: a finance sector speculating in assets, a supposedly productive (non-financial) sector doing the same; prices subject to boom and bust; and within all this the material and imaginative capture of those participating in home-ownership, alongside the implacable exclusion of those who are not.

AN OUTLINE OF AN ALTERNATIVE

It follows from our argument that an economy should be a means for fulfilling social goals, and not an end in itself, and that a means of deliberating and determining what such goals should be is essential to democracy. But our political institutions do not currently serve this purpose. Instead, governments define their primary role as that of managers and custodians of the national economy, sometimes even referring to the country and its people as Britain plc. There are two different aspects to the government's definition of this function. One is to facilitate 'economic growth', while leaving the nature and composition of such 'growth' largely to the market and to corporations to determine. The other is to maintain 'economic stability', measured not least by the rate of inflation, by the extent of borrowing and the size of the national debt. The principal interests which governments seek to protect here are those of the holders of assets. We have seen since the financial crisis of 2007-08, and measures adopted following earlier crises, that where the objectives of growth and stability are believed not to coincide, it is 'stability' which is given priority, even at the cost of economic contraction and large-scale unemployment.

The dominant conception of economic governance, in regard to the objectives of both stability and growth, generally seeks to limit the role of government to the maintenance of 'equilibrium' in what is supposed according to neoliberal economic theory to be an essentially self-regulating system. Thus government, through the Treasury and the Bank of England, monitors such indicators as the balance of payments, the level of government debt, the rate of inflation, and rates of growth in GDP, at an aggregate level; and 'news' of the economy consists largely of reported measures of this kind. On the changing composition of economic activity, its regional and local distribution, and its various component sectors, there is virtual silence, and a large degree of ignorance. Neither government nor the public has an information system available to it which would enable it to track the development of centres of production, and their manifold interconnections, even if they wanted to. Thus forms of planning which are completely essential to the operation of any large corporation, or indeed any other large organisation, have fallen under a neoliberal taboo when it comes to the development of the national economy. So deep has been the capture of society by neoliberal ways of thinking that it is a major task even to imagine an economy and society organised on a different basis, and to envisage how change could be achieved in such a direction.

Yet there are always cracks in the carapace. Hegemony has to be constructed and maintained and is thereby always open to challenge. And most of social reproduction in fact relies on non-financial relations, of trust, care and mutual responsibility. Not only is not absolutely everything captured, but those other feelings still resonate and resist. Elsewhere in the Manifesto we address a range of ways in which this can happen – through contesting vocabularies, cultural struggles around common sense, and appealing to people's desire for richer relations within society. Here we focus on what might be thought of as specifically 'economic' policies. Here too, however, we emphasise how 'economic policy' is itself – or can be – a part of cultural and ideological contest.

In what follows we offer some key elements of such an alternative, and of a transition towards it. These are given as broad outlines. All of them are elaborated in detail elsewhere in the (vast) literature that exists on potential alternative economic policies. The idea that is put about that the left has no alternative economics is entirely wrong, and is widely disseminated as part of a political attack.

1. Production and the role of the state

The point of departure must be that the sphere of production can no longer be taken for granted as the provider of resources whose distribution the state can then shift in a mildly progressive direction. This implies two aims: to build a productive base for the economy, and to re-think the role of the state within this endeavour.

First of all it is important to recognise that, contrary to apparent neoliberal ideology, the state is intimately and necessarily involved in the private sector. Indeed much of the private sector is utterly dependent, especially in our current economy, on the state and state activity. Many of the most successful modern economies have indeed developed as a consequence of alliances between private enterprises and governments, which, for example, provide the start-up costs for new investments, protect markets from premature competition, and provide markets for new products at crucial stages. The role of the military in supporting such development is familiar, but we could also note in Britain the role of public enterprises like the National Health Service (in regard to the pharmaceutical industry), the BBC (in relation to expertise in broadcasting), universities (in the development of scientific research), and leading professional schools in fields such as art and drama in developing the skills on which the 'creative industries' depend. Government also provides the framework of licences and franchises within which utilities and transport undertakings operate in Britain, thereby effectively limiting the competition to which they are subject, and making their environment predictable enough to encourage some amount of new investment.

Even more significantly, the state is the only agency that can invest, and take risks, in the long term, and it is this committed investment that is often necessary for major technological developments. Mariana Mazzucato has demonstrated that the idea that the private market sector of the economy is the primary source of scientific and technological innovation is largely a fallacy.[11] She has shown that the major scientific and technological innovations on which many of the most dazzling recent corporate successes have been based, even in the neoliberal United States (for example those of Apple, Google and Amazon), have come from government-funded laboratories, and from the later transfer of their discoveries to commercial use. The private sector is usually too averse to risk and uncertainty, she argues, to take on the costs of research and development on which innovative commercial products and services depend.

The interconnections between private corporations and governments in many spheres have become so extensive, but also so hidden from view, that the issue is not *whether* the government should intervene to enhance the workings of the economy, but *how* it should do this, and in particular in whose interests. What is needed is a major reassertion of the role of democratic institutions and practices in the organisation of the economy. Behind the project to build a serious productive sector in the UK economy, then, there must be a state that is creatively interventionist, that is publically recognised to be intervening, and that opens the nature of that intervention to democratic debate.[12]

2. Challenging 'finance'

Central to any rebuilding of the British economy must be a challenge to the character and dominance of the finance sector itself, and to the financialised common sense that it has helped engender. What is needed is a fundamental re-evaluation of the role and functions of the banking sector, such that it can come to serve the needs of the productive economy rather than functioning as a self-serving machine for the capture and sequestration of rents.

There are a number of steps that could be taken to improve the banking sector. These include: effective regulation of reward structures, to remove the gross excess of rewards now given to senior executives, and the misincentives to speculation and gambling which these engender; a tax on financial transactions, to reduce the relative profitability of the circulation of finance capital, compared to its productive long-term investment; bailed-out banks to be retained in public ownership and directed towards productive investment and socially-established objectives; registration of all new financial products; a programme to remutualise financial institutions operating in the housing market; the representation in the governance structure of the major banks of stakeholders who represent wider public interests; the regulation, where possible in agreement with other national governments, of 'offshore' financial operations, ensuring that all institutions operating in the market both meet their obligations to pay taxes and comply with other requirements of law and transparency; a strengthening of the regional presence and local engagement of banks, and the institution of a community reinvestment obligation.[13]

The aim of public-sector banking would in part be to do some of the jobs the current private sector does not do. But it could also be part of an ideological offensive – to challenge the financialised common sense of neoliberalism. The existence of a public presence within the financial system would strengthen the arm of regulation, facilitate genuine competition between providers, and potentially reduce the political influence of private finance. As Costas Lapavitsas has argued, public banks could operate as levers for the re-strengthening of the social and the collective at the expense of the private and the individual across the economy:

> If the public interest was fully represented and democratically expressed within finance, it could help re-establish public service as a superior motive compared to private gain across the economy in general. A re-strengthened spirit of public service would be a vital step to reversing the ascendency of finance in recent decades, while also laying foundations for a broader transformation of the economy in the interests of the many (op cit, p325).

In these ways, individual *policies* could be productive of a broader *politics*, and begin to address the wider ideological issue of financialisation.

3. Dampening the attraction of assets

Alongside the emphasis on rebuilding a production base for the economy, there should also be a firm address to the counter-attraction of assets. Some of the measures noted in relation to finance are also relevant here (the registration of new products, a transactions tax), but there is more that could be done. In particular, as we have noted, this must include an address to the land and property system, which could be achieved through a series of stages.[14] Council tax needs to be revalued in relation to current prices, in a system which ensures that liability remains in proportion to the value of properties, with revaluations at regular intervals to keep track of changing market values. At the moment council tax is massively regressive between owners – people in cheaper houses pay a far higher proportion of their house value than those in expensive houses. Revaluation would also have regionally redistributive effects, from South to North. This should be the precursor to a national Land Value Tax. The case for this is overwhelming.[15] It would work against boom and bust in the land and property sector, make planning and development more efficient, and work against the power of the property lobby. Only City firms are bigger donors to the Tory Party than the property industry (Inman, p24).

But there is also more to a Land Value Tax than that. As with the establishment of a public banking presence in finance, introducing a Land Value Tax is an economic policy that allows the opening up of much wider political discussion, as well as a challenge to current hegemonic vocabularies and common sense. Land is not something that is produced. Its price is often largely reflective of its location. And much of the value of a location, and increases in that value, is the result of activities and investments by all of us. The gains taken by the owner of the land are thus windfall gains – they are unearned, the private appropriation of socially-produced benefits. A Land Value Tax, as a measure to recoup this socially-produced value, thus opens up these areas to the political light, and to debate. 'Economic policies' are, or should be, more than purely economic policies.

POTENTIAL PRIORITIES FOR PRODUCTIVE INVESTMENT

We still need to address the question raised at the beginning of this chapter about what our economy would be *for*. The planning of 'production' in a modern economy needs to take account of the wide range of goods and services that contribute to well-being, both in their production and in their use, and to develop systems that can support these. Accordingly, we suggest here two examples of the kinds of priorities that such an approach would generate, namely ecological sustainability and the sustaining of collective care.

More generally, it is necessary to maintain Britain's competitiveness in economic markets, in order to ensure that adequate levels of employment are maintained. This is in part because paid work remains the primary source of individual and family incomes, and also because work is and should be an important means of human fulfilment and satisfaction. The arguments we made earlier for enhancing the government's role in the planning and generation of production address this dimension. The future of work is of particular concern in the modern economy, because of the tendency in the neoliberal system for skilled and fulfilling work in the productive system to be squeezed out (and this is now affecting many routine administrative as well as manufacturing processes). In this situation rewards are becoming polarised between a minority of very high earners, and an ever-larger number of low-paid workers.

Ecological sustainability: a Green New Deal

We support the Green New Deal Group's proposals for an interlinked package of measures that would include a systematic programme of large-scale investment in green infrastructure. This would benefit every community in Britain, 'providing skilled jobs, making homes warmer and keeping energy costs down'.[16]

The Green New Deal programme asserts and embodies a clear collective *vision* for economic policy. It would produce a huge number of jobs, demanding a wide range of real skills. It would create a whole new *productive* sector. It would necessarily be spread across the country (in sharp contrast to the way finance huddles itself into one small corner), and would be embedded in local relations. And – of course – it would begin to address some of the questions raised by climate change and environmental degradation.

The Green New Deal Group proposes finding the funding for this programme through: a more directed and regulated form of Quantitative Easing that would channel funds towards green projects; tackling tax evasion and avoidance; contributions from bailed-out banks; greater encouragement for general finance-sector contribution; releasing funds through enabling public bodies to buy themselves out of PFI commitments.

We could add to this list, for example through a more progressive taxation system and a Land Value Tax. But we also believe that the whole debate about taxation needs refounding. It is not simply a question of looking within existing parameters for ways of redistributing public funds. As we argued in Chapter 1, it is a political achievement of the right (i.e. it is not 'natural') that taxation is so disliked. We need to have the courage to make the case *for* taxation – tax is, or could be, part of what constructs our collectivity; and not just its level but also its purpose should be part of a rich debate.[17] A Green New Deal might be one way to galvanise such a debate. That could be even more true of our other priority ...

An economy of care and human development

Although it might be difficult to find anyone, at any point on the political spectrum, who did not genuflect before the idea that care and human development ought to be the central aims of economic strategy, it is quite easy to demonstrate that the current economic model is not at all directed towards these ends (and here we mean not just the post-crash austerity mindset, but the model that crashed, and which is now being rebuilt). We are being persuaded that paying bankers billions will somehow result, in the end, in better local health clinics, social services and pensions. It will not. Instead of waiting for this magical transformation we need a commitment to direct investment in social reproduction and the public realm more generally. That is, in education, health, training, social services, housing, public transport ... As we have argued elsewhere in this Manifesto, the obstacles facing such a commitment are not just financial (though we have also argued that financial constraint is itself a matter for debate); they also stem from the fact that our very language obstructs our view. In particular, the classification of public commitments to such provision and services are widely classified as *costs*, as a burden. Expenditure on wages and salaries for workers in these sectors is regarded as particularly burdensome, and this attitude has been exacerbated by the now customary denigration of public-sector workers and the undermining of the specific values and goals of these fields of activity (see Chapter 2, 'A relational society'). In fact, of course, a commitment to such spheres is the best *investment* a society could make. *This* is what an economy should be for.

Moreover, this commitment also contributes to the aim of developing a more ecologically sustainable economy. Our two priorities work together. If we are to rein in humanity's exhaustion of the planet's resources, we have to focus on 'growing better', that is, improving our lives by using our time to help each other directly instead of producing more things. We therefore have to see a service economy as a desirable goal, but not one based on services to businesses in pursuit of profit, rather one based on services to improve well-being – care in the broadest sense. The only way to save the planet, therefore, is for people to spend most of their time caring for each other. The need for labour and commitment remains undiminished in those spheres of life to which human relationships are fundamental. Governments may believe otherwise, but this is because of their misapplication of market logic. An economy whose purpose is to produce enhanced well-being will be one in which the attention given by people to one another's needs and purposes will become greater, and the society it serves will devote more of its resources to these ends. Such purposes would also include the cultivation of democratic participation itself, and a recognition of the time and work which this entails.

As we have seen, 'financialisation' has involved the increasing engagement of private finance in all these spheres of society, as public provision has been withdrawn or sold off. Conversely, a reassertion of the importance of care in the public sphere – in health, education, pensions and social care – will play a key part in confronting financialisation. The different elements of this strategy are thus intimately related.

Moreover, our defence and expansion of these sectors, while certainly focusing on the necessity of the services and jobs they provide, should also be expressed more generally in terms of the need for a strong public realm, and its centrality to building a good society. Here again, a specific element of economic strategy could work also to challenge and remould the hegemonic common sense. As we said at the outset, the economic and the cultural are not entirely separate spheres of society. Indeed, the cultural bankruptcy of the market model is everywhere evident in the public sphere. Film-maker and writer Patrick Keiller has long bemoaned the mean physical state of 'the physiognomy of our society', and argued for 'a more inclusive transformation of everyday surroundings'.[18] A key part of any confrontation with financialisation will be the reassertion of the public against the private, and a rebalancing away from the individual and towards the collective.

Such an approach to care would be embedded in and entail a wider politics. Thus, to take the specific example of care: prioritising care has the potential to transform some currently dominant notions of what is productive and what not, what is investment and what is expenditure. Furthermore, as Sue Himmelweit and Hilary Land argue, there is a strong gender dimension involved in the creating of a sustainable care system; amongst other things this would require addressing the issue of pay for care workers, as well as the question of working time.[19] There is a further whole world of politics here.[20] Working towards a sustainable and more egalitarian system would entail a reimagination and revaluation of what an economy should be about. As Himmelweit and Land also argue:

> Many people, largely women, are not getting the care they need. Many carers, also largely women, are not getting the support they need and the opportunities they deserve to take part in society. The paid care sector is failing to plug the gap through lack of funding, leading to recruitment and retention problems (p11).

Their proposals for change include: more support for family carers; the reduction of working hours; improvement in pay and conditions for paid care workers; and an increase in budgets. What's more, as they argue and their title emphasises, these proposals are perfectly 'sustainable'.

DEMOCRACY

Finally, running as a thread through all our arguments here is the issue of the democratisation of the economy. This must be integral to any new political economy. As many have argued, there is a fundamental incompatibility between the proclaimed values of neoliberalism and its results: most evidently, fierce inequality undermines genuine democracy. Streeck, for instance, has pointed out that: 'Since investor confidence is more important now than voter confidence, the ongoing takeover of power by the confidants of capital is seen by centre left and right alike not as a problem, but as the solution'.[21] He also argues – as have a number of other writers – that acquiescence in this state of affairs has been sought by borrowing from the future through a credit system that allows consumption at unsustainable levels, and he calls for a democratic departure from this 'life-threatening sedation' (p70). Any serious challenge to currently hegemonic understandings of the economy, including support for the prioritisation of real investment (which will take time to pay off), must be accompanied by a commitment to the people becoming stakeholders in the economy. A whole range of possibilities is available to achieve this – strengthening the trades-union movement, restraining the shareholder model, improving democracy within the workplace[22] – as well as enabling open public debate along the many lines we have indicated in previous sections. At the moment, as Christos Laskos and Euclid Tsakalotos argue, capital is treated as the universal class – its interests are assumed to coincide with those of society as a whole.[23] Democratising the economy, and debating what an economy is for, surely hold out the potential for challenging this.

NOTES

1. This is not the place to go into these arguments in detail. The chapters of the Kilburn Manifesto are not intended to be policy-briefings, or lists of policies. Rather, the aim is to argue for re-thinking the terrain and to set out broad themes and parameters. That is our aim in what follows in relation to the broad field of economic strategy. Many of the authors cited in this chapter include ideas on policy, and we hope that readers in search of policy ideas will follow up some of these. Other important sources of ideas include the work of Richard Murphy, and major contributions from groups such as nef, the New Political Economy Group and CRESC.

2. Costas Lapavitsas, *Profiting Without Producing*, Verso 2013, pp3-4.

3. Mariana Mazzucato, 'From bubble to bubble', *The Guardian*, 16.1.13.

4. Andrew Sayer, 'Facing the challenge of the return of the rich', in W. Atkinson, S. Roberts and M. Savage (eds), *Class inequality in austerity Britain*, Palgrave Macmillan 2012.

5. Doreen Massey, *World City*, Polity 2010.

6. N. Buck, I. Gordon, P. Hall, M. Harloe and M. Kleinman, *Working Capital: Life and Labour in Contemporary London*, Routledge 2002.

7. Colin Crouch, *Post-Democracy*, Polity 2004; and *The Strange Non-death of Neoliberalism*, Polity 2011.

8. See Neal Lawson, *All consuming*, Penguin 2009.

9. In this process value becomes more abstract. Marx explores this process in his 1844 *Economic and Philosophical Manuscripts*.

10. James Meek, 'Where will we live?', *LRB* 9.1.14; Matt Griffith, *We Must Fix It*, IPPR 2011.

11. Mariana Mazzucato, *The Entrepreneurial State*, Anthem 2013.

12. For more on industrial policy see Ha-Joon Chang, '"No industrial policy please, we're British" is out of date', *The Guardian*, 12.9.12; and *Industrial policy: can we go beyond an unproductive confrontation*, Annual World Bank Conference on Development Economics 2011.

13. The Green New Deal authors have put forward solutions along these lines – see www.greennewdealgroup.org.

14. Philip Inman, 'Could we build a better future on a land value tax?', *The Guardian*, 16.9.12.

15. Joseph Rowntree Foundation, *Tackling Housing Market Inequality in the UK*, JRF October 2011, cited in Inman, op. cit. Inman also reports support for a Land Value Tax from the Institute of Fiscal Studies and the OECD. See also material produced by the Labour Land Campaign.

16. Green New Deal Group, *A National Plan for the UK: From Austerity to the Green New Deal* (fifth anniversary report of the Green New Deal Group) 2013, p3. The first GND report was published in 2008 and was updated in 2013. Its authors are Larry Elliott, Colin Hines, Tony Juniper, Jeremy Leggett, Caroline Lucas, Richard Murphy, Ann Pettifor, Charles Secrett and Andrew Simms.

17. A similar case has been made in relation to hypothecation. See Geoff Mulgan and Robin Murray, *Reconnecting Taxation*, Demos 1993.

18. Patrick Keiller, *The View from the Train: Cities and Other Landscapes*, Verso 2013, pp22, 1; and see in particular his film *The Dilapidated Dwelling* (2000).

19. Sue Himmelweit and Hilary Land, *Reducing gender inequalities to create a sustainable care system*, JRF 2008: www.jrf.org.uk/publications/reducing-gender-inequalities-create-sustainable-care-system.

20. Anna Coote and Jane Franklin, *Time on our Side*, nef 2013.

21. Wolfgang Streeck, 'Markets and peoples: Democratic Capitalism and European Integration', *NLR* 73, Jan-Feb 2012, p65.

22. TUC, *A future that works: the TUC's Campaign Plan*, TUC 2013: www.tuc.org.uk/tuc-campaign-plan.

23. Christos Laskos and Euclid Tsakalotos, *Crucible of Resistance: Greece, the Eurozone and the World Economic Crisis*, Pluto 2013, p21.

8. Rethinking the Neoliberal World Order

Michael Rustin and Doreen Massey

Earlier chapters of the Kilburn Manifesto have focused on the impacts of neoliberalism on British society, and on how we might begin to conceive of feasible alternatives to that regime. But in thinking about the sphere of international relations, and the position Britain takes up within the world, it is necessary to take a more global perspective. We are taking as our starting point for understanding these issues the situation that emerged following the defeat of Communism and the end of the Cold War at the end of the 1980s. What is in the forefront of our analysis here is the continuing sequence of failures – catastrophes in fact – that have characterised the international policies of the west during that entire period, now of more than thirty years. There is need to understand the dynamic forces, and the ideological beliefs, which have brought this situation about.

We are going to focus particular attention on the sequence of crises that have taken place in the Middle East, and now in Europe. These include the disintegration of Iraq into warring sub-states and of Libya into warring fiefdoms, a bloody and unresolved civil war in Syria, the resurgence of the Taliban in Afghanistan as the strongest power, the ungoverned and self-destructive brutality of Israel in the treatment of the population of Gaza, and the descent of Ukraine into a state of civil war. And most recently there has been added the emergence of 'Isis', The Islamic State, which has swept aside resistance and is engaged in the establishment of a new theocratic state, or caliphate, occupying territories which were until now part of Iraq, Syria, and the *de facto* autonomous region of Kurdistan. Scarcely ever have governments the world over seemed less capable of responding with clear understanding and capability to the problems they encounter. It is not without significance that the situation in Ukraine called forth comparisons with the chaotic situation which led to the outbreak of the First World War and the end of the 'long peace' of the nineteenth century. We think of these events as a series of catastrophes not because of any particular commitment to the regimes and territorial arrangements which preceded these upheavals, but rather because of the huge losses of life, expulsions of populations, and disintegration of more or less peaceable conditions of social order, that have been their consequence.[1]

Our contention is that this has not been a contingent series of events, a random sequence of foreign policy accidents, but that they are in their own way systemic – a kind of organised disorder – and that understanding them is closely related to the task we have set ourselves in this Manifesto's analysis and critique of neoliberalism as a global system.

The politics of the post-second world war period seemed to have been so largely shaped by the Cold War that its end was expected by many to be a moment of opportunity. At least the risk of nuclear war had been significantly lessened, and several 'proxy wars' between the west and the Communist east (for example in Angola and Mozambique) were able to be resolved after the 'Second Cold War'.[2] The end of the apartheid regime in South Africa was hastened once the possible implications for the Cold War of the assumption of power by the African National Congress lost their significance. In Latin America, anti-communist perspectives which had legitimised interventions by the United States in several nations lost at least their overt relevance (for example the overthrow of Allende in Chile in 1973, the condoning of military dictatorship in Argentina from 1976 to 1983, and Brazil from 1964 to 1985, covert support by the United States for the subversion of Nicaragua's elected government by the Contras). For the first time for many decades major Latin American nations such as Brazil found space to pursue more radical agendas, with less interference from the United States.

Yet at a time when progressive development might seem to have become possible in several continents, including Europe (both east and west), the western powers, led by the United States, and with Britain as its most compliant ally, found themselves engaged in a gathering series of armed interventions. The central focus of these has been the Middle East, and the commitment of the western powers to retaining their hegemony in that region. While this drive is incomprehensible without reference to western powers' economic dependence on the Middle East's oil resources, we think that more than narrowly material interests are involved.

To understand this pattern of disasters it is important to remember that the end of the Cold War came about through the collapse of the Soviet Union and the end of European Communism, in what was seen as the total victory of the United States and its allies. This period saw the triumph of what was already by then a fully neoliberal system, which had followed the conservative counter-revolution led by Reagan in the USA and Thatcher in Britain. (We describe its effects within Britain elsewhere in this Manifesto – here we are examining its wider consequences.)

United States governments and their allies believed that this system could from now onwards exercise unquestioned hegemony over the entire world. The axiom of 'full spectrum dominance' was the military aspect of this ambition. The 'Washington Consensus', imposing the regime of neoliberalism through the instruments of international agencies such as the IMF and the World Bank, was its economic instrument. Universalist ideas of representative democracy, political and religious freedom, and human rights, were its ideological expression. This world-view was and is intolerant of other forms of political and economic organisation, and of cultures and beliefs different from its own. Thus support for Gorbachev's gradualist adaptation of the Soviet Union in the direction of social democracy was withheld, and 'shock therapy' and the gangster capitalism of Yeltsin preferred, the result being to weaken and impoverish Russia. This neoliberal system has to be understood in its entirety, in its economic, military, political and indeed psycho-social dimensions.

Within neoliberalism as a global project are a number of hidden or denied continuities with its antecedent ideologies and systems of power. These represent 'transformations' which have nevertheless left their preceding structures largely intact.[3] Thus the Cold War against the Communist enemy becomes the War on Terror, or the struggle against 'Islamic fundamentalism', even 'a War of Civilisations'. Under these umbrellas the military-industrial complexes and the security apparatuses that flourished during the Cold War were able to claim a new necessity and legitimacy, and the mentalities of antagonism and (at times) paranoia that the Cold War encouraged found new objects of fear and hatred. Colonialism – always ostensibly rejected by the United States because of America's original foundation in its Declaration of Independence, and supposedly repudiated by former European powers following their (mostly reluctant) acceptance of decolonisation – found a new lease of life, under the guise of humanitarianism and the advocacy of universal human rights.[4] The aim of economic domination survived after the apparent end of empires, though it took different forms.

The interventions and conflicts that have followed from the implementation of this neoliberal design in the Middle East have taken various forms. The support for Iraq in its war with Iran between 1980 and 1988 was aimed at preventing the emergence of a rival regional centre of power. Iran had been antipathetic to the west since the overthrow of the Shah, who had been especially strongly supported by the west after the coup against prime minister Mossadeq following the nationalisation of Iran's oil assets in 1951. The unconditional support of the United States for Israel, and its failure to insist that Israel comes to a peaceful settlement of its conflict with the Palestinians (e.g. the 'two state solution', which has probably now been destroyed as an option by successive Israeli governments), is another pillar of this neo-imperialist strategy. Political support for Israel within the United States is of great significance in US policy-making, just as support for 'white settlers' within threatened colonies influenced the imperial policies of Britain and France in different regions of Africa in earlier decades.[5]

The Cold War had provided the rationale for previous American intervention in the region, when they had supported the subversion of the Russian-backed government of Afghanistan, both before and after the Soviet Union's withdrawal from that country. But the unintended effect of this intervention had been to assist the rise of a new enemy, since the American-supported militant Islamic resistance to the regime subsequently turned its hostility towards the west: once their fight in Afghanistan had been won, the antagonism of the militants made no distinctions between communist and capitalist projects of atheistical modernisation. Thus it was that military and ideological structures in the west, which had for decades been directed against its Communist enemies, came to be redeployed for service against a new enemy that was in part its own creation.

Then, as an indirect consequence of the Taliban's takeover of Afghanistan, came the attack on the Twin Towers and the Pentagon in 2001. This, from the point of view of its perpetrators, was arguably the most successful act of terrorism in history. In provoking the United States into its own invasion of Afghanistan, al-Qaida succeeded in defining the terms of a new global conflict, named by the Americans 'the War on Terror', but prosecuted as a war on militant Islam, or on anything that looked remotely like it. 'Those whom the gods wish to destroy they first make mad', the Islamists of al-Qaida might have thought, as after 11 September 2001 the policy of America and its allies descended into a morass of irrationality, from which they have found escape extremely difficult. 'Terrorist' and 'terrorism' have become swearwords deployed by governments to demonise enemies of all kinds, and to legitimise the expansion of their apparatuses of security and surveillance to totalitarian proportions.[6] One may understand recent telecast executions of western journalists by ISIS as acts of provocation of similar intent: their purpose may be to elicit armed reprisals against which whole populations can then be mobilised.

What has become known as 'liberal imperialism' has become the rationale for this post-cold-war and ostensibly post-colonial version of the west's imperial project. With an attention to spectacle and sentiment characteristic of the media age, this doctrine often gives emphasis to 'humanitarian' conditions in its justifications of international policy. But according to Tony Blair (for example in his 2004 Sedgefield speech, in which he justified the invasion of Iraq), while such considerations had rightly extended the legitimate grounds for armed interventions beyond the norms of justifiable self defence against aggression, global threats of terror and global interdependence meant that there now existed much broader grounds for supporting military action to protect security.[7] It seems clear that within this framework more or less any form of military action could be justified on 'preventive' grounds (and that this can be seen as part of Blair's advocacy of a global, though regulated, market system – the international version of the 'Third Way'). Arguments by academics were promulgated in this period that proposed that earlier ideas of national state sovereignty (the 'Westphalia system'), which had restricted the grounds of justifiable military action against other states to self-defence, were now obsolete. It was argued that great powers such as the United States, with their 'coalitions of the willing', were justified in exercising military force against other nations without the authority of international law, or the agreement of the United Nations.[8]

Such conceptions have been deployed in the Middle East to justify several military interventions, in Iraq, Afghanistan, Libya, and less directly in Syria, not to mention various programmes of economic and diplomatic sanctions against other nations, such as Iran and now Russia, as well as the deployment by the United States of assassination by drone strikes to eliminate suspected terrorist groupings and their leaders, for example in Pakistan, the Yemen and Somalia.

There have been different models of explanation for these developments. Arguments concerning the defence of human rights and the prevention of terrorism have been deployed in the Middle East to rationalise the western powers' economic interests, particularly in regard to the oil resources. But a dominant 'realist' argument in International Relations holds that nations normally behave like the self-seeking individuals of market theory, to exert and extend their power to its feasible limits and beyond. In the international context, overarching forms of law, norms and governance are weak, and often fail to inhibit the actions of states, through their selective enforcement or non-enforcement. Within this perspective, least-bad outcomes are achieved when nation states can recognise each other's legitimate interest in security, and avoid undue provocations.[9] (Within this framework, more altruistic interpretations of the ways in which nation states might relate to one another are more or less excluded by the very way they define state and nation.)

Justin Rosenberg has argued that such 'realist' conceptions, focused on the power-seeking attributes of states, have in particular failed to explain the antagonisms of the Cold War, which he attributes largely to the conflicts between the competing social and ideological systems of communism and capitalism.[10] One could argue that this perspective, which gives emphasis to ideologies and the attributes of social systems in generating conflicts, has been refuted by the continuation of conflicts between Russia and the west after the fall of communism. But if neoliberalism – global capitalism at its most expansive – is recognised as the active force in determining the geopolitical strategies of western governments, it is evident that Rosenberg's theory of conflicting social systems retains its explanatory power. Conflicts based on ideological differences can and do persist, even after the defeat of a particular ideological enemy.

The post-cold-war imperial system chose to formulate its mode of operation in normative and ideological terms, attempting to mask the grounds of interest that motivated its actions – both of states and of sub-sectors within them (the military, the security apparatus, contractors and corporations). Following the ideological logic of the Cold War (defined as a conflict between the free and the unfree world, democracy and dictatorship), but now in a largely post-communist context, western powers have embarked on various projects of 'regime change' and 'democratic state-building', in nearly every case with catastrophic outcomes even for the promoters of these policies. This is certainly the case with the invasion and occupation of Iraq, and the invasion and occupation of Afghanistan, the countries in which the military commitment of the United States has been at its most overt. The first of these has descended into a state of civil war: Isis or the Islamic State is best understood as an outgrowth of Sunni resistance to the Shia domination imposed by the American invasion. And meanwhile in Afghanistan the Taliban are reported be regaining much of their lost ground, following the departure of the armed forces of the Americans and their allies.

Yet although Iraq had attacked Kuwait in 1990, and the Taliban of Afghanistan had offered some sanctuary for al-Qaida, the fact is that neither of these states had ever offered any violence to, or constituted any threat to, their invaders. For all the delusions and fabrications concerning 'weapons of mass destruction', the new imperial system was deploying its military power for different reasons and objectives than those by which it publicly justified its actions. Some of the grounds given for the overthrow of Saddam Hussein were those of justice and humanity, because of the extreme violence which had been perpetrated by his regime against Kurds and Shias and his political opponents. But whereas the intervention by Vietnam in Cambodia, against the Khmer Rouge, could be justified as seeking to stop acts of genocide, and timely intervention in Rwanda should indeed have had that purpose, the principal offences against humanity of the Iraq regime lay in the past at the time of Saddam's overthrow, which had the form more of punishment than preventive action.[11]

While the invasion of Afghanistan was provoked by the 9-11 attack as an act of revenge and punishment, it also embodied the neoliberal hubris of that time, the idea that western models of democracy could simply be imposed by an invading force and its retinues of contractors. The perpetration of 'war crimes' – for example the deliberate killing of civilians – has also become a frequent accusation made against regimes under attack, but the western powers' own repeated responsibility for huge scales of civilian suffering and death (e.g. in the Second World War, Vietnam, Iraq, etc) invariably remains unacknowledged.

In Syria, the mentalities of the Cold War remain present, but in the background. When the Assad regime deployed armed force against opposition resistance and consequent insurrection, and hostile outside powers (Saudi Arabia and some Gulf States on the one side, Iran on the other) intervened to arm and assist the opposing sides, the west aligned with a 'moderate' segment of the opposition, and Russia with the Assad government. Initially, western sympathies for the protesters were mobilised by the Assad regime's violent response, but as the dominant role of Islamic fundamentalists in the opposition has become clear, the depiction of the struggle as tyranny versus democracy has become untenable. Indeed it has become evident that one of the relative virtues of the Assad regime was its toleration of religious minorities, including Christians. In this case western governments, their fingers burned by earlier interventionist failures, have provided only limited assistance to their allies in the 'moderate opposition', and not enough to make a difference to the outcome of the civil war.

In Egypt, the outcome of mass protests was initially more positive, from a liberal perspective, than in Libya or Syria. Protesters were protected by the military against their repression by Mubarak's security forces, and Mubarak was removed from power. An election then took place, but the liberal elements of the opposition were defeated by the Muslim Brotherhood, a moderate Islamist movement which had much deeper social roots than those of the urban liberal opponents of the regime. However, within a year there was a popular rising against the Brotherhood government, followed by an army coup, and military rule was once more restored. The new military government, led by former head of the armed forces Abdul Fattah al-Sisi, is even more oppressive than that of Mubarak, and is seeking to destroy a movement – the Muslim Brotherhood – with which the Mubarak regime had co-existed. But the Americans have given their support to the Sisi government, and continue to provide it with substantial military aid (while Tony Blair has gone out of his way to endorse the new regime). The weakness of the west's supposed standard-bearers in Egypt, the democrats who were initially prominent in the demonstrations in the public squares, has been revealed by the support which many liberals have given to Sisi's overthrow of their elected government.

Meanwhile the autocracies of Saudi Arabia and the Gulf States remain uncriticised allies of the western powers, despite their covert role in promoting Sunni fundamentalism throughout the world. It is clear that the place of democratic values in the formation of the policies of western governments' policies is almost always subordinate to their broader strategic interests.

EXPLANATIONS: CONTINUITIES WITH THE COLD WAR

How can we explain such a disastrous series of catastrophes? Why have the NATO powers engaged in so many interventions which have failed in what they set out to do? Part of the explanation lies, as we have suggested, in the nature of the system or regime which emerged following the outcome of the Cold War, and in the victory which America and its allies thought they had achieved with the collapse of the Soviet Union and the end of European Communism.

There are important continuities with the earlier organisation of the capitalist world in its confrontation with Communism. Thus the system has always deployed humanitarian and libertarian arguments in its stance, and during the Stalin years especially these had considerable force. The west has also always claimed that its 'free markets' are superior to other forms of economic organisation, and its preferred model of government has been democracy. Its constitutional democracies may have only ever given limited expression to democratic norms, and the system may have always been willing to tolerate and even promote 'exceptions' to its own values – for example the sponsored and supported dictatorships in Latin America in the 1970s and 1980s, and contemporary support for autocracies in Saudi Arabia and the Gulf Emirates. But nevertheless, its norms were, and remain, significantly embodied in its own political systems, and have been important in maintaining the allegiance of its citizens, especially when it was in competition with its Communist rival.

The strategy of the west has also continued in its earlier methods of international operation. The strategies of covert and overt military intervention which were routinely practised (on both sides) during the Cold War have been adapted for use against mostly new enemies in the post-cold-war period. It is important to see these continuities between the two epochs of the west's geopolitical strategy. In the moment of triumphalism which followed the collapse of the Soviet

Union, parallels must have been drawn between the democratic transformations which had just taken place in Russia and Eastern Europe and those that were now deemed to be desirable in other regions of strategic value, notably the Middle East. And of course there was a vast 'military industrial complex' built up during the Cold War which had no intention of demobilising itself now that battle was won.[12] From its point of view, new enemies could only be welcome. In terms of the social psychology or group mentalities of the west, there was also a problem to be solved. How could a society which had organised itself around a paranoid fear and hatred of its communist enemy (nuclear policy had after all declared a preference for universal destruction over ideological defeat) function in the absence of a defined antagonist? Al-Qaida and the War on Terror fulfilled this requirement perfectly.[13]

Thus equivalences were perceived between the transitions which had taken place from one-party state socialist rule to versions of democracy in Eastern Europe, and projects for transformation which were imagined (or fantasised) to be feasible in nations ruled by authoritarian regimes, such as Iraq, Syria, Libya and Afghanistan. This project had begun before the end of the Cold War, when the United States sought to undermine the Soviet-controlled regime in Afghanistan, through mobilising and supporting mujahideen – Islamic guerrillas – recruited from the tribal regions of Pakistan. This was the 'bear trap' which American cold war strategists set for the Soviet Union, as a payback for their own earlier defeat in Vietnam. Even when the Soviets withdrew from Afghanistan, leaving local communist leader Najibullah in power, the Americans saw no reason to desist from their project of subversion.[14] The access to power of Islamic fundamentalists in Afghanistan – the Taliban – was an unforeseen consequence of this cold war intervention, and an early instance of how little this regional and cultural context of operation was understood by the Americans.

It seems likely that the current regime in Syria and the over-turned regimes of Libya and Iraq – all secular state dictatorships – are also conceived in the minds of western policy-makers as hangovers or affiliates of the defeated communist system. Syria was a long-term ally of the Soviet Union. Iraq had attempted its own aggrandisement, in its invasion of Kuwait, while its regime and that in Syria were led by rival sections of the Arab Socialist Ba'ath Party. Gaddafi in Libya had sought be the successor of Nasser as the anti-western leader of the Arab world, and to take a role independent of both the east and the west. In this era of American triumphalism, each of these countries seemed to be candidates for transition to the west's model of a 'modern' state. Furthermore, many of the leading figures in their liberal opposition movements lived and worked in the United States, and were able to present themselves as potential leaders of alternative ruling groups who, once installed in power, would be sympathetic to western interests.

Interventions in Iraq and in Afghanistan after the Twin Towers attack were initially punitive in their nature: their projects of 'democratic state-building' followed only once the previous structures of government had been swept away. In Syria and Libya, the protest movements of the Arab Spring were seized upon as opportunities for the west to encourage the changes which both its ideology and its strategic interests required. Two further military interventions or support operations therefore followed, although, in the light of earlier harsh experience, more cautiously in the Syrian case.[15]

Then there is Ukraine, which can even more clearly be seen as unfinished business of the Cold War. Ukraine is perceived as having yet to make its full transition to the western, neoliberal model, being still divided between its Russian and its European Union affinities. When a movement emerged to overthrow a pro-Russian government, the Americans and West Europeans supported what was in effect a coup, and found themselves once again involved on one side of a virtual civil war. As in many of these conflicts, including for example in Kosovo, the initial agenda was established by militant factions, which were then able (on various grounds of liberal sympathy, humanitarian concern or cynical geopolitical interest) to draw western governments and publics into giving them support, and even into fighting for them.[16]

There are two principal reasons why this project of liberal imperialist transformation has had such disastrous outcomes, in particular in the Middle East. The first is that military intervention, civil war and the breakdown of social order destroy the basis of social trust on which the west's sought-after democratic structures depend. In the states of fear to which people are reduced by civil violence, local forms of affiliation and security are often sought, to replace those which were previously given by the state and its laws. In the Balkans, populations defaulted to ethnic and even religious identifications that had been imagined to have lost their potency in post-war Yugoslavia. In Afghanistan, Libya and Syria, populations have returned to religious and tribal sources of identity, as their states have collapsed or have become largely criminal and gangster-infested in their operation.[17] Furthermore, the institutions and values which the west ostensibly sought to advance through its armies, special agents, contractors, bombings and drones were discredited by the means by which they were being imposed.[18]

A second factor is that these societies always had much more complex and deeply rooted forms of life than the west's liberal colonisers understood, or chose to understand. They were also in certain respects already more 'western', more capable of moving themselves in 'liberal' directions – for example in such matters as education, emancipations of gender, technology and science – than their colonisers and modernisers wished to recognise. Thus Tony Blair's government was for once right in its view that Gaddafi's government might be persuaded to engage in peaceful relations with the west, if diplomatic efforts were made to bring this about.

The west also commonly exaggerates its own virtues when it sets its liberal society up as a model for others. Its own forms of democracy are limited in their scope, and are distorted by the interests of property and capital, as this Manifesto has documented. Its cultures of individualism and consumption are often both crude and violent, by comparison with other forms of social life. Forms of government that may not be democratic according to the norms and procedures of western constitutionalism, may nevertheless have their own means of taking account of the wishes and interests of their citizens, and may be more responsible, for example in regard to the crisis of global warming, than some capitalist nations.

In fact, some reappraisal is being imposed on the west's rulers by the many policy failures of the post-cold-war period, and the misfortunes they have brought to a major region of the world. Few any longer believe that a new order is about to be imposed on the world by the United States, as its policy-makers envisaged two decades ago. The 'new imperialism' of invasions, assisted insurrections and regime change has been to some degree discredited. The current climate of opinion regarding international relations is one of anxious uncertainty. We hope that this provides an opportunity to set out different principles and objectives for this sphere, just as we are proposing in regard to the economy and culture of neoliberalism.

Before we discuss what such principles and goals should be, we should say something about Britain's specific involvements in the global nexus of international relations, which we see as an aspect of the system of neoliberalism.

BRITAIN IN THE GLOBAL SYSTEM

Many elements have contributed to Britain's integration into the global strategies of the neoliberal west in the post-cold-war period. One of the most significant of these are the residual mentalities of Britain's position as the former centre of a world-wide empire. Even after decolonisation had supposedly taken place, Britain fought wars in Malaya, Kenya and Cyprus to retain its influence, and invaded Egypt in an attempt to overthrow Gamed Abdul Nasser and to retain control of the Suez Canal. In Afghanistan, Britain was re-entering a territory which it had previously fought to control (without success) in the nineteenth century. Britain and other western powers had at the end of the First World War drawn up many of the frontiers in the Middle East which are now in dispute. One can also see the prolonged 'Troubles' in Northern Ireland as resulting from a British commitment to hold on to what was originally an imperial province. The British government has sought throughout the post-war period to retain its status as a 'Great Power', despite its diminished economic and military resources; indeed the main purpose of retention of its nuclear deterrent is to maintain this position of supposed parity with other 'nuclear powers'. Thatcher's Falklands/Malvinas adventure in 1982 was a manifestation of a continuing belief in Britain's imperial mission, determined in this case by the democratic rationale of the islanders' 'right to self government' – and by the unsavoury attributes of the Argentine dictatorship at the time.[19] Victory in the Falklands was a significant factor in Thatcher's election victory in 1983; popular identification with this late imperial achievement, and with the naval and military prowess which it demonstrated, outweighed the sufferings that the harsh economic policies of the government had brought during its first years of office. Tony Blair's doctrine of 'liberal imperialism' was thus the reinvention of a long tradition, set out with a new focus on humanitarian concerns. These have been brought to the centre of attention by mass media coverage, including through the (understandable) attribution of hero or heroine status to modern aid workers, and even journalists, who work in far-off situations where there is extreme suffering. Liberal imperialism in fact presents itself with two different identities. One is that of the dedicated aid worker. The other is that of the British soldier – often speaking from a situation of danger, and representing in its most responsible and capable form the activities of the military in seeking to bring 'peace' to another region of the world.[20] Thus public identification with Britain's continuing imperial mission is doubly sustained.

British governments were able to maintain public support for military interventions across the globe (in the Falklands/Malvinas, in the former Yugoslavia, in Sierra Leone and in the first Iraq War) for a considerable period. Few seemed to object to successive British prime ministers and foreign secretaries lecturing other governments on their offences against human rights, or their threat to world peace, as if this was the natural prerogative of a leading nation such as Great Britain. It is only more recently, as the disappointing or catastrophic consequences of these interventions have become evident, that support for such military action has diminished. Ed Miliband plainly judged the public mood accurately when he opposed military intervention in Syria.

A second major continuity in British policy has been with the strategies and mentalities set out during the Cold War – as described above – and this has strongly maintained Britain's integration within the neoliberal international system. It is important to remember here how the Cold War imposed itself on British politics after the Second World War, diverting its course for the worse. The rearmament consequent on the Korean War divided the post-war Labour government, leading to the resignation of Aneurin Bevan and his allies, and weakening that government in its later years. The Wilson government of 1964 struggled with the political consequences of the Vietnam War, as well as its hyper-inflationary economic consequences in the 1970s. The morphing of 'imperial' into 'Cold War' interests was used to confer legitimacy on what were in reality still colonial struggles during this period: Vietnam is a prime instance of this displacement and misdefinition of goals.

A third aspect of Britain's integral involvement in this western global strategy has been the distinctive 'financialised' form of its economic development. The genesis of neoliberalism in Britain is closely linked to Britain's imperial history and to the predominant role of finance capital in its economy – which is in considerable part a residue of the empire. Rent from the ownership of and trade in land and other forms of property, whether held within Britain or abroad, has been more important in the mentality and practice of Britain's ruling class than industrial production. The outcome of the political and social crisis of the 1970s, in the arrival of Thatcherism, reinforced these long-established tendencies. (We discuss these issues in Chapter 7.)

One has a depressing sense of déjà vu in returning to the debates of the 1960s, 1970s and 1980s, on the redirection of the British economy away from finance and shareholder power, and towards manufacturing and industrial production, as well as towards more responsible forms of corporate governance. This was in effect an argument for a turn from the 'aristocratic' domination of British society, symbolised by the social origins and persona of Sir Alec Douglas-Home. The complexion of the current Tory leadership shows that little has changed since. (Except perhaps that there are even fewer people of working-class origin within the system of government than in the 1960s; and today's ruling class, though still founded on inherited property, has become more meritocratic in its formation, taking advantage of its access to private education and elite universities to maintain its power.) The financialised British economy has been a major pillar of neoliberal economic orthodoxy, which opposed statist and corporatist methods of economic organisation.

The consequence of all these factors is that Britain has firmly aligned itself with the United States throughout the post-war period, and it is from the United States that the main direction of its international policy has come. Support for the Americans' cold war positions led to Britain being allotted a subordinate space in which it could retain some of its post-imperial commitments. We saw in Blair's proximity to President Bush in the second Iraq War how valuable to both parties this association could be. Continuing nationalist illusions have also turned Britain away from the European Union, which could have provided an alternative, more 'industrial', less militarised and more consensual framework for development.

In Europe the class interests of British governments were also to the fore in the campaign to convert the EU from being a potential social-democratic bulwark towards being a haven for, and promoter of, the interests of capital. Their commitment to the 'widening' rather than 'deepening' of the European Union reflected this free-market priority. Its latest manifestation can be seen in the Trade and Services Agreement, the numerous Bilateral Investment Treaties, and, most threateningly, the proposed Transatlantic Trade and Investment Partnership. Together these will create an even more aggressively deregulated environment for business, and, most importantly, they constitute a further attack on democratic rights – the interests of companies are to be given the power effectively to restrict the policy-making options of elected governments. The current Coalition is an enthusiastic supporter of these trends.

ALTERNATIVE PRINCIPLES AND COMMITMENTS

The failures of the west's international strategies in the post-cold-war period give rise to the need to rethink these orientations in a fundamental way. In this Manifesto we have developed a critique of the neoliberal system in regard to its economic and social effects. Below we suggest some of the principles that should guide Britain's role in the international sphere:

1. Policy should be based on the recognition that war is nearly always the worst of man-made disasters. The first concern of international policy should be their avoidance as a means of pursuing conflicts, for the reason that these seem nearly always more harmful in their consequences than the 'evils', real or imputed, that they purport to remedy. Military interventions should never be supported unless sanctioned by the United Nations and for the implementation of international law, which includes the prevention of genocide. A leading criterion for such intervention should be the preservation of lives, those of by-standers and even enemies, as much as those of fellow nationals.

2. To this end, Britain's longstanding over-investment in its military power should be reduced. Its nuclear deterrent should be abandoned, and it should reduce its economic reliance on arms manufacture. Indeed, the main purpose of retaining substantial armed forces at all should be to provide a resource that can, should need arise, contribute to peace-keeping forces mandated by the United Nations. A commitment to a concept of an active and creative peace should take the place of the anachronistic attachment to the idea of war that lies deep in the British national tradition.[21]

3. Britain needs to emerge from the shadow, and unfinished business, of the Cold War. Russia should not be regarded as an enemy, and the aim of policy should be to increase its social and economic exchanges with the rest of Europe. There is no good reason to advance the powers of NATO or its penetration of Eastern Europe, and this organisation's quest to find a new military and ideological role for itself should be resisted. Indeed there may now be good reason to advocate its dissolution since its ideological justification as a bulwark against Communism has vanished.

4. The idea should be rejected that access to raw materials, such as oil, depends on occupation of the territories where they are produced, or the domination of those who produce them.

5. In so far as British governments wish to promote their own liberal, democratic, or even at some point democratic socialist values, it should do this by example, and by rhetorical, political and economic support for progressive efforts elsewhere.

6. The undermining of democracy by market forces and corporate interests, far from being encouraged, should be actively opposed.

7. Britain should be strongly committed to European integration, despite the failure of the European Union so far to fulfil the social democratic possibilities which it once seemed to possess, and despite its failure to respond progressively to the financial crisis of 2007-8 and the deeper contradictions of neoliberalism which this revealed. We support an enlarged economic, social and political role for the European Union in such spheres as infrastructural investment, the redistribution of resources between regions, the support of the rights of minorities, environmental protection and economic planning. Integration in these strategic spheres should be compatible with measures of democratic devolution.

8. Britain should support the strengthening of the United Nations as an instrument for the resolution of national and sub-national conflicts, and for international co-operation. It should encourage the adjustment of its governmental institutions to take account of the present-day balance of populations and powers in the world. It should thus support the reconstruction of the Security Council, such that its permanent members come to include large nations such as Brazil and India, and allow its own representation as a Permanent Member to be replaced by the European Union.

9. An urgent commitment must be made, as we argue in other instal-

ments of this Manifesto, to the environmental sustainability of the globe, which calls for a commitment to radically reduce the production of CO_2 and other harmful greenhouse gases, and to economic models that seek to reduce the consumption of the world's scarce natural resources.

In this Manifesto, we have developed an analysis of neoliberalism and of its harmful impacts on many aspects of social and economic life in Britain. In this chapter we have sought to extend this argument to the sphere of international relations, and to a consideration of Britain's role in the world. Neoliberalism, we argue, is indeed a global system, and needs to be understood and opposed as such.

NOTES

1. We have for reasons of space had to omit other crucial developments, such as the rise of China and other large emerging nations and economies, and the decline in the relative power of the United States and Europe which is its consequence. The state of recurrent war and crisis which we describe, and the rightwards political movements in several nations which have accompanied it, has this underlying loss of influence, and reactions to it, as its backdrop.
2. Fred Halliday, *The Making of the Second Cold War*, Verso 1983.
3. This is analogous to how Gramsci had described the politics of 'transformism' in Italy – here apparent shifts of power between centrist political factions concealed the preservation of the status quo.
4. Of course major anti-colonial political movements were active in some of the imperial nations.
5. Analogous has been the influence of Cuban exiles in American politics in preventing any reconciliation with the government of Cuba after the overthrow of Batista in 1959, who had ruled over what had been a quasi-colony of the United States.
6. At the time of writing another consequence for the United States of this mentality has become highly visible, in the crisis of race relations and policing which has arisen in Ferguson, Missouri. Unwanted weaponry from the Iraq War has been released by the Pentagon to municipal police services in the United States, leading them to confront their urban black populations in the manner of an occupying military force.
7. Tony Blair, Speech 4.3.2004: www.theguardian.com/politics/2004/mar/05/iraq.iraq.
8. See P. Bobbitt, *The Shield of Achilles: War, Peace and the Course of History*, Knopf 2002.

9. Within this perspective, see John J. Mearsheimer's 2014 critique of policy in Ukraine, 'Why the Ukraine is the West's fault: The Liberal Delusions that Provoked Putin,' *Foreign Affairs* September-October 2014.

10. Justin Rosenberg, *A Critique of the Realist Theory of International Relations*, Verso 1994.

11. Some might draw up a more favourable balance-sheet in regard to the west's interventions in the former Yugoslavia, first to defend Bosnia-Herzegovina and its Muslim population against Serbs in 1992-95, and then to defend the Kosovo Albanians against Serbia in 1998-99. But the non-viable ward states of Bosnia-Herzegovina and Kosovo that have emerged are hardly a positive outcome of these interventions, compared with the condition of Yugoslavia before its break-up. Would it not have been better for the western powers to have supported the preservation of Yugoslavia as a federal state, and not to have lent their support to the different secessions and attempted secessions from it? Earlier traditions of imperial interference by the various European powers were in play here, as well as residual hostility to what had been a relatively successful Communist state.

12. Nevertheless, there are political conflicts over priorities, and relative military expenditures in western countries have fallen in the post-cold-war period.

13. H. Segal, 'From Hiroshima to the Gulf War and After', in A. Elliott and S. Frosh (eds), *Psychoanalysis in Contexts*, Routledge 1995.

14. Once Russian support was withdrawn in 1991, Najibullah was doomed. He was publicly hanged by the Taliban in 1996. A dramatisation of this history by the Tricycle Theatre gave a memorable account of his fate: *The Great Game: A Cycle of 12 New Plays*, first performed in April 2009.

15. The only country of the Arab Spring which has escaped military intervention, and where there has been a relatively positive outcome, is Tunisia. This may be explained by its lack of either significant oil resources or strategic significance. By contrast, the Saudis moved to put down the protest movement in Bahrain in 2012.

16. The idea that governments find themselves endorsing initiatives which begin outside their control has a precedent in the displacement of Native Americans, in which 'settlers' often ignored treaties which had been made by the United States government, but whose expansionary actions were subsequently endorsed and legitimised by the latter.

17. Another example of this process of 'regression' to quasi-tribal affiliations and antagonisms is that of Northern Ireland during the Troubles. It was the unpredictable acts of violence, from both sides in the conflict and from the security forces, which undermined what trust there had been between the cohabiting communities.

18. There is much to be said for Hobbes's view that nothing is worse than the breakdown of peace.

19. Michael Foot, then Leader of the Opposition, supported the expedition, on grounds of the rights of the Falklands islanders and because of the dictatorial nature of the Galtieri regime.

20. Identification with British military traditions remains an important element in the national psyche, as the contested commemorations of the centenary of the Great War once more reveals. Adam Hochschild, in his 2011 book *To End All Wars: A Story of Loyalty and Rebellion* (Houghton Mifflin Harcourt) describes how the traditions of fox-hunting in England were once closely connected to the aristocratic culture of the cavalry, for which some generals saw a military future even after 1918.

21. See John Gittings, *The Glorious Art of Peace: from the Iliad to Iraq*, Oxford University Press 2012.

9. ENERGY BEYOND NEOLIBERALISM

Platform

The NHS was designed in 1948 by scaling up the Tredegar Medical Aid Society – a mutual health provision organisation in South Wales set up by miners and their families that had run for over fifty years. By scaling up this local community-controlled structure, the founders of the NHS fundamentally transformed the economy and politics of healthcare nationwide. Today, we need a comparable transformation of energy provision. Could Eigg in Scotland – an island owned collectively by its inhabitants and entirely supplied by renewable electricity – be the Tredegar Medical Aid Society of energy?

This article seeks to explore energy alternatives that break with the foundational assumptions of the neoliberal order. Our argument is that, rather than begging for small palliative scraps, the left must make the argument for a new energy and economic settlement. This is necessary for survival, and for justice. We need a fundamental change of direction on energy.

ENERGY CORPORATIONS, FINANCE AND THE STATE

In Nigeria 72 per cent of people are forced to use wood for cooking, while their country exports 950 billion cubic feet of gas every year. Much of it is shipped to Britain. Yet when Platform invited Niger Delta activist Celestine AkpoBari to London, he was astounded to hear that Britain suffers the worst levels of fuel poverty in Western Europe, with one person dying of cold every six seconds last winter. So who benefits from this disparity? The answer lies in record energy company profits. Together, the big five oil companies – BP, Chevron, ConocoPhillips, ExxonMobil and Shell earn more in one minute than 90 per cent of UK couples earn together in a year.

A century-long strategic alliance between fossil fuel corporations and Western governments has fostered an energy system that has been structured by imperial, extractivist and then neoliberal power. Global neoliberal extractivism – based on the exploitation of non-renewable natural resources – is now trying to solve the dwindling of easily accessible oil reserves by violently pushing for new reserves to be exploited. Cue Arctic drilling, fracking and efforts to extract from beneath the pre-salt ultra-deep waters off Brazil. Once discovered and measured, geological deposits are represented as 'proven reserves' and they then become financial assets that are tradable and valued on the FTSE.

This process thrives on accumulation by dispossession: the expulsion of people from their land, the occupation of villages by soldiers, and the poisoning of groundwater. Military, diplomatic and financial support from states to corporations is key to its facilitation. The aim of Western states is to maintain imperial power by keeping their corporations in control of fuel flows. London is now a centre of both financial and energy imperialism.

Neoliberal common sense persuades us that there is little we can do about this. We are addressed as individual passive consumers of energy, purely as 'customers' – and this serves to obscure our other identities, as Doreen Massey argued in Chapter 1. We are encouraged to believe that BP and Shell, British Gas and EDF are the organisations best placed to 'efficiently' extract, process and generate energy, and that the market will deliver the best prices to us as the big companies compete among themselves for our custom. Our choices as customers supposedly influence this market. But in practice, the dominance of a small number of multinational corporations annihilates the possibility of any choice that could generate significant change. As Beatrix Campbell writes in Chapter 4, global capitalism 'deploys the language of freedom, choice and competition to oust solidarity, co-operative creativity and equality'.[1]

As a result of these companies' dominance, itself the culmination of successive privatisations by Conservative and Labour governments, Britain's fuel poverty rates are now among the highest in Europe. One in five households was in fuel poverty in 2010; 10,000 people died in winter 2013-4 from cold homes. Yet the Big Six energy companies take £1 billion per year in premiums that are charged predominantly to disadvantaged users.[1]

As even a study commissioned by the Oil and Gas UK lobby group admitted: 'the market has not delivered the most efficient outcome for UK gas consumers'.[2] Meanwhile, under the liberalised regime in which the industry operates, the upward volatility of gas prices – which is partly due to breakdown in the ageing UK gas supply infrastructure – is allowed to feed through into immediate price spikes.

The ability to pick between different energy suppliers is a false freedom. Those who use the energy are excluded from influencing decisions on how any surplus should be invested – into fossil fuels or renewables, imported fuel or local sources – or on how to structure prices.

Nor does the government make these decisions on people's behalf. Under the market fundamentalist regimes of both the Conservatives and New Labour, the UK government gave up this power to corporations. Even though energy regulator Ofgem has been slightly re-empowered in recent years, it still has no role in such decisions, or any capacity for investment into energy infrastructure.

In an earlier period decision-making power over North Sea oil was also largely handed over to private oil and gas corporations. Moreover, since the 1980s, taxes on their profits have been consistently cut, leaving Britain with by far the lowest effective tax ratio of the four North Sea oil and gas extracting countries; its tax regime is the second most generous to private oil companies in the entire world, after Ireland.

The outcome has been a dramatically reduced government take, and a fiscal regime that has been described as 'a vehicle for the delivery of corporate welfare on a grand scale'.[3] In the six years prior to 2008 the UK lost out on £74 billion. As companies used the cash flow from the North Sea to subsidise drilling in other parts of the world and oil prices rose further, the government succumbed to demands for ever more subsidies. Enormous revenues were accumulated by oil companies and recycled through the City of London.

Fossil fuel corporations have woven around themselves a Carbon Web – the set of legal, cultural, financial and government institutions that enable them and prevent democratic control. Decisions made behind closed doors in corporate headquarters, Whitehall and at £1500-a-ticket conferences lock us all into decades of fossil fuel use. Individuals and wealth flow through the revolving doors between the state, oil and finance. Britain has become a petrostate, and London an oil city, extracting wealth from fossil fuels from Nigeria to the North Sea, from Azerbaijan to Egypt.

Financial holdings in the City are concentrated into fossil fuels, with 20 per cent of the FTSE 100 made up of just BP and Shell. As London's role as a central node in a global fossil fuel economy has grown, so Britain's body politic has become increasingly skewed, at the expense both of the de-industrialised regions of the UK and front-line communities in the Global South.

The big energy companies work hard to convince us that they are essential to the functioning of modern society. In a plastic world, we all use synthetic fabrics, petrol and gas heating. How could we cope without BP and Shell to provide for us? How could national cultural institutions like the Tate or the British Museum function without oil funding? (Hint: Less than 0.5 per cent of their income comes from BP.) This is aimed at creating a perception of dependency, that will allow the continued intense accumulation of wealth by corporations and elite classes.

RE-IMAGINING OUR ENERGY FUTURE

> There is always more in reality than one can experience or express at any given moment. A greater sensitivity to the latent potential of situations may encourage us to think about things not only as they are, but also in terms of what they may become.
>
> Javier Medina[4]

Individual consumption does not begin to encompass the manifold relationships we have to energy. We take buses, we work in heated offices, we buy frozen icecream. Our public wealth is used to subsidise oil companies, our cultural institutions to launder their image, and our government sends troops to support resource grabs. We have political and economic relationships to North Sea oil, wind turbines in the Thames estuary and carbon dioxide molecules in the atmosphere.

The whole relationship of society to energy needs to change. We need to shift power away from the entangled interests of finance and the big companies, and challenge the current monopolised energy system, so that these relationships can become intentional and active, so that energy consumers can become producers, distributors, owners, sharers and collective users of energy. We need to democratise energy. This means commoning resources, dispersing economic power and ending dependence on the multinationals that exploit public resources for private profit.

How can we increase our sensitivity to the 'latent potential' of our energy structures? We need to be able to envision and describe a functional energy system that provides for people's needs and does not entrench exploitation or rely on constant expansion. To do this we need to articulate a new common sense that builds on what Gramsci called 'good sense' – working with the grain of existing values and collective practices. One way of doing this is by learning from positive, albeit contested, experiences elsewhere, including Bolivia, Denmark, Venezuela and Norway.

New strategies also need to interact with present struggles, like those of frontline communities in Lancashire and Yorkshire who are blocking fracking rigs; or the Greater London Pensioners Association and Fuel Poverty Action who are using direct action casework to fight for warm homes and democratically-owned, renewable energy; or the Hackney housing estate residents, Islington councillors and Balcombe villagers who are setting up locally owned energy schemes.

Zero Carbon Britain have laid out concrete ideas for achieving the rapid shift away from fossil fuels that is necessary for planetary survival, through already existing wind, solar and biomass technology. But as they comment, 'the necessary transition is at the very boundary of what is politically thinkable'. The left's job is to make this transition thinkable by grounding it in redistribution of power and in diversity.

The social democratic settlement was grounded in redistributional justice, i.e. in equitably sharing out economic resources; but it failed to transform underlying power structures, ultimately allowing capital to continue to thrive. Without participation in decisions over the allocation of surplus and investment into energy or housing, people remain excluded from shaping and defining their community.

Solutions need to be grounded in a politics that is sensitive to autonomy and local variation, and committed to decentred decision-making.[5] We need countervailing initiatives located in broad-based institutions and networks that have an interest in challenging over-centralisation or private appropriation of power. These could include networks of rural producer-user energy co-operatives, borough-run electricity grids and regional mutual pension funds. We can learn from the commons: resources controlled by and available for use by a whole community. And by combining commons-based energy structures with more centralised institutions, we can ensure a lasting diversity of collective social relations that can prevent a resurgence of corporate power.

ENERGY COMMONS

The commons as a form of collective ownership and use of resources has a deep history in Britain. But the concept regained increasing international popularity following the Zapatistas take-over of San Cristobal de la Casas on New Year's Eve 1993. Commoning – producing and reproducing a commons – means developing non-capitalist ways of managing resources that are democratic, horizontal, participatory and respectful of local difference. But 'beyond the state and the market' does not necessarily mean 'without state and market': a state can still be used progressively to expand our spaces for community life, while commons are also at risk of being subjugated to broader market mechanisms.[6] They create space for autonomy and democracy – but do not exist in isolation.

There is no commons without community – but in a progressive approach to the commons, 'community' should be 'a quality of relations, a principle of cooperation and of responsibility to each other', rather than 'a gated reality'.[7] The commons should represent a commitment to a broad and relational imaginary of place, not a return to exclusionary traditions.[8]

We all regularly engage with and use land, water, air, digital commons – they are so widespread that they're largely invisible, taken for granted. But they are also part of our existing experience of the world, and this means that the idea of the commons forms part of the stratified deposits of 'good sense' that are available to us for challenging neoliberal common sense.[9] Such is the 'pull' of the commons that some resources are even experienced as common (for example fresh water lakes and rivers) when they are actually private. Corporations may own many of the UK's waterways, but their history as collective, communal resources cannot so easily be erased. So how do we imagine commoning energy?

Commoning energy is already a reality elsewhere in Europe. Most notably, it underlies Denmark's remarkable success in ending dependence on imported fuel, which has in large part been replaced with local renewables. Denmark's wind power revolution has been described as 'a grassroots, community-based initiative, underpinned by decentralised, cooperative and municipal ownership alongside small-scale private ownership'.[10]

This came about after an intense political struggle over energy policy in the late 1970s, when a coalition of leftists, greens and conservative rural interests united in distrust of proposals based on centralised forms of energy (oil and nuclear-based). Instead they promoted an alternative vision of a more localised and decentred non-nuclear future based on renewables and more radical democratic practices. And they achieved remarkable success. Within twenty years the country went from dependence on oil imports for 90 per cent of its energy demand to self-sufficiency in energy. Crucially, 80 per cent of wind turbines in Denmark are owned by co-operatives or families. This starkly contrasts with Britain, where community ownership of renewables is miniscule.

This transformation was achieved through a combination of targeted government subsidies to support the fledgling wind sector, a renewables quota for electricity distribution companies, and 'residency criteria' laws that limited ownership of wind turbines to those living in the local municipality. Community participation in ownership and development meant there was little public opposition to the placement of wind farms. Ownership of the electricity distribution system is also decentralised in Denmark, with 55 per cent of the grid owned by user-run co-ops, 12 per cent by municipalities and 26 per cent by Denmark's state oil company. The state played an enabling role by setting targets, rules around ownership, and prices.[11]

Germany's energy economy is currently being transformed by its policy of *Energiewende* (Energy transition), supported by both main political parties, but during the process neoliberal power and more democratic forces are battling to assert themselves. On the one hand land grabs by private equity firms in former East Germany are turning collective farmland into privatised solar plants. On the other, Germany is witnessing a mass movement towards community and city-controlled renewables. From Berlin to small villages, a re-municipalisation effort is seeking to bring energy generation and distribution back under collective ownership.

These examples do not necessarily constitute a purist energy commons, but they are commoning energy, drawing on non-state and non-market approaches. Britain has the potential to follow the Danish model, making use of local wind and solar potential as an important move towards energy commons. But a significant barrier hindering UK renewables is the role of national right-wing politics in shaping and exacerbating local opposition to wind farms, taking advantage of local suspicion of imposed industrial projects. Too often the response of those on the left has been to deride this opposition as NIMBY and right-wing. Those looking to common the UK's energy should also hear in these complaints an experience of disenfranchisement, of exclusion from decisions and their benefits by a London elite. It should be remembered that renewables can also be subjected to enclosure and wealth extraction – ultimately benefiting private equity interests in the City.

Such suspicion can be countered by enabling communities to take control of and benefit from new energy infrastructure. The Isle of Eigg in the inner Hebrides undertook a historic community buy-out in 1997, and took control of their land. In 2008 the community switched on the island electrification project, making 24-hour power available for the first time to all residents and businesses on the island. Hydro, wind and solar energy now contribute over 95 per cent of the island's electricity demand. Eigg has also inspired energy co-operatives in England, ranging from places resisting fracking such as Balcombe and Barton Moss, to inner city estates in Hackney and Brixton.

Expanding the energy commons beyond such small communities requires attention to the 'material requirements for the construction of a commons-based economy'.[12] Some commons are easier to conceptualise than others. An area of land is stable through time and needs a known amount of work to be useable for activities such as foraging or grazing cattle by a community. The use of a digital commons like Wikipedia is limited only by the technologies of connectivity that maintain it as well as the work of its moderators: its user community is distributed across the world. It seems that energy is easier to imagine as a commons on a localised scale – as we have done here – but we need to develop the vocabulary and concepts of energy commons that are necessary to address bigger scales.

Silvia Federici has argued that scaling up means posing the question of how to bring together the many existing and proliferating forms of commons, so that they can begin to cohere and help provide a foundation for evolving new models of production and distribution.[13] This is most obviously necessary when we try to grapple with questions like climate change or regional inequality. Locally-managed commons-based energy systems are good at empowerment and enabling variation, but they can't answer all the challenges we currently face. We need to be able to co-ordinate, share and allocate resources at a higher level.

FROM OFFSHORE OIL TO OFFSHORE WIND

$2°C$ remains the official international target for limiting the damage caused by climate change, despite increasing recognition that this would still bring devastating consequences. And according to the International Energy Authority (a conservative source), if the world is to achieve the $2°C$ goal, no more than one-third of existing proven reserves of fossil fuels can be consumed prior to 2050. Clearly, moving beyond extractivism means coming to terms with leaving fossil fuels in the ground.

The most recent figures from DECC show the UK as having around 2.9 billion barrels of proven oil reserves, implying a maximum 'burnable carbon' total of 954 million barrels. At the current breakneck rate of extraction of 518 million barrels per year, the UK will reach this limit within two years.[14] To avoid contributing to catastrophe, Britain must completely change direction and move to rapidly replace fossil fuels with renewables (as well as significantly reducing its 1700 TWh demand for energy). Britain has the capacity to generate vast amounts of electricity from offshore wind, wave and tidal energy. In the deep waters off Cornwall and Scotland, floating turbines could be anchored to the ocean floor by cables. In 2010, the Offshore Valuation Group estimated that Britain could generate more than 1500 TWh per year from floating wind turbines alone, close to the UK's total energy demand, including transport.

But the urgent need to upscale renewables infrastructure must not lead to multinationals once again picking Britain clean of its energy wealth. Instead of becoming another sphere of accumulation, offshore electricity generation must be based on long-term planning that balances energy needs with biodiversity and local jobs. The lessons from the neoliberal experiment with oil are clear. Privatisation saw a drastic reduction in the state's take in oil revenues after 1982, and

Conservative governments entirely depended on company-provided data for assessing tax rates and production costs. Energy economist Ian Rutledge compared the negotiation process to asking a small child whether it could think of any persuasive reasons why it should be given a large ice cream.[15]

How can a new social settlement ensure public benefit from renewables? One useful step would be to set up a national renewables company that owns and operates a significant stake in offshore wind. While increasing government revenues, the most important function of such an entity – as with state-owned oil companies – would be to improve the state's bargaining potential and regulatory process. By acting as the 'eyes and ears' of government within the offshore industry, a national energy company could make available considerable insider information.[16] In making this argument Vickers and Yarrow were discussing the privatisation of Britoil and British Gas, but the argument also applies to offshore electricity, where the rents will be similarly enormous, and thus also the economic value of information.

This does not mean that all offshore wind needs to be owned by a centralised entity. In Denmark, major offshore wind projects have been built by various public companies, ranging from state oil company DONG to municipality-owned entities. In South America, innovative public-public partnerships in the water sector have seen city councils bringing in expertise from worker-run co-operatives in other countries.[17] Other public-public partnerships can be created to access finance. A large wind farm off the coast of Copenhagen was built by the city council-owned utility company together with a co-op comprising 10,000 local residents. The rapid growth in Denmark's wind turbine manufacturing industry benefitted from the absence of patenting of prototypes, allowing companies to quickly innovate and improve the technology, the result of a fortuitous nineteenth-century century law banning rural technology patents. Institutional blocks to the privatisation of technologies and information will be important to decentralising power over the UK energy system, and developing it fast.

If the state holds major equity holdings in offshore wind, this opens the potential for an Offshore Wind Fund, taking inspiration from Norway's oil fund. If based around participatory and decentred decision-making rather than diktats by elite technocrats, such a fund could disperse economic power. By enabling community bodies to allocate funds to local energy generation or saving projects, new energy structures would be democratised. Funds could be limited to energy projects that meet rigorous local content and local, common ownership guarantees. This would boost regional and community economies in both urban centres and peripheral rural areas. Combining revenue reform with land reform would ensure that renewables generation is not dominated by a small number of already wealthy landlords.

TAKING FINANCE BACK FROM THE CITY

Just two companies – BP and Shell – make up almost 20 per cent of the value of the FTSE 100. Shares in these companies form an average 30 per cent of most pensions; their shares are seen as offering a hypersecure long-term investment, similar to a government backed bond.

However, the corporations' actual share value is largely predicated on their proven reserves. As new oil fields are discovered, the value goes up. Yet, as we have noted, the International Energy Agency argues that to prevent a 2°C increase, two thirds of proven fossil fuels must be left in the ground. That means our struggle to shut down most extraction is also a struggle to wipe out most of BP and Shell's share value. Planetary survival is pitted against pensioners' future income.

Unless we change the basis of those pensions. If we wrested back control over our financial resources, we could also pay for the transition without falling hostage to exploitation by international finance. As it stands, neoliberal power builds dependency and puts limits on collective action through institutionalised gatekeeping, which restricts who can access investment, and in what form. This bottleneck kills many dreams. Community-owned renewable energy projects across the country are on hold, unable to access the funds to build.

The solution is not to go begging to the City, but to work to pool our resources and re-appropriate the wealth that we ourselves have produced, and to enlarge the sphere of production that exists outside market relations.[18] Much of the country's wealth is already ours – it is theoretically public – but control over it has been handed to private companies and asset managers. They use our wealth to speculate on assets largely unrelated to the real economy of goods and services, seeking to increase privatisation and generate ever higher levels of accumulation.

Ethical investment mechanisms in themselves are not enough; where such considerations do exist, they are often applied only as a filter to weed out the apparently 'worst' of the best-performing company stocks. However, a growing climate divestment movement is beginning to force money out of fossil fuels. The Rockefeller heirs joined in September 2014, Glasgow University in October. But if our aim is to breach the walls of neoliberalism, this movement needs to go beyond persuading disinterested asset managers to move money from fossil fuels to privately owned mega-renewable projects.

The recent decades have seen wealth extracted from Britain's regions and centralised in the City of London, through pension contributions, insurance payments and public-private partnerships. Divesting from extractivism depends on taking back control over capital from the City. This could mean local authorities re-investing their pension funds locally to build new council housing or renewable energy, as in Enfield in North London. It also means creating a financial infrastructure that is able to redistribute, and give ex-industrial regions the power to rebuild, by recycling their wealth in the local community. In an economy no longer driven solely by shareholder interests, low-return but secure investments into infrastructure could be prioritised.

Pressure is building to divest from fossil fuels. But the ultimate aim is to divest from neoliberalism itself. By commoning finance, we could break the grip the City holds over the rest of Britain, and create the basis for a new financial architecture, dedicated to economic and energy democracy.

WORKERS AND POWER

Alliances between labour unions and environmental movements can play a key role in transforming the neoliberal energy settlement. The fundamental change in energy infrastructures needed to address climate change in Britain could create 1.33 million full-time equivalent jobs in wind, marine, solar power, geothermal, synthetic gas and support services according to Zero Carbon Britain. Issues around synthetic gas have yet to be fully worked through, but it does open the door to retooling some of the existing downstream fossil-fuel infrastructure, including the Grangemouth refinery, where in 2013 workers were battered into accepting worsening employment conditions in order to save their jobs. Such retooling would provide these workers with a long-term role in our energy future.

The transition will transform what jobs are required and where. The Energy Democracy Initiative, a global trade union network for a just transition, has argued that organised labour needs to look beyond its 'traditional job-protection focus' to join with other sectors in campaigning for the creation of economic development models–based on decentralised renewable energy systems. The National Union of Metalworkers of South Africa (NUMSA) are an exciting example of such 'social movement unionism', and are building a practical, just and socialist response to climate change. One of the largest unions in South Africa, NUMSA represents almost 300,000 workers in energy intensive industries, and in 2011 it established a worker-led Research and Development Group on renewables and energy efficiency, including workers from solar panels and wind turbine factories. NUMSA has been trying to build international networks for just transition, guided by the idea that labour should contribute to a common good.

NUMSA's efforts carry echoes of the attempt to restructure Lucas Aerospace in the 1970s. Engineering shop stewards sought to convert the company from manufacturing missiles to producing socially useful products. They won a lot of support for their alternative corporate plan, which included plans for the production of ecological vehicles, energy conservation machinery and equipment for the disabled. However, with the exception of Industry Minister Tony Benn, the Labour government opposed the plan, and the vision for Lucas Aerospace was not realised.

This example points to the potential role of democratic worker control and involvement in restructuring towards a low-carbon economy. As well as mobilising trade unionists in support of sustainability, movements pushing for transition need to ensure that community-based energy projects create skilled, stable and unionised jobs. The interests of workers need to be centrally embedded in how we shape proposals for our energy future.

Concrete policy steps to achieve this could include legal requirements to meet significant 'local content' quotas: these could nurture domestic industry for the long run, build a new skills base and invigorate local economies. Feed-in tariff programmes could specify wage levels and union requirements, and incentivise local manufacturing of material components. The local content elements of Ontario's feed-in tariff has created 20,000 jobs and was on track to create 50,000 – until the EU challenged it for breaching WTO rules.

We also need energy authorities and bodies to have strong elected worker representation on their boards as in Norway and Denmark. Effectively combating the climate crisis will be greatly aided by workplace democracy, with workers and trade unions centrally involved in planning and structuring the transition.

DECOLONISING ENERGY

Fuel flows through pipelines and along shipping routes from Nigeria, Azerbaijan and Kuwait to Britain. Except, of course, that neither crude, nor the far lighter gas, flow of their own accord. The web of pipelines and tanker routes is not a rain catchment area where mountain streams head downhill, joining tributaries and rivers to provide water to the city in the valley. Fossil fuels require pressure to be forced down a pipeline, while political and financial forces determine the route along which it is transported. The global oil market didn't evolve into this form of its own accord. The transfer of fuel is the product of wars, labour and political struggles, costly infrastructure, mass displacement, imposition and arming of undemocratic regimes and intensive corporate lobbying.[19]

In a 1993 meeting with BP directors, Foreign Secretary Douglas Hurd emphasised that 'there were some parts of the world, such as Azerbaijan and Colombia, where the most important British interest was BP's operation. In those countries he was keen to ensure that our [the FCO's] efforts intertwined effectively with BP's'. This statement neatly sums up Britain's external energy policy: the interests of the state (often also framed as 'security' of energy supply) are seen as ensuring British corporations' control of fossil fuels. This prevents crude from being managed and exchanged by countries outside the neoliberal consensus: it keeps the oil *flowing*. David Cameron's broader instruction to British diplomats to prioritise British exports only underscores the point: 'every submission and every brief for a visit now has to include the commercial interests'. As well as diplomatic support, external energy policy mobilises UK export credit finance and DfID, the Ministry of Defence and the European Bank for Reconstruction and Development. Carbon colonialism means that oil executives and shareholders in London's City are reaping rewards from militarisation, repression and poverty, as well as the catastrophic consequences of climate change in the Global South.

New gas pipelines promoted by the EU on behalf of oil companies (such as BP's Euro-Caspian Mega Pipeline from Azerbaijan to Italy) require continued pressure in the flow for another four or five decades. To counter concerns over the carbon and political impacts of such projects, state and corporate PR strategies deploy the 'energy security' argument as a way of setting parameters for media and public debate. The rhetoric of 'keeping the lights on' re-asserts a politics of demanding oil, gas and other fuels for 'us' – and not 'them'. 'Security' also privileges top-down and militaristic solutions that disempower and exclude the majority. When government identifies 'energy security' as a priority, progressive and green campaigners – aiming for short-term victories – are sometimes tempted to adopt these frames in the hope of opening doors to decision-makers. But accepting this framing further consolidates the power of the neoliberal energy consensus. It helps executives like Shell's Jan Kopernicki in his demand that Britain redirects billions towards building new warships, on the grounds that 'the UK's economic security depends on energy security: without enough energy, the economy simply cannot keep going'. Kopernicki wanted more navy frigates to escort Shell tankers off the coast of Somalia: 'I don't want to be alarmist but I provide transport for essential oil and gas for this country and I want to be sure that the lights are on in Birmingham, my home city.'

Assisted by concepts like 'energy security', carbon colonialism keeps the violence of oil extraction invisible or distant from privileged publics in the Global North. Despite the appearance of an increased global interconnectedness, we remain oblivious 'to the blood in the food we eat, the petroleum we use'.[20] We need to overcome this invisibility by establishing a different relationship to the sources of our energy.

Norway has made some efforts in this regard: well-resourced Parliamentary committees investigate the international impacts of Statoil, actively engaging civil society in a process of collective learning. This has its limitations, but the outcome is a more deliberative politics of energy, a geography of responsibility that is different from Britain's colonial practice. In decolonising energy, we can also learn from recent attempts to create more reciprocal energy relations in Latin America.

Venezuela has developed a practice of energy solidarity of sorts, including its 2007 provision of cheap fuel for London's buses and subsidised heating oil to fuel-poor and indigenous communities in the US.

Dismantling energy colonialism and replacing it with energy solidarity means doing more than building new energy models grounded in justice, democracy and sustainability in Britain. First steps towards reparations for theft and abuses of the past should include support for grassroots climate adaptation plans and welcoming climate migrants (i.e. granting migrants the same employment and welfare rights as British citizens); cleaning up the toxic legacy of oil spills in the Niger Delta and elsewhere; support for projects like Yasuni-ITT in Ecuador, in which oil would be left in the ground in exchange for compensation from rich countries; and support for public-public partnerships in which public institutions build services for public needs, rather than exporting energy and water privatisation camouflaged as 'services'.

MOVEMENTS: BUILD AND CONFRONT

A new social settlement cannot be built solely from the top down. Social movements and forces must articulate, demonstrate and embody the values, discourses and frames that make up its underlying common sense. Contending but allied social forces can tell different stories, animating the imaginary and proposing new models of social relations. Resilient movements in debate with one another can build strategies for radical and lasting change. The political activity of the left cannot be reduced to the conquest of institutions – we need to aim to transform reality itself.[21]

Despite the neoliberal hegemony, we can invoke the ever-present critical and healthy nucleus within our common sense that opposes injustice, to articulate counter-hegemonies and re-work assumptions: Why subsidise BP and Shell, some of the most profitable corporations in the world? Why invest billions into searching for new fossil fuels when burning them would make the planet uninhabitable? Why ask the fuel-poor on pre-payment meters to subsidise the rich? Why import oil and cause devastation in the Niger Delta, when we could meet our energy needs domestically? Why not run renewable energy on a collective and public basis, rather than replicating the North Sea giveaway to corporations? Why not use council pensions to fund energy efficiency retrofitting and new council housing stock, rather than hand them over to City investors to finance deep water drilling? Why not begin today the inevitable work of dismantling the fossil fuel industry?

Culture is essential to politics: we build energy democracy in radio plays and ownership structures, toys and electricity grids. But language and ideas are not enough in themselves to change the energy basis of society. We need to create the necessary political space and build the infrastructure, institutions and practices that will make an alternative energy system.

'Alternative' must mean more than a small-scale off-grid utopia. Nor does it mean an alternative but separate system, in parallel with neoliberalism. If we were to proceed on this basis elite groups – including new elites – will in all likelihood seek to recuperate, to take over, to concentrate power, and subject collective projects to their private interests. This is what happened in Norway, where deliberative processes were subverted and technocrats enforced their will against democracy.[22]

To prevent this, movements need to dismantle existing power structures at the same time as building our energy future. We should aim to take space and make demands that force the hand of neoliberalism and authoritarianism; to strangle corporate power by denying it what it needs – possibilities for ever greater accumulation; to build the future while we confront the present.

CONCLUSION

The Labour Party may be busy developing alternative energy policies, but there's no sign that it is breaking with the neoliberal framing of debates, or challenging the taken-for-granted assumptions listed earlier. To break the neoliberal energy consensus, we need both bolder policy proposals (like an Offshore Wind Fund and public-public partnerships) and social movements pushing back against fossil fuel corporations and pushing forward visions for a just energy economy.

With CO_2 in the atmosphere having passed the 'safe' 350 parts per million mark, the scale of the rapid power-down necessary to prevent runaway climate change is alarming. The ambition to provide energy for everyone's needs may come into conflict with such a rapid power-down and we have no easy answer to this conflict. But if energy resources available to us as a population are to shrink, we need institutions that will prioritise energy justice, and which give access and decision-making power to those who have been marginalised and excluded by our energy and political system.

Sooner or later climate change is going to force a collapse in the current social settlement. What will take its place is still up for grabs. In a different climate, it is not only energy infrastructures that will be reconfigured; so too will be border and migration regimes, welfare and flood defence, food and water supply. The future settlement could take the form of an even more isolated and paranoid Fortress Britain. But this is not the only possibility. Energy systems help shape our economic and political structures, and an energy future grounded in democracy will create the potential for more just outcomes.

A paradigm shift is necessary: 'from consumptive energy to productive and regenerative energy, from capital-intensive energy to low-cost energy, from labour-displacing energy to livelihood-generating energy', from the use of fossil fuels to meaningful work.[23]

This is a call for energy democracy. Not energy security or energy separation. These are too rooted in the neoliberal common sense, and serve to empower militaries and heavy-handed governments over a passive population. A survivable and just energy future means breaking the grip of elite interests on our energy systems, ending dependency, increasing autonomy, building diverse power structures through which we can hold one another to account, and leaving fossil fuels in the ground. Energy democracy would put an end to fuel poverty and create conditions for economic democracy; and it would take power out of the hands of unaccountable elites. We are not limited to a single unitary model – a resilient energy future will be composed of diverse energy commons, solidarities and practices. We believe energy democracy can be realised by scaling up from decentralised, community-controlled renewable energy projects, and using the state's institutions to pool and redistribute resources.

Referring to the pioneering Tredegar Medical Aid Society, NHS founder Aneurin Bevan described the creation of the NHS as 'We are going to Tredegarise you', Seventy years later, could Britain's energy be Eigg-ised?

This essay was written by Platform. *We combine research and art, education and campaigning to drive social and ecological justice and challenge the power of the oil industry. Platform consists of Farzana Khan, Mika Minio-Paluello, Sarah Shoraka, Emma Hughes, Anna Galkina, James Marriott, Jane Trowell, Sarah Legge, Mark Roberts, Tanya Hawkes and Adam Ma'anit. We tweet* @platformlondon.

NOTES

1. Brenda Boardman, *Liberalisation and fuel poverty* in Ian Rutledge and Philip Wright (eds), *UK Energy Policy and the End of Market Fundamentalism*, Oxford University Press 2010.
2. Ian Rutledge and Philip Wright (eds), *UK Energy Policy and the End of Market Fundamentalism*, Oxford University Press 2010.
3. Juan Carlos Boué and Philip Wright, *A requiem for the UK's petroleum fiscal regime*, in Ian Rutledge and Philip Wright (eds), *UK Energy Policy and the End of Market Fundamentalism*, Oxford University Press 2010.
4. Gustavo Soto, *La espuma de estos días*, 2010.
5. Andrew Cumbers, *Reclaiming Public Ownership*, Zed Books 2012.
6. Gustavo Soto Santiesteban and Silke Helfrich, *El Buen Vivir and the Commons: A Conversation Between Gustavo Soto Santiesteban and Silke Helfrich* in David Bollier and Silke Helfrich (eds), *The Wealth of the Commons*, The Commons Strategy Group 2012.
7. Silvia Federici, *Feminism And the Politics of the Commons*, the commoner 2010.
8. Doreen Massey, *Geographies of responsibility*, Geografiska Annaler 2004.
9. Quotations from Gramsci are from *Selections from the Prison Notebooks*, Lawrence and Wishart 1972.
10. Cumbers, op cit.
11. Ibid.
12. Federici, op cit.
13. Ibid.
14. Extracting a fraction of the proven reserves at a much slower pace is possible. In the early 1970s Norway enacted legislation to cap extraction at a controlled 'moderate pace'. It was only the growth of a domestic oil-industrial complex in alliance with globalised capital that saw the cap abandoned in the 1990s.
15. Ian Rutledge and Philip Wright, op cit.
16. John Vickers and George Yarrow, *Privatisation: An Economic Analysis*, MIT Press 1988.
17. Cumbers, op cit.
18. Federici, op cit.
19. James Marriott and Mika Minio-Paluello, *The Oil Road: Journeys from the Caspian Sea to the City of London*, Verso 2012.
20. Maria Mies and Veronika Bennholdt-Thomsen, *Defending, Reclaiming,*

and Reinventing the Commons, Canadian Journal of Development Studies 2001.
21. Marta Harnecker, *Rebuilding the Left*, Zed Books 2007.
22. Helge Ryggvik, *The Norwegian Oil Experience*, Tik-Centre 2010.
23. Vandana Shiva, *Soil not Oil: Environmental Justice in a Time of Climate Crisis*, South End Press 2007.

10. Race, migration and neoliberalism

Sally Davison and George Shire

As Stuart Hall and Alan O'Shea argued in Chapter 3, common sense is a form of everyday thinking that offers us frameworks of meaning with which to make sense of the world:

> It is a form of popular, easily-available knowledge which contains no complicated ideas, requires no sophisticated argument and does not depend on deep thought or wide reading. It works intuitively, without forethought or reflection. It is pragmatic and empirical, giving the illusion of arising directly from experience, reflecting only the realities of daily life and answering the needs of 'the common people' for practical guidance and advice.[1]

This understanding about how common sense operates is particularly useful in trying to unpack the complex articulations between race, migration and nation that inform current debate, and the particular ways in which these ideas are mobilised within neoliberal ideology.

The common sense of a society contains within its mix of ideas 'stone age elements' and 'prejudices from all past phases of history': previous ways of understanding the world leave their mark on popular ways of thinking.[2] Each political formation draws on a repertoire of elements to create its own forms of hierarchy and patterns of exclusion and inclusion. In Britain especially, common sense on race is suffused with relics from its past imperial history, though it also draws on other elements, such as feudal beliefs about the divine right to rule, or a Shakespearean celebration of the happy few at Agincourt. These and other accretions have left what Gramsci describes as 'stratified deposits' in our ideas about Britishness, Englishness, ethnicity and difference.

The long centuries of global domination have left many traces. Racism in contemporary Britain remains heavily influenced by the colonial period, when it was seen by Europeans as natural that white men ruled black people, and the civilising mission was the white man's burden. And the contemporary global inequality that is a direct legacy of colonial history strongly reinforces these attitudes, since it does in fact reflect a continuing reality about who holds power and wealth in the world. Openly racist ideas are rarely expressed in western discourse in the twenty-first century, but race is nevertheless omni-present within its culture (most notably in much of the rhetoric of the 'war on terror'). Media images of over-crowded boats and immigrant bodies washing up on the Mediterranean shores of the EU, or shrouded, anonymous and abject prisoners in Guantanamo or Abu Ghraib, or the pictures of Ebola victims that reproduce the ubiquitous imagery of African victimhood – none of these is overtly presented as being 'about race', but they are carriers for common sense ideas about the natural order of the world.

Ideas about British values and the general inferiority of foreigners are mobilised most often in current debates in the notion that 'our small island' is being over-run by immigrants from Europe, but one of the reasons this view is taken up by the media and populist politicians so readily is that they have a long tradition to draw on: a treasure trove of familiar stories about the good old days – Blighty, imperial adventure, autumn mists and beer – as well as a well-stocked supply of horror stories about people who don't belong – muggings, gangs, people speaking foreign languages on trains, veiled women on the British high street.

The broad outlines of the story – there are too many of them, 'they' are not like 'us', they are a threat, they are criminal, they are illegal, they will swamp us, they are taking things that rightfully belong to us – have been deployed in the same but different configurations for every wave of migration to Britain (almost always driven by the desire for cheap labour). These stories have particular embellishments in particular periods, but they go back at least as far as the industrial revolution, and start with the vilification of the Irish (of course the long history of anti-semitism stretches back even further). Migration tends to be accompanied by tales of people who, because they are not like us, are not seen as fully human – or certainly as not entitled to the same rights as us.

Other countries have their own versions of these stories. As Agri Ismail observes of Swedish right-wing populists, 'their definition of what deviates from the norm always corresponds to those who have arrived most recently'. Ismail illustrates this point with a story about Swedish migrants to the US, who had their own experiences of not being considered white. He quotes a 1901 letter from a lumberjack who complains about his workplace because there are 'probably 15 white men here to 60 Swedes'; he describes the Swedes as 'beasts' who smell of herring: 'Walking behind a string of Swedes is something impossible to a person with a delicate nose'.[3] Being in the wrong place at the wrong time can apparently make any ethnic group – even the Nordic Swedes – seem not white enough. As this example illustrates, it is those of lowly status who tend to be regarded as lacking whiteness.

Conversely, the term immigrant is not often associated with more affluent migrants, for example Americans (of whom more than 200,000 currently live in Britain), or Germans (more than 300,000). The rhetoric that surrounds immigration and race most often finds its pariahs in over-crowded hostels or sweat shops.

Broadly speaking, whiteness is associated with higher status and wealth, while blackness is associated with poverty and abjection. In this sense race forms part of an ideological repertoire that asserts the rightness for the job of ruling of those from the rich white world – and the lack of qualification for such a role of the poor majority. Race is as much about whiteness as blackness – and ideas about white superiority are most often expressed these days in terms of western civilisational superiority.

RACE AND NEOLIBERALISM

Though theories of the market, neoliberal or otherwise, are not them-selves racialised (not least since they deal in inputs of labour rather than human beings), the functioning of the contemporary global economy is deeply embedded in the histories and practices of racism. The operations of the market are always underpinned by unequal power structures; and the maintenance as far as possible of unequal global power relations has been a key concern of the global elite throughout the postcolonial period. The continuance of a dominant common sense of the whiteness of power as natural – including who is entitled to intervene internationally and which societies best embody a specific normative set of western values – has been a crucial part of securing consent for these unequal relations.[4]

Common-sense ideas about British and/or western values have much to contribute here. For example western ways of fighting are regarded as much more civilised than those of jihadis: death by drone is seen as a more modern means of despatch than beheading. Similarly, lack of democracy is more acceptable (often invisible) when it is part of the British story: thus, for example, the complete absence of democracy under British rule in Hong Kong is forgotten in the current debate about the lack of democracy under the People's Republic.

The way migration is discussed fits into the same hierarchy of entitlement. It is assumed that people from the rich west can go wherever they want, but the poor will by and large stay where they are. The supreme example of this one-way view of migration is the invisibility in much contemporary discussion of the mass European/white settler migrations of the nineteenth century, especially to North and South America, the Antipodes and Southern Africa, which led to the dispossession, subordination and sometimes eradication of whole populations, with all the consequent inequality and violence that this has brought to the world. Today, as neoliberal capitalism spreads its grip across the globe in search of new sources of raw materials and new markets, it produces levels of dispossession and displacement even greater than those that caused the nineteenth-century emigrations. But for twenty-first century victims of capitalism's great destructive capacity, moving away for a better life follows a very different pattern. The movement of populations that has characterised the whole of the modern period is called into question when the periphery seeks to come to the centre.

There is of course no such thing as a pure market. Liberals may dream of the free movement of goods and people, but securing the conditions in which this can happen requires massive intervention and investment. This is why liberals and conservatives have so often ended up in coalition together. Through their uneasy alliance the necessary law and order is secured by the conservative/authoritarian/populist wing to enable the liberals to pursue their free trade. The contradictions this involves are seen very clearly in debates on immigration. The lure of cheap labour has to be balanced against the need to patch together the necessary alliances of populists and conservatives that will keep the system afloat. The ideas about race and nation that are submerged just beneath the surface of this debate – and which seek to hold together an alliance between the wealthy and a working class addressed in national rather than class terms – are usually unmentioned but are nevertheless present. In Britain the Liberal Democrats, unsurprisingly, are the strongest enthusiasts for liberal policies such as support for the EU and fewer controls on immigration, but in the Labour and Tory parties there are major divisions between conservatives and liberals (as there are indeed in most of the smaller parties).

Discourses of white/English/British superiority can thus be seen as a resource deployed to help secure cross-class alliances between disaffected sections of the working class and the authoritarian populist right. As well as helping to secure consent for western dominance at the global level, they therefore play a key role in domestic politics.

NEOLIBERAL MERITOCRACY

A third key way in which racialised forms of common sense help sustain neoliberal hegemony is the role they play in naturalising privilege. We are encouraged not to notice that the biggest factor in determining people's life chances is the relative wealth of the families they are born into. Racialised thinking is thus closely related to another stalwart of neoliberal common sense – meritocracy. The idea that those who are at the top are there because of merit necessarily implies that those who are under-represented lack merit in some way. (And the corollary is that lack of success must be linked to a failure to work hard, or to personal flaws such as laziness, criminality or parasitism.)

The refusal to acknowledge the existence of the networks of advantage, patronage and power that maintain the rich in their position is damaging to everyone whose life is structured by inequality – whether this is connected to race, class, gender or other forms of structural inequality. As David Theo Goldberg has argued, meritocracy refuses any acknowledgement of the role racism plays in everyday structures of society; it masks racism through its apparent espousal of a moral commitment to opportunity for all.[5]

The current dominance of exclusionary language in political discourse (where it is also used as a means of whittling away support for universal forms of welfare provision) feeds into institutional racism and the assumptions it makes about people who are 'like us' or 'not like us'. It harms people who are somehow deemed not to have the right qualities to be leaders. It makes assumptions about who does and doesn't belong in the top institutions.

SHIFTING SETTLEMENTS

Another way of tracing the relationship between discourses on race and migration and neoliberalism is to see how they have changed over time, as the social democratic settlement has been gradually dismantled. An over-arching feature of this change has been the shift from an emphasis (however imperfectly executed) on equality and tackling structural inequality towards a focus on individual rights and equality of opportunity.

Stuart Hall's innovative analysis in both *Policing the Crisis* and his later work on Thatcherism showed the important role played by race in the shift towards 'authoritarian populism' at the end of the 1970s.[6] In *Policing the Crisis* Stuart and his co-authors produced the earliest conjunctural analysis of what we first thought of as Thatcherism, then Thatcher/Reaganism and ultimately neoliberalism. As part of this endeavour they analysed the political terrain that produced the 1970s moral panic over 'mugging', and showed how this newly created and strongly racialised category of crime tapped into common sense feelings about Britishness and law and order.[7] This sense of law and order as being part of the traditional British way of life helped to build a new populist alliance in an era in which the world as we knew it seemed to be collapsing, after the '1968 moment'. Traditional values were portrayed as being under threat from strikers, protesters, hippies and immigrants – and 'alien black elements' were seen an integral part of the enemy within (*Politics of Thatcherism*, pp24-5).

References to race and immigration have been a consistent part of the mobilising repertoire of the authoritarian aspect of neoliberalism since the 1970s – in fact they began as far back as the Powell period, which first put this set of ideas into political play. (Powell was an important precursor of aspects of Thatcherism.) Stuart wrote of the 'magical connections and short-circuits that Powellism was able to establish between the themes of race and immigration control and the images of the nation, the British people and the destruction of "our culture, our way of life"' (*Politics of Thatcherism*, p38). Paul Gilroy wrote: 'The right has created a language of nation which gains populist power from calculated ambiguities that allow it to transmit itself as a language of "race"' (*Ain't No Black*, p29).

There was of course, opposition to this populist mobilisation of concerns about race and migration. Black organisations, and movements of solidarity between black and white people, were also developing during this period, and people were also trying to develop new theories about cultural identity and belonging. The 1970s also saw the beginnings of discussions about multiculturalism – an idea frequently derided by all mainstream parties these days, but one whose origins lay precisely in the recognition of the fact that society was becoming more multicultural – and that this was something to be welcomed rather than feared. The GLC, under Ken Livingstone's leadership from 1981 to 1986, represented probably the most successful coming together of all these strands, though other centres of municipal socialism, with similar policies, also flourished at this time. The movement for Labour Party Black Sections also took off in the early 1980s and this led to the election of four black Labour MPs in 1987. These can be seen as rear-guard actions to defend an old-style politics of equality in the face of the emerging new regime.

Race was at the heart of political battles during the transition to Thatcherism. The 'loony left' was a term invented in the mid-1980s to disparage both the left and the new movements for equality: by being associated with each other, mad shop stewards, mad feminists and mad anti-racists could each add layers of looniness to the others' image. The term 'loony left' thus always resonated with a message about race. The defeat of the left by Thatcher, which led to the eventual defeat of the left within Labour, was also a defeat for anti-racism and black politics, as was perhaps most obviously seen in the Thatcher government's abolition of the GLC and the Metropolitan County Councils.

When Labour was elected in 1997, the supporters of equality in the party had not yet lost all influence, and New Labour had not yet evolved its own distinctive take on these issues. The government at first seemed quite promising. In 1998, only one year into government, it instituted the Macpherson report into the murder of Stephen Lawrence, and in 2000 it introduced the Race Relations (Amendment) Act, which strengthened legislation on equality, including some changes recommended in the Macpherson report. Also in 2000, however, the New Labour leadership, with Home Secretary Jack Straw taking the lead, disassociated themselves from the Parekh report on the future of multi-ethnic Britain, which they themselves had commissioned. This was a signal of Labour's shift away from an 'Old Labour' position on race and migration. As Ben Carrington has put it, 'state multiculturalism lasted about three years in Britain'.[8]

As the New Labour clique started to consolidate its grip on the Labour Party, they began to move away from framing the debate in terms of equality and began instead to argue for a more liberal, rights-based, 'modernising' approach. As Judith Squires pointed out in a 2004 *Soundings* article, some important shifts in the New Labour approach to equality could be seen in the debates that led up to the establishment of the single equality commission, the Equality and Human Rights Commission.[9] In particular Judith points to a new location of equality issues within the modernising agenda, with an increasing emphasis on their importance for economic productivity – equality was 'good for business as well as individuals'. She quotes Barbara Roche (who was a minister in the Blair government from 1997 to 2003, including a stint as Minister of State for Asylum and Immigration from 1999 to 2001) at the 2002 TUC: 'a diverse work-force gives employers a competitive edge'. Barbara Roche is still a strong defender of the value of immigration to the national economy, and as Chair of Migration Matters continues to define this in purely economic terms: 'plugging skills gaps, boosting output and bolstering our recovery'.[10]

A further consequence of the establishment of the Equality and Human Rights Commission was a running together of the six kinds of inequalities it was set up to deal with – three of which (gender, race and disability) had previously had their own bodies, now abolished; all these specific issues were now to be addressed through the discourse of 'rights', with far less consideration being given to the specific histories and cultures that had generated particular forms of structural inequality. This too can be understood as part of the shift towards seeing problems of inequality in individual terms.

COMMUNITARIANISM

The Cantle report of 2001 was central to another major shift in Labour policy. Published after the Oldham race riots in the same year, the report correctly noted the problems of segregation in Oldham, and to a certain extent the problems of racism faced by the local Pakistani community; but it saw the solution to the problem as policies to promote 'cohesion', rather than an effort to address the material causes of poverty and segregation, or to tackle racism. And in the end the responsibility for cohesion came to be placed upon the Pakistani population, who were asked to try harder to integrate.[11] This emphasis on cohesion reflected the communitarian turn in Labour thinking, which was also eventually taken up by the Tories under David Cameron. Communitarianism is good social cover for neoliberalism because it is an amorphous, seemingly neutral concept that has no links with political economy: it allows for discussion of social issues but without making any connections to the material forces which shape them.

New Labour's communitarianism had been directly conceived of as a repositioning from 'old' Labour ideas (the new clause 4 can be understood as replacing the concept of class with that of community). Its policies on cohesion were in the same spirit – and involved not only a disavowal of the need to address structures of inequality, but a shift of responsibility from national government on to individuals or 'communities'. In 2004 David Goodhart added a further twist with the idea (shocking then, but everyday now) that Britain was possibly 'too diverse to sustain the mutual obligations behind a good society and the welfare state'.[12] 'Community' thus first displaced equality, and then became itself the grounds for exclusion. Indeed the common-sense concept of community has become increasingly exclusionary as it has become ever more entangled with a politics of us and them that seeks to defend the local against the global.[13]

SHIFTS IN EUROPE

The European Union has also made a big shift in the neoliberal direction since the 1980s, particularly with the Maastricht treaty of 1992 (whose 'social chapter' however, was still too much for the Major government, which negotiated an opt-out). Successive British governments have played a leading role in pushing change in this direction. In particular Britain was a strong supporter of the major expansion in 2004, when ten new countries, mainly from the former communist block, joined the Union, which had the effect of a further massive dilution of social Europe. For the existing EU member states, the new

East European members were seen as offering a source of new markets, cheap labour and investment opportunities, and the pre-accession treaties made privatisation and liberalisation central to the negotiations.[14] The effect of the 'shock therapy' administered by the west during the 'transition time' of these countries has been to create a zone of peripheral economies within Europe whose main enterprises are now owned by international companies, and whose competitiveness is based on cheap labour – and this has had a knock-on effect throughout the EU. There is now a large supply of cheap labour, which causes downward pressure on wages across the EU, while the intensification of privatisation in the East has helped entrench the domination of business interests across the union; what's more, the local populations have often expressed their discontent with the rapid dissolution of their security through support for the populist and far right parties, which has strengthened the political representation of this tendency within European institutions.

As is now well known, the accession of the Eastern European economies in fact led to greater migration to Britain than had been expected, which meant that the decade to 2011 saw record levels of net immigration to Britain (an annual average of 197,000 over the decade). This represented a shift from earlier patterns of migration, which had mainly been from countries that had formerly been British colonies, and migration now became linked in the popular imagination with Europe.

Flexible labour markets that keep down wage costs are at the heart of the neoliberal project. Neoliberal governments usually disavow this intention, however: for them migration is good for growth – another term devoid of human content.[15] However, in order to create an alliance that will keep them in power they very often have to find a way of securing the consent of those whose ways of life are being destroyed by globalisation – who, in the words of Carl Rowlands, 'want to escape modernity'.

This is when migrants become people – people who are taking jobs and overwhelming the welfare state, the visible representatives of globalisation on a street near you. In populist rhetoric Europe has now become the symbol of everything that threatens UK security. As James Meek argued after his recent visit to Thanet, a place where a very large part of the local economy – including utilities, shops and public services operated by private contractors – is run by large companies whose headquarters are overseas: 'There's plenty of evidence in Thanet to support UKIP's general proposition that local power is being diminished while the power of remote, faceless authorities is growing'.[16] But, as Meek also points out, the success of UKIP and other populist politicians has been to identify those faceless authorities with 'Europe' and to associate 'Europe' with immigration.

As Ed Miliband has correctly identified, the problem of migrant workers being used to undermine local wages and conditions is a real one, to be addressed by measures to defend minimum levels of wages and conditions. In other words this is a problem of unequal relations between capital and labour, to be addressed by state and or collective intervention (not that he is able to express it in this way). But this kind of argument is very difficult to make in the current climate. In the Tory party, Boris Johnson and a diminishing band of others continue to support migration on business grounds, as do the CBI. But this is not the case the left should be making. (The rest of the Tories seem to have decided to give up on their move away from nastiness, though re-reading Ben Carrington's piece reminded us of what now seem impossible scenes at the Tory party conference of 2007. After Cameron had attacked Gordon Brown's call for British jobs for British workers – 'we've got to be better than that' – his standing ovation was accompanied by the playing of Jimmy Cliff's 'You can get it if you really want', in what was a consciously multicultural gesture, albeit with a song that was lyrically on message.)

Debate takes place on two completely separate levels: the macroeconomic level, where there is argument over the economic effects of migration; and the common sense everyday level, where exclusionary discourses are so well entrenched that there is scarcely any contestation. Iain Duncan Smith recently dismissed a report by UCL academics Christian Dustmann and Dr Tommaso Frattini – which defended European immigration between 2001 and 2011 on the economic grounds of the fiscal benefits to the UK – on the grounds that it was 'silly'. Summarising the report as 'Oh look in tax terms they have contributed more', his riposte was: 'First of all you have to take them all the way through to when they get older and they actually start taking from the state'; and then: 'You don't account for the fact that often in many communities they literally change the schooling because so many people arrive not speaking English. You have then got problems you know with local services, transport all that kind of stuff'.[17]

(Perhaps this is where Nigel Farage got the idea of blaming immigrants for the state of the M4.)

This response frames migrants as being unentitled to normal services and benefits even if they have paid tax all their lives, and is also located within a wider stance that seeks to characterise the welfare state in terms of people 'taking' things. It makes no attempt to engage with the statistics, in the confident knowledge that no-one in the mainstream press will be remotely interested in such niceties. (There are many complex arguments to be made about the economic effects of immigration but there is not space here to engage in them in any detail. There were indeed some problems for service provision in areas most affected by the bulge in migration after European expansion in 2004, but these were largely due to the unplanned and unregulated nature of the flow of labour, which took place without any consideration of the human needs of either those who migrated or existing residents.) In fact this IDS attempt at common sense shows neoliberalism at its starkest. It is obvious that a flow of people will require services, that some will have children, and some will become ill or even grow old. But the ideal of neoliberalism is a worker with no rights and no social or familial existence. Cheap overseas labour could be even cheaper if workers could be denied the usual rights of citizens (and there is an additional benefit if they can be blamed for the underfunding of public services and lack of affordable housing). Thus with one claw neoliberalism beckons workers in, while with another it seeks to strip them of their humanity.

LABOUR, UKIP AND CLASS

In 'The Great Moving Right Show' Stuart also discusses the contradictions in Labour that mean it tends to acquiesce in populist discourses. He argues that once Labour became established as a governmental force it had to change its articulation from one that was 'class-to-party' to one that was 'people-to-nation' (p27 *Politics of Thatcherism*).[18] It had to seek solutions for the crisis (in this case the 1970s political crisis) within the already existing framework – 'within the limits of capitalist survival'. Stuart makes these points in discussing how the national interest could be set against 'sectional interests' of all kinds, including 'greedy' trade unionists. But forty years later, including two decades of New Labour, we can see that this disarticulation from class has had wider ramifications, particularly given the widespread adoption of a communitarian sensibility in discussions about the nation.

The problem for Labour is that the mantle of speaking for the working class has been taken on by UKIP. As Ewa Jasiewicz has written:

> When you take class identity out of who we are, when you take away any pride in the working-class history of resistance that has won us our rights at work and more, then class becomes not a 'them and us' of workers and bosses, but entwined with race, insiders and outsiders, the hardworking deserving poor and the hardworking, immigrant undeserving poor.[19]

As she argues, people who talk about 'foreigners taking jobs' are not necessarily racist. But the problem is that they don't ask who it is that is giving these jobs to 'cheaper, casualised, more compliant workers'. UKIP, through 'addressing British-born victims of neoliberalism' – talking to workers about work but without talking about power and wealth – are seeking to yoke these sentiments to an exclusionary politics that discourages investigation of underlying power structures. The left needs to do something different: to construct a popular national politics that recognises the value of human diversity, and builds an alliance that brings together a popular majority that can encompass class and other forms of inequality, and is capable of challenging the unaccountable power of the elite. In doing this we could do worse than revisit some of the inclusive politics of the GLC and Metropolitan Councils. The resort to a defensive politics of belonging is an understandable response to the impersonal forces of globalisation. We need to challenge this with an inclusive politics that makes a more accurate identification of those remote, faceless authorities.

Thanks to Lynda Dyson and Doreen Massey for their input into this article.

NOTES

1. The notion of common sense has been a recurring theme in this manifesto and in the work of Stuart Hall more generally. See Chapter 3 on common sense neoliberalism, and the seminal text produced by people from the Centre for Contemporary Cultural Studies, *The Empire Strikes Back: Race and Racism in 1970s Britain*, published in 1982.

2. Antonio Gramsci, *Selections from Prison Notebooks*, edited and translated by Quintin Hoare and Geoffrey Nowell Smith, Lawrence & Wishart 1971, p324.

3. Agri Ismail, 'The pioneers of global gentrification', first published in *Glänta*, February 2014 (English version in Eurozine: www.eurozine. com), quoting Philip J. Anderson and Dag Blanck, *Swedes in the Twin Cities: Immigrant Life and Minnesota's Urban Frontier*, Minnesota Historical Society Press, 2001, p17.

4. See Michael Rustin and Doreen Massey's Chapter 8 'Rethinking the neoliberal world order', and see also the section in Beatrix Campbell's Chapter 4 on postcolonial violence.

5. David Theo Goldberg, *Racist Culture: Philosophy and the Politics of Meaning*, Blackwell 1993.

6. Stuart Hall, 'The Great Moving Right Show', *Marxism Today*, Jan 1979, available at www.amielandmelburn.org.uk, *Marxism Today* section; also in Stuart Hall and Martin Jacques (eds), *Politics of Thatcherism*, L&W 1983. The key chapters in *Policing the Crisis* (referred to by Stuart in the *MT* article) are 'Exhaustion of consent' and 'Towards the exceptional state': Stuart Hall, Chas Critcher, Tony Jefferson, John Clarke and Brian Roberts, *Policing the Crisis: Mugging, the State and Law and Order* 1978, reprinted by Palgrave in 2013.

7. Paul Gilroy develops this argument in *There Ain't No Black in the Union Jack* (Hutchinson 1987), in his chapter 'Lesser breeds without the law'. The pattern of policing of black communities established in the 1970s and 1980s remains deeply entrenched today. So too does the routine reporting of the ethnicity of non-white perpetuators of crime – as in 'Polish rapist', 'Asian paedophile', 'foreign criminal'.

8. Ben Carrington, 'Where's the white in the union jack', in Mark Perryman (ed), *Imagined Nation*, L&W 2008, p117.

9. Judith Squires, 'Equality and New Labour', *Soundings* 27, autumn 2004.

10. www.migrationmatterstrust.co.uk.

11. The background of 9/11 and the 'War on Terror' clearly also fed into changing attitudes towards multiculturalism, but the main focus of this chapter is on the relationship between neoliberal politics, race and migration: it has not been possible to give full consideration here to the equally complex relationships between liberal interventionism and race.

12. David Goodhart, 'Too diverse', *Prospect*, Feb 2004.

13. For more on this see Nira Yuval Davis, 'The double crisis of governmentality and accountability', *Soundings* 52, autumn 2012, pp94-5.

14. See Carl Rowlands, 'Europe's periphery', *Soundings* 46, winter 2010.

15. On the emptying of human content from economic discussion see Doreen Massey in Chapter 1, 'Vocabularies of the economy'. It is in particular notable that in economic discussion the impact of migration is most often

discussed in terms of GDP or growth, which are indices that are less and less connected to any notion of the general well-being.

16. James Meek, 'In Farageland', *LRB*, October 2014.
17. Quoted in *The Guardian*, 16.11.14.
18. This is not necessarily a bad thing, but the notion of the 'people' is complex and needs to be politically constructed – see Ernesto Laclau, 'Why constructing the people is the main task of radical politics', in *Critical Enquiry* 32, summer 2006; and *On Populist Reason*, Verso 2005.
19. Comment is free, *The Guardian*, 29.5.14.

11. DISPLACING NEOLIBERALISM

Doreen Massey and Michael Rustin

The project of the Kilburn Manifesto grew out of earlier work by *Soundings* writers to understand what we called (following Gramsci) the 'conjuncture', in the light of the financial crisis of 2007-8. We were trying to work out what had brought about this crisis of the system of neoliberalism, or unrestrained globalised capitalism, which had come to dominate the western world during the previous three decades. Might there be an opportunity, arising from the damage caused by the crisis, and the discrediting of the institutions – banks and governments in particular – that were responsible for it, for the development of some significant forces for change? Was there a chance for some revival of the progressive projects that had been greatly weakened by the neoliberal ascendency, and by the determined assault by capital and its political agents on labour and its collective forms of representation and self-defence?

Some of us had considered that a degree of recognition of failure by the dominant elites might be forthcoming, and there might indeed be some concession by them to more enlightened kinds of regulation of the market economy. But such hopes were short-lived. Across Europe, the remedy very quickly adopted for the failure of the neoliberal system was to insist that it be imposed with even greater rigour on economies and societies already ruined by the crisis.[1] The 'structural adjustment programmes' (lowering of wages, programmes of privatisation, reductions in public spending) which had in the 1980s been imposed with disastrous effects by the IMF and the 'Washington Consensus' on debt-burdened economies in Latin America and Africa were now to be visited on Europe itself. The 'solution' to the debt problems imposed by the banking crisis on nations such as Greece, Spain, Iceland, Portugal, Ireland and Italy was to be the restoration of competitiveness to their economies, even though, in a context of general austerity, and with a single European currency valued by reference to Germany's superior competitive advantage, this was always going to be impossible to achieve.

The fact is that the causes of the 2007-8 financial crisis have been deliberately misrepresented, and with considerable political effect. Its underlying causes were a state of growing inequality and the weakening of the relative position of labour over a long period. (The average real incomes of the American 'middle class' – i.e. working population – have been stagnant for decades, while the wealth and income of the rich have soared.) And the decisive 'symptom' of this situation, which led to the near-breakdown of the financial system, was the sub-prime mortgage crisis in the USA, based as it was on the packaging of unaffordable loans for house-purchase. 'Globalisation' – in the form of the exposure of western labour markets to competition from lower-cost producers – and the assault on the protective institutions of the working population (trade unions, welfare provision) were the means by which this change in the balance of economic power had been brought about during the 1980s and 1990s.

This crisis of 2007-8 was in fact the second major destabilisation of the post-war period. In the first decades after the second world war governments had acquired, through pressure from below and the emergence of a progressive consensus, the power to regulate and stabilise the market economy, and to maintain some balance of power between social classes. This settlement broke down at the end of the 1970s, and neoliberalism was installed as its conservative remedy. But the breakdown of 2007-8 represented the failure of neoliberalism itself. However this crisis was misrepresented just as the first one had been, as essentially a crisis of governmental profligacy and excessive social protection. Despite 'bleeding the patient' having failed to achieve stability over the three decades of neoliberalism, it was decided that the remedy for the second crisis must be further bleeding.[2] The consequences of this continuing disaster are still unfolding, though in relatively slow motion. There is no prospect of success for these policies because without increased demand for goods and services, there can be no enhanced production or investment. The dominant economic policies are indeed nothing but a recipe for a never-ending recession.

So far, the political consequences of this crisis have been scarcely more positive than the economic. There have indeed been significant upsurges of radical protest, for example in movements in the USA and Britain such as Occupy, and in the rise of new radical political parties such as Podemos in Spain and Syriza in Greece. Should either of these two parties come to power in general elections, they may indeed be the catalyst for a new stage of the crisis, and for recognition that solutions are needed in which financial capital can no longer call the shots. But more potent than the rise of these new formations of the left has been the upsurge of nationalist and xenophobic movements of the right in many countries, which systematically misidentify structural problems – which are essentially those of impoverishment and class relations – as issues of national and ethnic identity. The control of migration, and the suppression of the cultures of migrant communities, has been widely presented as the central issue to which governments must respond, although migration has only a peripheral relation to the economic problems of European nations. We take strong issue with this definition of the problem in the Manifesto's chapter on race. Although migration has adverse consequences for some sections of the population (for example in competition for jobs), its overall consequences when judged in terms of economic growth and development are probably positive.

The economic situation that currently prevails across all of Europe needs to be understood in its larger international context. The broader condition which this situation of stagnation and political regression reflects is that of the decline in the relative power and wealth of the west, and especially of Europe. For a brief moment, with the collapse of the Soviet Union and of East European Communism, the situation seemed quite the opposite. Never, it seemed, had the west been stronger. We draw attention in our chapter on the international context of this crisis to the catastrophic outcomes of the moment of western triumphalism. We chart the resurgence of a new form of so-called liberal imperialism (so 'liberal' that it restored systematic torture as an instrument of policy), and the contribution this has made to reducing a whole series of states and former states (much of the former Yugoslavia, Afghanistan, Iraq, Libya, Syria, Ukraine) to disorder and barbarism. This has been a politics of misunderstanding and delusion parallel to the failures of economic governance described above. The repeated error of western governments has been to believe that if dictatorial governments could be undermined or overthrown, sometimes by direct invasion (Iraq, Afghanistan), sometimes through overt or covert support to dissidents and rebels (Syria, Libya, Ukraine – whose first insurgents were the 'pro-Europeans' of western Ukraine), the consequence could be expected to be their replacement by pro-western capitalist democracies. In reality, the major principal outcome of policies based on this belief has been states of civil war, the breakdown of peace and order, and the rise of fundamentalist theocratic movements, deeply hostile to the west and its supposed values. In the Middle East, the west has in fact become an ignorant and unwitting agent in a conflict between branches of Islam that in some ways resembles the Thirty Years War between Protestant and Catholic powers of seventeenth century Europe.

This pattern of military and paramilitary interventions by the west or its proxies in regions of its former imperial influence or domination shares some features with the interventions which took place during the 1980s to overthrow or subvert radical governments in Latin America (Chile, Nicaragua, Argentina, Brazil) and in Africa (Angola, Mozambique). But it is different in one significant respect. These earlier neo-imperial interventions, for the most part, in their own reactionary terms, succeeded at the time in either defeating and replacing progressive governments or at least in holding back their advance, for example in Africa (though many of these changes have now finally been once more reversed, after having caused decades of suffering to the citizens of the countries concerned). The west's military interventions of the period since 1989 have, however, almost uniformly failed to achieve their objectives. What is being disclosed, over and over again, in this sequence of disasters, are the limitations of the west's power. What was trumpeted by the United States after 1990 as 'full spectrum dominance' turns out to be a continuing failure of military and para-military interventions to achieve their intended goals.[3]

This situation must surely be understood in the context of the rise of new economic powers, in particular but not only that of China, and the loss of the west's comparative economic advantage over its competitors. The prolonged European, and Japanese, economic recessions must be seen against the contrast of much higher rates of economic growth in the 'emerging markets' of the former 'Third World'. What we see in the flailing adventurisms of neo-imperial policy, and in the imposition of 'structural adjustment' programmes on its own peoples, is a system in decline. This is indeed the sign of the unravelling of the current settlement and a reshaping of relations of power across the world.[4] The political movements to the right that have taken place in many nations are in response to people seeing their economic well-being under threat, their former sense of status, superiority and power diminished, and their governments largely powerless to influence the situation for the better. This has some alarming similarities to the developments which took place in Europe in the 1930s, following the disaster of the First World War and the crisis of the existing social order which followed upon it.

One may wish to reflect on the changing subjective relationships to the institutions of government that are being brought about by this situation – to which each of our own personal responses may be some kind of witness. One can perhaps identify periods prior to the 2007-8 financial crisis in which the dominant system seemed to be solidly based and even in its own terms effective – certainly in comparison with the current era. But in virtually every nation of Europe there currently seems to be a general disenchantment and loss of belief in governmental capacity, and a major symptom of this has been disaffection with what were formerly the major political parties. One factor that has contributed to this state of affairs is the evident immunity of financial institutions, corporations, and the very rich, from the jurisdiction of states.

Indeed we made an assessment in our earlier writing about the conjuncture (see *The Neoliberal Crisis*) that the current situation was likely in reality to be beyond the capacity of any elected government to contain or regulate.[5] In *Policing the Crisis*, Stuart Hall and his co-authors described the governmental situation of the 1970s in just these terms, documenting the disintegration of the post-war settlement just as it was happening.[6] During this decade, weak governments – of different nominal hues but attempting similar remedies – succeeded each other, until in 1979 the right found its opportunity to embark on a radically different path, which, after its second election victory in 1983, enabled it to decisively change the political and economic landscape in Britain. At the time of writing we face a general election whose outcome could well be as indecisive as those of the earlier 1970s. This is not merely because it is possible that no single party will obtain a decisive majority; it is because there will be no clear alternative proposed to present policies. Even if the Labour Party manages by default to find itself in a position to form a government, there is little indication that it holds within its still closely-guarded locker of policies any remedies adequate to the problems we now confront.

To develop such an agenda of feasible alternatives to the misguided and destructive politics of the last thirty years is now the project which faces us. The connected account which this Manifesto has been able to provide of the shape of the dominant neoliberal system can only be the beginning of this. In this conclusion, we try to identify ideas and themes which suggest a way forward, and a new progressive course.

WHAT WE HAVE TRIED TO DO

We have now come to the end of the sequence of planned instalments of the Kilburn Manifesto, though not of our project to think, discuss and seek to engage broader publics. What we have been attempting here is an exploration of the current moment, primarily within the UK, but set also within an international context, in an analysis that resists both the demand for immediate policies that simply respond to electoral pressures and the temptation to read the present situation merely as a symptom of long-held first theoretical principles. We need both a full recognition of the specificity of these times and a wielding of 'theory' that does not collapse into reductionism. We also need to be able both to engage current popular and political debate in its own terms, and when appropriate to challenge those terms of debate as precisely part of the problem.

Soundings, the journal from which this Manifesto sprang, has always been committed to analysis informed by such considerations, and there are a number of reasons for this. Most immediately we believe it is necessary to engage with both wider publics and potentially sympathetic political parties. Both parliamentary and extra-parliamentary politics are vital in any future process of change. A political party that has any intention of being bold needs to know that there is support 'out there'. Although it should certainly show political leadership and not be a slave to already-constituted 'public opinion', it equally needs to feel that there is some possibility of purchase among the wider public for its challenges to received wisdom, and that there is extra-parliamentary pressure to buttress it against the conservative forces it has to operate within when 'in power'. It is as a result of this understanding that we have stressed so much the importance of addressing issues of common sense, hegemony, culture, language. The debate about economic policy, for instance, is hemmed into its current narrow and unquestioning terms both by the vocabularies and understandings of the economy itself, and by the shape of wider society – the way we think about issues of 'fairness', or of gender, or the state, or the environment, to mention but a few examples from the foregoing chapters.

Moreover, even insofar as we are addressing potentially progressive political parties, it is also the case that even the most immediate and 'practical' of policies on particular issues necessarily entails, and should explicitly be set within, a broader debate and vision for society. Drawing out these underlying principles can make possible a different kind of appeal to people, interpellating them in ways that a technical policy discussion fails to do. (Thomas Frank, in *Pity the Billionaire*, makes the same point in critique of the Democrats in the USA.) Individual policies can be used to raise bigger issues of principle and to establish genuine political frontiers. Likewise a scattergun array of individual policies will neither add up to much nor make much gut appeal (or sense) to the general public without a framing political project.

Tom Crompton wrote about this in *Soundings* 54. Starting from the famous quotation from Thatcher that the object was to change the approach, and that in turn meant it was necessary to touch 'the heart and soul of the nation', he explores the 'expressive function' of policies, their 'affect'.[7] This is crucial. Even individual policies need not only to address practical, material, issues but also to touch on and help shape underlying values and identities. This is part of the struggle over common sense. It recognises that political constituencies do not just exist, out there, ready-made; they have actively to be constructed. As Stuart Hall and Alan O'Shea write in Chapter 3, here in specific reference to the Labour Party: 'Labour must use every policy issue as an opportunity, not only to examine the pragmatics, but to highlight the underlying principle, slowly building an alternative consensus or "popular philosophy"'. This is an injunction that applies to policy discussion among the extra-parliamentary left as well, and in so far as the chapters in this book have addressed particular policies they have tried to do so precisely in this manner.

All of this meshes with the kind of analysis we have tried to produce here: the moment presented itself to us – or at least the question we asked of it did – in conjunctural terms. It concerned the articulation of the different instances of the social formation; how they provide (or do not provide) the conditions of existence for each other. The glaring fact in the aftermath of the 2007-8 financial crisis was not just that the political right was using the economic crisis to reinforce a neoliberal political agenda (this was common currency on the left), but rather that, while there had been this extraordinary crisis in the economic sphere there were no major political fractures, no serious unsettling (after the first few moments) of the established (neoliberal) ideological hegemony, no significant ruptures in popular discourse. Our aim has been to ask what enabled that to be possible; to argue that what is necessary is a thoroughgoing change in the terms of debate (i.e. an ideological rupture), and perhaps to begin to suggest ways of changing those terms of debate.

Two things are immediately evident from this framing. First, it is clear that there is no place here for assumptions of a simple economic determinism. Of course the economy is utterly crucial, but it is equally the case that the current politically engineered economic trajectory, which is doing so much damage to so many people and to so many aspects of society, could not possibly be pursued without support (ideological cover, cultural assumptions, political discourses …) from other instances of the social formation. Second, and in consequence, serious attention must be paid *to* those other instances and to the structuring role that they play. We have, inevitably, only begun that analysis here, but it is in recognition of its significance that the first chapters of the Manifesto after the opening salvo in various ways take on these questions.

'Vocabularies of the economy' (Chapter 1) challenges the very language we use to talk about the economy, which itself settles our understanding of it, and sets the terms of the debate about economic policy. (This is then carried into the chapter on economic policy, Chapter 7.)

'A relational society' (Chapter 2) takes on a conceptual centrepiece of the whole neoliberal world view – the 'idea of an autonomous, self-seeking individual as the foundational "atom" of the human world' – and demonstrates that it is ill-conceived. Rather, the chapter argues, there must be more recognition of our inevitable relatedness and inter-dependence, and of the fact that these relations each have their own specificities. There needs to be a proper recognition, and a politics, of relations. This would not only challenge a central tenet of neoliberalism, but begin to point – as the chapter does – to alternative ways forward. (The building of a sustainable system of care must be central to economic strategy. And the argument for a dialogic state, in the chapter 'States of the imagination', also puts this question of human relationships centre-stage, arguing for the recognition of the affective dimensions of our different relationships with state institutions and practices: 'the complex clusters of relationships through which the state (that strange abstract idea) is brought to life. Each cluster of relationships … is highly political'. Likewise 'States of imagination' picks up the question of language and 'the need to renew and remake public discourse in order to constitute new forms of public solidarity', in order to work towards creating a state that can contribute to the reinvention and expansion of public culture.)

The third of this opening cluster, 'Common-sense neoliberalism', explores the nature of common sense, pointing to the fact that it is always contradictory and contested, and argues that challenging the currently hegemonic, neoliberal, common sense must be central to our project. Questions of language (discourse), of human relationships other than the market-based commercial transactions of the isolated individual, and the significance of understanding and contesting the ruling common sense, run throughout the contributions to the Manifesto.

Conjunctural analysis is also partly about periodisation (see Stuart Hall, 'The neoliberal revolution' in *The Neoliberal Crisis*). Yet it is a periodisation of society as a whole that takes its shape out of the interweaving of different elements (social, cultural, economic), which often individually have different temporalities. This is evident in the current moment (see John Clarke, 'What crisis is this?', *Soundings* 43, reprinted in *The Neoliberal Crisis*).

Thus it was over decades preceding the neoliberal conjuncture that the *economic* and *social* changes began that undermined and fragmented what had been thought of as the natural (in other words taken-for-granted) base of the Labour Party. The intersection of that long-term erosion with a more immediate dynamic within the *political* sphere – in which Blair and New Labour chose to interpret those shifts in a manner which actively disconnected the party from those traditional political roots (indeed on occasions set those roots up as the other to be opposed) – was also absolutely crucial. It transformed the political terrain. It did so not only by shifting the centre of that terrain to the right, but also by erasing the possibility of alternatives to neoliberalism and by reducing the political field to questions of technical competence, of who could manage the system better. Each of these threads in the weave (economic, social and political) had its own dynamic and its own temporality (and indeed its own spatiality – the economic being inherently global for instance), but each provided conditions for the other. Their articulation, and the nature of their articulation, was crucial.

Likewise, the explosion of impatience and frustration with the social-democratic settlement, an explosion that erupted over half a century ago, in the 1960s, set off a host of challenges and changes especially in the cultural field very broadly defined. Their intended dynamic was progressive and broadly to the left, but they were taken up with delight by the right and incorporated into their ascendancy from the 1980s onwards.[8] So what had been in the 1960s a claim for the recognition of diversity and a challenge to the tendency in social democracy towards monolithic structures was (and this is not in any way to deny the genuine gains that were made by means of these claims and challenges) slowly transmuted towards its endpoint of individualism. The claim for greater flexibility was likewise co-opted into being primarily a labour-market principle whose effects would be borne by workers. And so on.

Some of the atmosphere and tenor of the cultural movements of the 1960s even contributes, in the same distorted fashion, to the success of the hegemony of finance today. The sector's apparent lightness and fleetness of foot, its (again apparent) ease of flow, mesh comfortably with the cultural feel of the present moment (see Doreen Massey, 'Ideology and economics in the present moment', *Soundings* 48, p33, reprinted in *The Neoliberal Crisis*).

These longer, differentiated, and intersecting temporalities and spatialities are crucial to understanding the character and dynamics of the current conjunctural moment. If there is a particular articulation that is a fulcrum of the present balance of forces it is surely that of financial interests with those in land and property. Both have long histories, both have been and continue today to be central pillars of the class-structuring of UK society, both have changed in form over the centuries and both have persisted. Financial interests have for long been internationalised, from the days of empire through to the finance-dominated globalisation of today. Though located in the UK, and dominant in its economy, society and geography, the relation of finance to the productive economy of the country has often been semi-detached. The landed interest has been, historically, more home-based; the battles over its power and the elite ownership of vast parts of the country are part of national history. The past forty years have seen the coming together to dramatic effect of these two class interests. On the one hand the structural dominance of finance has gone along with the invention of a new mode of financial imperialism. On the other, land and property have become the perfect vehicle for storing financial flows (a recent report on London house-price data writes that 'properties in the capital [are] seen as a "global reserve currency" for overseas investors as well as wealthy locals').[9] And, as the quotation indicates, 'the landed interest' is now itself an element in a thoroughly globalised economic sector. The intermeshing of these two class interests, along with the transformation of each, and of both together, is a central thread in the story of the current moment.

And added to that are the interests of big oil, long globalised and now a significant part, not only of the FTSE, but also of people's pension holdings – in other words big oil is also integral to the power of finance (see Chapter 9). Indeed, in the case of energy, the articulation of contrasting temporalities and spatialities is even more marked. The alliance between energy corporations and finance, much strengthened over recent decades under neoliberalism, has worked to its immense advantage an inheritance of global reach built on a centuries-long imperial history. Neoliberal measures, including privatisations, the backing-off of governments from big decisions over energy policy, and a favourable tax regime, have further strengthened the power of big oil; and the dominant vocabulary of 'customers' positions us as dependent, able only to influence the final market (if indeed that), rather than challenge the structures of production – and of power over the continued extraction of strata deposited hundreds of millions of years ago (and irreplaceable) – that are at the heart of the issue. It is, as Chapter 9 demonstrates, a deadly constellation.

There are good reasons for taking seriously the nature of these intersecting histories and geographies. Doing so helps unpack the structure of what can seem like an overwhelmingly monolithic situation. It aids recognition of the significance of different strands, both in their relatively independent development and in the way they do or do not provide the conditions of existence for other threads in the weave. Such a process of conceptual disentanglement helps to clarify the different forces we are up against, and to set particular individual conflicts into a longer historical context. A battle over the 'redevelopment' of a housing estate, for instance, stands in a long line of confrontations going back to the enclosures and the clearances and beyond, over who is to own and have control over 'the nation's' land. Maybe it helps – politically, intellectually, emotionally – when struggling in an occupied building, or standing for hours with one's protesting poster, to do so in the knowledge of that longer lineage of contestation. What's more, an analysis of the articulation of these different histories, how they work together today, could be a basis for the recognition of common interests between forces opposing the dominant order, and for possible alliance.

So what kind of a moment is this? Since 2007/8 there has clearly been a crisis of the economy which is as yet unresolved. This applies to the UK, the EU, and globally. But could there be crises in other aspects of society that could bring this to a head, to 'fuse in a ruptural unity' as Althusser once put it? As Stuart wrote in 'The neoliberal revolution': 'Crises are moments of potential change, but the nature of their resolution is not given. It may be that society moves on to another version of the same thing (Thatcher to Major?), or to a somewhat transformed version (Thatcher to Blair?); or relations can be radically transformed' (pp60-1). The present moment would seem to be different from either of those two transitions within neoliberalism. Firstly, there has been a major economic implosion, brought about internally to the system rather than by political opposition, and, even though ideological and political hegemony have been restored, the waters have certainly been disturbed. The hostility towards banks, and to a whole range of big corporations, remains. Tax, and its various forms of non-payment, is a toxic issue. There is more talk of posh boys running the country. The word 'privatisation' now widely comes trailing clouds of negativity and suspicion. Any and all of these could provide a way in to deeper issues. And there is, of course, austerity. Things *are* different from before the financial crisis. And second, the economic crisis and the lack of an alternative response have been seized upon politically by the LibDem-Tory Coalition to unleash what Stuart called 'the most radical, far-reaching and irreversible social revolution since the war' ('The neoliberal revolution', p27). And yet he argued, in the same piece, that 'the present situation *is* a crisis, another unresolved rupture of that conjuncture which we can define as "the long march of the Neoliberal Revolution"' (p13). A crisis is always also a moment of opportunity. One can ask of this moment in particular if the trajectory is sustainable. Economically the basic issue of sustaining sufficient demand, given such a shift from labour to capital, is clearly evident. Ecologically, as Platform write in Chapter 9, 'sooner or later climate change is going to force a collapse in the current social settlement'. And if those moments of potential difficulty for the neoliberal system are successfully staved-off, will that be by increasing degrees of inequality and authoritarianism, which might provoke a serious political challenge? The impressive rise of left-wing social movements and parties in Greece and Spain (to restrict ourselves here to Europe) gives cause for hope, just as the rise of right-wing parties points to a failure of what have been perceived as 'mainstream' electoral politics, one that is much more serious than a mere decline in voting levels. In the ambivalent responses to these moments of difficulty is there an emerging crisis of the political? Maybe a return to 'business as usual' is actually no longer possible.

A NECESSARY SENSE OF CRISIS, AND A WAR OF POSITION

Crisis can be an over-used term. Nevertheless, the essence of the analysis of the Kilburn Manifesto is that a continuing crisis *is* what we are living through. It needs to be insisted on that the programmes and discourses which now dominate the politics and policy making of Britain, and more generally of the west, are inadequate to the situations to which they purport to respond. Thus, austerity is *not* a solution to the problems of economic instability, inequity and lack of growth. Thus, the expansion of NATO and the institution of a neo Cold War against capitalist Russia is not a solution to the problems of the west's security. Thus, neo-imperial military and paramilitary interventions in the Middle East, to bring about regime change, and to guarantee the west's energy supplies, merely make worse virtually all of the problems (whether of terrorism, or energy security, or the protection of human rights and democracy) which they seek to remedy.

It will be seen even in the time frame of the next five years that the opposite strategy – of reconciliation and open exchange, such as is now being pursued by the United States in relation to Cuba – has far more beneficial consequences than the ostracism, sanctions and siege of the previous five decades. A similar redirection of policy needs to take place in relation to both Iran and Russia.

It is thus necessary for voices to be heard, however unwelcome they may be, which insist on this fundamental mismatch between the 'official' parameters of policy-making and the realities of the situation. Only then can pathological political symptoms (such as the resentment mobilised against migrants from Europe, or of 'Islam' in general) be recognised as the epiphenomena they are.

Gramsci memorably differentiated the preconditions respectively of a 'war of manoeuvre' and a 'war of position'. The former were those circumstances in which a decisive change in the balance of social and political power could be achieved, at one stroke, so to speak. He had in mind conditions of revolution, but one could also describe in those terms the coming to power of Labour in 1945, or of Thatcher in 1979 (even though in the first case momentum was lost during the years of governmental office, whereas in the latter it picked up). A 'war of position' is one in which no sudden or rapid changes in the balance of power are feasible, but where nevertheless gains over the long term can be made.

We believe we are presently in a situation where a 'war of position' needs to be prepared for. The value of the victory of a Labour or a Labour-led coalition government in May 2015 is not that it will by itself transform politics or society, but that it can establish a situation in which new thinking and new kinds of political action may again become possible. The creeping individualisation, privatisation, and consumerisation of society which has taken place over the past three decades and more will not be reversed by five years, or even ten years, of the compromising and hyper-cautious social democratic rule that we are most likely – at best – to see. But, in that context, at least it should become a little more possible to develop forms of agency, new centres of power, different kinds of identity, and resistances to the market, from which a better social order can emerge. We think that in the current political conjuncture, it is emphatically necessary to take a long view.

EMERGING THEMES

What has gone

The process of producing the Manifesto has brought home just how thoroughly social democracy is over. This is not so much in terms of formal structures – there will still remain in place, though much transformed, mechanisms of redistribution and elements of the welfare state. Rather we mean it in terms of ethos and spirit; how the 'common sense' of social democracy has been fractured and fragmented. How our language has been transformed. Stuart wrote in 2010 (in 'Interpreting the crisis', *Soundings* 44, reprinted in *The Neoliberal Crisis*) of 'the cleansing of political discourse', of the erasure of the language of class, of the substitution of 'market forces' for 'capitalism', of 'community' for 'society'. For many, the very temporal structure of our self-positioning in the world has been imploded. Where once there was a feeling of living in a longer history in which there would be progress, to which we might contribute (whatever our background reservations of this awkward double belief, and our subsequent critiques of deterministic Grand Narratives), now there is constant change, especially technological, but it is small change.

Big change, historical change, seems too difficult to imagine. And although the previous imaginary most certainly had its downsides (its often monolithic nature, the very constraint of living within an assumed trajectory), it did have a feeling of historical locatedness, and of optimism (however misplaced). Today, as many have observed, the very notion of a future seems to have been cancelled.

All that atmosphere of social democracy, it seems to us, has gone. Beatrix Campbell's exploration of the changing contexts of feminism (Chapter 4) provides a vivid example. This could be read simply as loss, and as depressing, but what it brings home to us in the Manifesto is rather different. Firstly, it forbids nostalgia: we must address the radically changed here-and-now. We can't go back. And secondly we must reinvigorate a sense of prospective time, a grounded sense that things could really be different (as opposed to a rather deracinated invocation that another world is possible). And for that, we must shift the terms of debate, redesign the political terrain. These are insights that permeate the Manifesto.

Financialisation: an alliance against finance

Central to that here-and-now, we would argue, is 'financialisation'. This has been a thread in many of the chapters here, and its importance is evident, not only in the obvious economic sense but also in the manner in which it has weaselled its way inside our heads, our imaginations, and structured the culture more widely. It is arguable indeed that it is the crucial fulcrum of articulation of the different instances in the current, neoliberal, hegemony. It is part of what holds the thing together. By the very same token it is consequently a possible basis for recognising common themes among a myriad different struggles in UK society today; it is the 'common enemy' of a host of apparently rather different skirmishes. Could opposition to financialisation be the key to constructing chains of equivalence that link at least some of these struggles together, constructing a common political frontier, an 'alliance against finance'? Such an alliance is in fact proposed in the Green New Deal, and as well as supporting this we would suggest broadening the scope of what is proposed there.[10] The aim of such alliances is to maintain the specificity of the different struggles, and their grassroots constituencies, while linking them in demands that question the deeper power structures of the social formation, opposition to which they share. Of course, the 'deepest' such power structures are even bigger things – imperialism, capitalism. But, as Chantal Mouffe has argued, in constructing practical on-the-ground analyses one needs recognisable points of power, ones that are conjurable in the imagination.[11] We would suggest that financialisation is one such in the current conjuncture.

Tapping into 'good sense'

However, if finance/financialisation is one of the 'enemies' a challenge to which might help undo some of the worst aspects of the present settlement, it is also necessary to identify some of the good things we have got going for us. There are indeed many specific struggles, though somewhat disconnected in their particularities – hence the need for alliances as argued above. But there are also potential feelings and attitudes, sentiments perhaps barely recognised still less openly aired, which are – we believe – quite widespread. In Chapter 3 Stuart Hall and Alan O'Shea explored the notion of common sense – a concept key to conjunctural analysis. As well as stressing the internally composite and often contradictory nature of common sense, and the fact that it is a site of political contestation, the authors point also to the fact that common sense always contains '"the healthy nucleus" which deserves to be made more unitary and coherent' (p54, citing Gramsci). This is Gramsci's 'good sense': 'Good sense provides a basis on which the left could develop a popular strategy for radical change – if it takes on board the idea that common sense is a site of political struggle' (p54). There are many potential elements in the current good sense that could be appealed to, and, once drawn out, woven into a wider and more explicit narrative.

We might pick up on that widespread dislike of being constantly called, and therefore positioned as, a 'customer' or a 'client'. Students hate being called clients; passengers on trains comment with scorn on being addressed as customers; fans of the football team one of us supports have a banner asserting their identity as 'supporters not customers'. What is going on here is a popular rejection of the reduction of all identities and relations to those based on commercial transactions (Chapter 1). Could not this be drawn upon, and a political discourse developed which recognises the specificity of relations and the crucial importance of having a politics of relations (see especially Chapters 2 and 6)?

In their chapter, Stuart and Alan explore the element of 'fairness' in all its complex and contradictory articulations and conclude that 'while neoliberal discourse is increasingly hegemonic and setting the agenda for debate, there are other currents in play – empathy for others, a liking for co-operation rather than competition, or a sense of injustice, for example' (p65). Likewise, in Chapter 6, Janet Newman and John Clarke document 'how attached people remain to their identities as members of a wider public'. And Platform, in Chapter 9, point to questions that might be asked of energy policy that would touch on and potentially draw out that 'healthy nucleus within our common sense that opposes injustice'.

One of the clearest examples of such a possibility, where a sense of fairness could be drawn out and integrated into a progressive politics, concerns the oft-invoked notion of 'the something-for-nothing society'. This is particularly significant because debate over its meaning gets right to the crux of the neoliberal settlement.

The something-for-nothing society

There is no doubt that the Coalition government is very aware that people are susceptible to notions of fairness. They touch upon it constantly in ways that are designed to foment antagonisms among those who might otherwise oppose them. Cameron works himself up into a manufactured rage against what he calls 'the something-for-nothing' society. He is usually referring to people without jobs. He knows he can trigger people's sense of (un)fairness. Why should I work when others lounge around on 'benefits'?

An immediate and easy response is to enquire as to precisely what it was that *he* did to earn all the wealth he was born into. But there is an even more structural response, for he and the Coalition government of Tories and Liberal Democrats have presided over the formation of an economy and society in the United Kingdom that is *precisely* about getting something for nothing. Much of the economy today is not about the production of new things, it's about buying and selling assets (land, art, property, derivatives of various sorts, commodity futures) in order to extract rent and/or to make a profit on sale. Money is 'made' simply out of the ability to *own*. As was argued in Chapter 7, this is wealth extraction not wealth production, and its immediate economic effect is redistribution towards the owners of assets. In shorthand it is often called a rentier society. It is also a something-for-nothing society. And in the chapter 'Energy beyond neoliberalism', the mechanisms, and the 'unfair' appropriations, that this involves are seen through a wider geographical lens, in the private monopolisation of parts of the earth and its resources. What is at issue here is *unearned* income and wealth. Is this not also an issue of 'fairness', and can it be drawn upon? Can it be triggered in directions very different from those pointed to by Cameron et al?

There are clearly difficulties. For one thing, people have bought into it, both imaginatively and materially. What are rises in house-prices or in the shares in one's pension but the private appropriation of socially-produced value? Yet the right, and the rich owners of assets, are also aware of the potential precariousness of what they are up to. As Andrew Sayer has pointed out, the very distinction between earned and unearned income went curiously out of use just as unearned income rose to its new prominence, and he writes of how the history of finance has seen continual struggles over the use of favourable and unfavourable terms for its practices: ' ... "investment", "speculation", "gambling", "fraud" ...'.[12]

There is clearly a contest to be ignited here, just as Stuart Hall and Alan O'Shea argue, over how that component of 'good sense' that is appealed to in the idea of fairness is to be articulated and understood politically.

At the time of writing, the battle over the New Era estate in London has been in the news (it is in truth one of many such battles). The sale of the estate, which previously provided homes at affordable rents, to an international investment group that proposed huge increases in rents, can be seen as an 'event' that crystallises much about the current conjuncture. The buildings and the land the estate stands upon have been transformed from being thought of as primarily use-values making a modest return to being regarded as purely financial assets. And this transformation is a product of that new articulation of landed capital and finance, and the globalisation of the land/property sector under the neoliberal hegemony, that was discussed in the opening chapter: a particular event that emerges from the constellation of long, and more recent, histories, and changing geographies. However, the point here is that it has become a cause célèbre, and ideas about fairness have been central to the battle.

Indeed the campaign has touched such a nerve that even London's Tory mayor Boris Johnson has offered support – in spite of the fact that as this particular confrontation was already brewing he was welcoming to London 'Le marché international des professionnels de l'immobilier' (MIPIM), the world's biggest property fair – precisely the kind of force through which the estate's tenants stand to lose their homes (the fair itself also attracted considerable grassroots opposition). It was a perfect moment for entering the contest over what we mean by 'fairness', for raising challenges over gains from ownership of land and property, for bringing into mainstream political debate the whole issue of unearned income. That the goal was open for such an intervention is evident in the very fact that Johnson felt he had to say something: he – if not opposition politicians – was all too aware that this touched painfully upon that healthy nucleus of 'good sense' that is waiting, not to be smothered by platitudes and sympathy for the individual, but to be drawn out in order to raise more structural, political, arguments; to be mobilised as part of the contest against the hegemonic common sense, in order to help a challenge to the material interests and structures that promulgate it. As the book was going to press it was announced that the owners had sold out to a foundation providing affordable homes. A round in the battle heroically won; a bigger case to be made.

What's more, this is an arena which is ripe for perfectly possible and potentially extremely effective 'policies'. In Chapter 7 on 'reframing the debate' on the economy we wrote about the necessity for a land value tax – a policy that would not only work (among other things) to dampen the frenzies that result in profiteering on housing estates such as New Era, but would also be the perfect vehicle for raising the bigger political issues of (un)fairness and unearned income. A policy, in other words, that is more than a policy, one that could be part of an alternative narrative and the drawing of political frontiers.

Lines of social division

There is one other element in this rise of the new rentier society which is rarely mentioned but that is important to the left. This is that it changes class relations.[13] The main mechanisms of exploitation and of appropriation of the surplus are no longer so clearly located in relations between capital on the one hand and workers on the other. Value is also appropriated through rent, capital gains and interest. This means that the locations of expropriation have multiplied, often to places that are less transparent and less easily contestable than the places of production to which we are accustomed (or where contest does not have an established history). This is another important shift, one that is more recent than the decline of manufacturing and mining that is so frequently referred to, but which has also contributed significantly to the fragmentation of working-class forces.

Moreover, other lines of social division are also important to the structuring of the current moment. Lines of division around gender/sexuality and race/ethnicity, for instance, structure social relations in distinctive ways. As we argued in the framing statement that opens this volume: 'When these social divisions operate within a capitalist system, they are, of course, profoundly shaped by it and articulated to it. But they retain their "relative autonomy"'. What has been important to our kind of analysis in the Manifesto, therefore, has not been the documentation of the inequalities, discriminations and exclusions that follow these lines of divide (though these are important), but rather trying to understand how these relatively autonomous systems of division and subordination articulate with those of neoliberalism. We have addressed just three such lines of division in the Manifesto so far. And each, as it turns out, is distinct in the nature of its entanglement in the current settlement.

Attention to the divide along generational lines is a response to the immediate political and economic characteristics of the post-crisis situation itself. There are both clear material deprivations of young people and a political discourse that aims to set the generations against each other. In part, this latter has been constructed in order to divert attention from class divides. But it would not have had any political purchase if it had been entirely untrue. Like many a diversionary political narrative, it reaches in, and touches on, a felt reality. Chapter 5 resets this understanding. What is manifested as intergenerational inequality is in fact integral to the construction of a new class settlement, of inequality and insecurity. A 'new' generation is emerging, with the potential for a collective identity, precisely as a marker of shifts in the social settlement. The younger generation can be understood in part as a crucible within which post-social-democratic norms can be experimented with and embedded. It might be seen as a temporal equivalent of the 'crucible' that, on the spatial dimension, is Greece.[14] Both are forcing grounds for the sharpening of neoliberal principles. Understanding the intersection of class and generation in this way gives us new tools for understanding the current conjuncture, reorientates the political frontier away from being a simple intergenerational conflict, and points towards the potential for new political agency.

As well as there being parallels with Greece, the 'generation' question is set within discourses and movements that span much of Europe and North Africa. The line of social division that runs along gender and sexuality, however, is shown in Chapter 4 to have global dimensions. It also has a longer structural history, and the nature of its articulation with the dominant economic order has changed over time. As the chapter argues, in Europe, the social-democratic sexual contract, centred on the progressive movement towards, for instance, equal pay, is dead. It had its own limitations, being overwhelmingly concerned with redistribution rather than with the transformation of human relations and hegemonic identities, but it did produce progress. In the matter of gender equality the chapter confirms the argument that we have reached the end of that social-democratic narrative of improvement. It was a historic defeat. In its place we have a new articulation of neoliberalism and patriarchy. Both capitalism and patriarchy have their (relatively) independent dynamics; there is no logical or necessary association between them. Rather they feed off each other in their conjunctural association, further transforming and enabling each other. Under neoliberalism this mutual enabling and moulding is startling. From the attacks on the welfare state in the west (and in China), to the 'new wars' and militarised masculinities that are no longer confined to war zones, to the impunity which protects sexual violence, to the male-dominated sexual settlements that structure capitalism in Asia (and, we might add, the hyper-masculinities of the so-called 'advanced' economic sectors in the west – finance and technology) … all these are utterly imbricated into the character and functioning of neoliberalism. 'The new global settlement is nothing if not a new sexual settlement.' What this means is that a strong feminist movement not only 'intersects' with other struggles against the current order (the need for the social solidarity of some kind of welfare state, the need to address complex social relations, the need to address this within an internationalist frame, the need to confront violent sexualities …); it is also crucial in *undermining* that order. Neoliberalism has constructed itself in such a way that it *depends* on forms of male domination. Maybe that could be, given a strong feminist movement, also a fault line along which it can be attacked.

Chapter 10 analyses some of the – rather different – mechanisms through which racialised discourses and practices have been articulated with neoliberalism. Indeed, as it argues, race was at the heart of many of the shifts, and the political battles, that marked the initial transition to the new settlement. Since then racialised forms of common sense have been key to the functioning and the sustaining of neoliberalism, whether in the maintenance of unequal trade relations or in the construction of cross-class alliances.

What the chapter also highlights, however, are contradictions at the heart of these articulations. 'Neoliberalism' has long relied for ideological support upon conservative discourses which in formal logical terms are contradictory with it – for example Margaret Thatcher deployed family and nation. Such contradictory combinations are integral to the functioning of hegemonic common sense. They can be seen clearly today in the co-functioning of neoliberalism and racism. One question is therefore whether the contradictions can be prised open to enable a way in for alternative formulations that could refigure the political frontier, away from racial lines to those lying between an alliance that can 'encompass class and other forms of inequality' on the one hand and 'the unaccountable power of the elite' on the other.

SITES OF RESISTANCE

We have argued since the inception of *Soundings* that politics is, and needs to be, far more than 'politics' alone. (Indeed this is even one of the lessons which needs to be drawn from the rise of neoliberalism, which is not merely a political programme of governments, but has involved the conquest of an entire society and the 'common sense' of its age.) It was this conception of politics that inspired the New Left from its beginnings in 1956, and which we sought to renew when *Soundings* was founded in 1995. Thus the struggle over how society is organised, how its members are to relate to each other, and what will emerge as its central values and symbolic representations, needs to take place in a multiplicity of locations.

Nevertheless, there are certain key domains on which political argument must be concentrated.

Inequality and poverty

One of these concerns the deepening inequalities brought about by the regime of neoliberal capitalism, and the poverty which accompanies that. Growing inequalities are not merely a matter of incomes and the differential abilities to spend that are its most conspicuous features; they are also about the distribution of wealth and power. The grossly unequal distribution of wealth in societies such as Britain signifies that a small minority has control over investment, and the allocation of capital. The financialisation and over-investment in landed property which we have characterised as the misdirection of the British economy is integral to this inequality of power. Even where capital is ostensibly owned by large numbers of citizens, through pension funds and the like, there is no effective mechanism to ensure that such resources are allocated to socially responsible purposes.[15] In the context of the distribution of capital and its growing inequality, programmes of privatisation (endorsed by New Labour in office) have been highly significant, since they have transferred resources hitherto in common ownership (however indirectly and remotely managed) to individuals possessing significant private wealth, who are in fact a small minority of the population. The distribution of economic power in this society is becoming almost feudal.[16]

A consequence of the neoliberal pattern of economic development is not only deindustrialisation in Britain and many other nations, but more widely the diminution of the demand for skilled employment. This is the result in part of the substitution of capital for labour, now reshaping clerical and administrative work too, and also of the export of investment to low-wage regions of the world. Its effect is to weaken the power of those who must live by their labour, which is the majority of the adult population. This itself brings about a further redistribution of power in favour of the propertied. This phenomenon of the 'squeezed middle' is manifest in the USA in the stagnation of 'middle class' (as we have seen, a Marx-phobic euphemism for working class) incomes, over two decades. A similar phenomenon is evident in Britain. It is given a hypocritical political expression in Tory appeals to 'hard-working families', which appear to identify with them even as they are being damaged by neoliberal economic policies. Labour's 'squeezed middle' is its rhetorical counter-slogan, which is weakly linked to the idea that the super-rich and tax-avoiding corporations should make a larger contribution to the well-being of the majority.

There are many reasons why an economic strategy distinct from the finance- and property-led model of neoliberalism is needed. For one thing, maintaining living standards and avoiding another financial crisis depends on this. But for another, the balance of power between classes – between that of labour and property – depends on the availability of productive and creative forms of work. A renewed public sector has a crucial part to play in such a development, both in stimulating and guiding new productive investment, as Mariana Mazzucato, has argued, and in providing contexts for humanly rewarding work.[17]

In political terms, the crucial issues of poverty, growing inequality, and the irresponsibility and misuse of corporate power, call for a politics of witness, critique and attack. Injustice to the poor, indefensible privileges and impunities for the rich, the escape of financial and corporate institutions from the effective jurisdiction of governments – all these need to be exposed as, in Edward Heath's words, 'the unacceptable face of capitalism'; and political mandates must be won for moves towards more equitable economic arrangements. Where egregious misconduct occurs (rule-breaking or cheating by banks or by outsourcing companies, evasion of liabilities to taxation), advantage must be taken of what should be seen as political opportunities.

It has been demonstrated in recent years, by among others Richard Wilkinson and Kate Pickett, that high levels of inequality are destructive of social well-being, not only for the poorest in society, but for the quality of life of society as a whole.[18] It seems that the steeper the gradient of material inequality in society, the more numerous the 'morbid symptoms' and social unease that arise from widespread experiences of disrespect, humiliation and anxiety – or, in an earlier formulation, 'relative deprivation'.

Democracy and democratisation

Similar in its fundamental importance is the issue of democracy, and the goal of achieving a more democratic form of society. Enforcing the narrowest interpretation and restricted meaning of the idea of democracy has always been one of the principal means by which capital and property has retained its power, in the historical context of a long process of democratisation which led to the achievement of a universal franchise only in the 1920s, less than a century ago. Casting a vote in national, local, and European elections every so often, and having the opportunity (in fact exercised by only a diminishing minority of the population) to participate actively in electoral politics, is a minimal form of exercise of democratic power, usually amounting to little more than a right of popular veto over really unpopular policies and decisions.

Under the sway of neoliberalism, the cause of democracy has for the most part lost ground. Colin Crouch has described its 'hollowing out', through the increased influence of corporations and financial institutions on government, through lobbying, and through their financing of political parties and opinion-forming more generally.[19] The shrinkage and diminished power of trade unions, and of elected local governments, have been a further cause of the weakening of popular democratic agency in our age.

In fact, democratic power and responsibility is most effectively exercised in circumstances close to people's experience, where they have most knowledge and understanding of what is at stake for them in decisions. The most important area of people's lives which is excluded from formal, and often from informal democratic processes too, is the workplace. A precondition of a deeper democratisation of society is the instituting of democratic rights and responsibilities in the economic sphere, through the representation of employees on company boards, and in decision-making procedures, and through the countervailing powers of trade unions and professional associations. Not only would such a development deepen the culture of democracy in society, and people's experience of democratic practice, but it would also make many corporate and governmental organisations more efficient and competitive, through enabling them to mobilise greater initiative, responsibility and commitment from their members.

The referendum on Scottish independence has been a momentous event in British political life, in showing what intense levels of commitment and activity are possible when citizens feel that something important is at stake for them. This debate has led to a fresh consideration of issues of devolved power in the rest of the United Kingdom, including England. The reality is that the United Kingdom, prior to Scottish and Welsh devolution, has the most centralised apparatus of government in Europe. The de-industrialisation of much of Britain, and the reduction of power of its local authorities, have contributed to increasing inequalities by region, compounding the inequalities of class and ownership which have grown under neoliberalism. Without responding to a romantic localism, a significant devolution of powers within a framework of norms and of redistribution would offer a possibility of redressing this balance, and of creating new centres of democratic agency, such as have emerged from devolution in Scotland. It is necessary also to revisit the issue of the electoral system, whose first-past-the-post system for Parliamentary elections seriously inhibits the democratic process.

The issues of inequality and democratic empowerment are central to any contestation of the power and legitimacy of neoliberalism as a system. Whatever constraints an alternative government may face on coming into office, a crucial measure of its effectiveness will be the progress that is made by those two measures – the direction achieved towards the lessening of inequality, and towards the enhancement of democratic power and practice.

Environmental issues

In *Soundings* 51 Guy Shrubsole recalled that Robin Cook once said that environmentalism was the 'sleeping giant of British politics'.[20] As an immediate issue, it has had its ups and downs, bursts of activity around roads protests, GM foods, climate change and the selling-off of public forests being separated by periods of relative quiescence. But his article also points to a distinction between opinions, attitudes and values. The first refers to the immediacy of policy issues, attitudes to the currents below the surface, and values to the deep tides of public mood. It is at the level of attitudes and values that the Manifesto has been wishing to argue. One of the approaches to addressing this, as Guy Shrubsole argues, is to take on our estrangement from the natural world – recognising and valuing our relationship to it. This too, is absolutely of a piece with our approach here.

One of the crucial things that our chapter on energy makes clear is that environmental issues are not part of some separate sphere but are utterly connected with all the other political struggles we have been addressing. Its relevance to debates about democracy is central to that chapter: it argues the need for both social movements and state intervention, and a more diversified and flexible set of arrangements in which local specificity and initiative is crucial without relapsing into a facile or exclusivist localism. The issue of land ownership, too, is important to changing our energy system, both to enable the necessary changes of use and to prevent gains and grants going to rich landowners. The furore which greeted the proposed sell-off of public forests is an indication that there are progressive feelings to be tapped into here. And the question of energy is also utterly tied up with that of finance, and with the development of London especially, which is not just a financial hub but also an energy city. This raises in turn huge questions of the UK's historical and global responsibility. Could there not be a politics which specifically addressed this role of London within the global world? To ask what London stands for? It is not so long ago that London was a radical city.

So issues of 'environmentalism' are not only basic to our very survival; they are also integral to the rest of our politics, an arena in which a myriad of different political frontiers can be opened up.

MULTIPLE SPHERES OF ACTION: FINDING UNITY IN DIVERSITY

The nature of conjunctural politics is that one cannot predict the locations of antagonism and potentiality which might prove most significant in the struggles to supplant neoliberalism from its current position of ideological dominance. We have argued in this Manifesto that neoliberalism has become a shared common-sense, indeed has been deliberately constructed to have this force, by many different agencies. We have pointed in this Manifesto to existing sites of resistance. For example our argument against individualism, in support of a relational concept of human nature (in Chapter 2), is rooted in most people's experience of dependency and connectedness as a condition for development through the life-cycle. Against the pressures to interpret relationships in market terms, doctors, nurses and teachers go on seeing those for whose well-being and development they work as patients or pupils or students, and not as mere customers. The resistance to market and corporate definitions of these spheres of work is thus central to a different concept of a good society. The revealing commitment by the Conservatives to reduce the role of the state and of public services to a residual minimum, something not seen since the 1930s, now exposes the full meaning of neoliberalism, but perhaps lays out a terrain on which it can be successfully fought.

But there are many other spheres of life in which the values of neoliberalism, and the forms of power which it mobilises, need to be contested. In Chapter 9 we discussed the significance of environmental issues, and the mobilisations around them, as a crucial instance of this. These questions involve the future well-being of the entire human community, and demand a perspective that is not merely individual and short-termist, as in the dominant neoliberal kind. Developing responsible programmes to respond to the dangers of climate change entails a fundamental shift in values, which may even now be taking place, even if too slowly.

Or consider the more specific field of post-school education. It has been reported that half a million young people entered their first year of university in 2014, the largest number ever. The experiences they have, the curricula they follow, what and how they learn, must in their own way be formative for the social order which is inevitably re-made by every generation. There are questions to be asked concerning what it is to be 'political' in this context? How can university teachers and 'support staff', and their students, give to their work a meaning which resists its reduction to the mere achievement of credentials and competitive advantage, whether for themselves or their increasingly 'corporate' organisations? Here is a location where the invention of a 'prefigurative' form of politics, in which learning and social relations take the form one would wish them to have in the future, may be as important as more regular forms of political action. These desirable relations are rather far from the present state of affairs, of universities dominated by managerialism, competitive grading, and an underlying awareness that many graduates will not find work which makes good use of their education and capabilities. But for such a prefigurative approach to become possible, there needs to be a critical analysis of what are now the widespread disappointments of this sector.

One cannot predict where, even engaging in the most joined-up and multi-faceted political analysis, the need and opportunity for political contestation and debate may open up. For example, leading sports organisations like to claim that they have 'nothing to do with politics', when in fact sports provide society with some of its most influential representations of its meanings and values. Thus it would make some difference to society's sense of itself if followers of football, the dominant British national game, claimed some stake of ownership and decision-making powers in the teams they support. Or if international sporting federations, like FIFA or the IOC, were freed from oligarchic control and corruption.

Or, to take another apparently minor instance, we have seen that the setting of history syllabuses in schools has serious political meaning, in so far as they construct and impose one version of national and social identity – most recently that of Michael Gove – rather than another. We need to remember the addition to the vocabulary of socialism which was accomplished through the writings of Raymond Williams among others – the recognition that cultural practices and institutions (for example the press) are crucial in defining the limits of possibility, and are themselves a crucial field of conflict.[21]

The argument we are making, by reference to these various instances, is that a politics which seeks at least to contain capitalism within a limited, accountable and democratic space needs to have many dimensions, some of which may not seem recognisably political in the usual senses of that term. There are, as Deleuze and Guattari have put it in their different idiom, 'a thousand plateaus', that is to say an almost infinite number of sites of multiple intersection within which a society's future can be imagined, fought over, and determined.[22] Indeed, in a good society there would be many co-existing and contending forms of power, and not exclusively those of property and capital on the one hand, nor of governments and political organisations on the other.

The challenge, after these years of neoliberal ascendancy, is to develop ways of thinking and feeling which can bring about connections between different kinds of action, and identifications between those engaged in them. There needs to be both respect for diversity, for the specificities of each sphere of life, and a recognition of what need to be fundamental guiding conceptions of fairness, equality, and 'deep democracy'. The task is to create and sustain a new consensus around such values, which elected governments would over time find the confidence to give force to through their decisions.

We in *Soundings* will continue, now the Kilburn Manifesto is concluded, to develop this analysis and these arguments.

NOTES

1. In the immediate aftermath of the banking crisis Gordon Brown played a positive role in staving off a financial collapse, but this is now largely forgotten.
2. Martin Wolf has memorably pointed out (' Reform alone is no solution for the Eurozone', *Financial Times* 2.10.2014) that the effects of the weakening of social protection in European economies have not been to enhance competitiveness, but merely to extend poverty more widely. His Keynesian analysis is fully set out in *The Shifts and the Shocks: What we've learned – and have still to learn – from the financial crisis*, Allen Lane 2014.
3. The shallowness and underlying weakness of the American imperial project has been noted, from different political perspectives, by Niall Ferguson (in *Colossus: The Rise and Fall of the American Empire*, Allen Lane 2004); and Michael Mann (*Incoherent Empire*, Verso 2005).
4. We acknowledge here Justin Rosenberg's contribution to the development of the ideas we set out in Chapter 9.
5. Sally Davison and Katharine Harris (eds), *The Neoliberal Crisis*, published online in 2012, and as an L&W paperback in 2015, as a companion volume to this one.
6. S. Hall, C. Critcher, T. Jefferson, J. Clarke, B. Roberts, *Policing the Crisis* [1978], republished by Palgrave Macmillan in 2013.
7. Tom Crompton, 'Thatcher's spiral and a citizen renaissance', p37, *Soundings* 54, summer 2013. Quote cited from *The Sunday Times*, 3.5.1981.
8. Luc Boltanski and Eve Chiapello, *The New Spirit of Capitalism*, Verso 2005.

9. H. Osborne, 'Round the bend: the crescent where house prices average £16.9m', *The Guardian*, 12.12.2014, p21.

10. See www.greennewdealgroup.org.

11. See, for example, Chantal Mouffe, *On the Political (Thinking in Action)*, Routledge 2005.

12. A. Sayer, 'Facing the challenge of the return of the rich', in W. Atkinson, S. Roberts and M. Savage (eds), *Class inequality in austerity Britain*, Palgrave Macmillan 2012, p107. See also M. de Goede, *Virtue, Fortune, and Faith: A Genealogy of Finance*, University of Minnesota Press 2005; and Chapter 7 of this volume.

13. Sayer, op cit.

14. See Christos Laskos and Euclid Tsakalotos, *Crucible of Resistance*, Pluto, 2103; and, by the same authors, 'Out of the mire: arguments from the Greek left', *Soundings* 57, summer 2014.

15. Robin Blackburn has proposed that a democratic transfer of power could be achieved if the nominal popular ownership of pension fund assets could become a substantive one. See his *Age Shock: How Finance is Failing Us*, Verso 2011.

16. The crucial text on patterns of unequal ownership and their significance is Thomas Piketty's *Capital in the Twenty-First Century*, published in 2014. The best-selling impact of this book suggests that this problem is becoming recognised by a significant body of opinion, beyond the left.

17. M. Mazzucato, *The Entrepreneurial State*, Anthem Press 2013.

18. R. Wilkinson and K. Pickett, *The Spirit Level*. Penguin 2010.

19. See Colin Crouch, *Post-Democracy*, Polity 2004; and *The Strange Non-Death of Neo-Liberalism*, Polity 2011

20. Guy Shrubsole, 'Waking the sleeping green giant', *Soundings* 51, summer 2012.

21. R. Williams, *The Long Revolution*, Chatto and Windus 1961.

22. G. Deleuze and F. Guattari, *A Thousand Plateaus*, Continuum 1987.

Notes on Contributors

Beatrix Campbell is a writer and campaigner, and the author of many books, including *Wigan Pier Revisited* (1984) and *Agreement!* (2008).

John Clarke is Emeritus Professor of Social Policy and Criminology at the Open University. He has written widely on the state, and co-authored *Publics, politics and power* with Janet Newman (2009).

Sally Davison is co-editor of *Soundings*.

Stuart Hall was a founding editor of *Soundings* and a regular contributor to *Marxism Today*.

Ben Little is co-editor of *Soundings* and is Senior Lecturer in Media and Cultural Studies at Middlesex University.

Doreen Massey was one of the founding editors of *Soundings* and is currently Emeritus Professor of Geography at the Open University.

Janet Newman is Emeritus Professor of Social Policy and Criminology at the Open University. She has written widely on the state, and co-authored *Publics, politics and power* with John Clarke (2009).

Alan O'Shea is Emeritus Professor of Cultural Studies at the University of East London.

Platform (@platformlondon) is a London-based collective that combines research and art, education and campaigning to drive social and ecological justice and challenge the power of the oil industry. Farzana Khan, Mika Minio-Paluello, Sarah Shoraka, Emma Hughes, Anna Galkina and James Marriott co-wrote our essay.

Michael Rustin was one of the founding editors of *Soundings* and is currently Professor of Sociology at the University of East London.

George Shire is a member of the *Soundings* editorial board.

The Neoliberal Crisis:

A SOUNDINGS COLLECTION

Eds Sally Davison and Katharine Harris

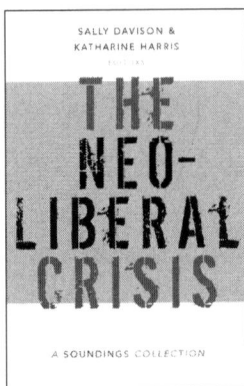

The neoliberal revolution, which began in the 1970s, was an extremely successful attempt to roll back the gains of the post-war welfare state and of liberation movements, and to restore the dominance of business interests across the world. In recent years, many *Soundings* articles have interpreted these developments through conjunctural analysis and this volume brings together some of those contributions, from Stuart Hall, Doreen Massey and Michael Rustin – the founding editors of *Soundings* – John Clarke, and with an introduction by Sally Davison and Jonathan Rutherford.

The Neoliberal Crisis is being re-released as a companion volume to the Kilburn Manifesto, to provide background and context to the Manifesto's more wide-ranging analysis.

To buy, go to: www.lwbooks.co.uk

ISBN: 9781910448076

Price: £11.99